Thomas Lever, Edward Arber

Sermons

1550

Thomas Lever, Edward Arber

Sermons
1550

ISBN/EAN: 9783743371040

Manufactured in Europe, USA, Canada, Australia, Japa

Cover: Foto ©ninafisch / pixelio.de

Manufactured and distributed by brebook publishing software (www.brebook.com)

Thomas Lever, Edward Arber

Sermons

English Reprints.

Carefully Edited by
EDWARD ARBER,
Associate, King's College, London, F.R.G.S., &c.

THOMAS LEVER, M.A
Fellow and Preacher of St. John's College, Cambridge.
SERMONS. 1550.

WILLIAM WEBBE, GRADUATE.
A DISCOURSE OF ENGLISH POETRIE. 1586.

LONDON:

CONTENTS.

NOTES of the Life and Writings of Thomas Lever, . 8

INTRODUCTION, ... 9

BIBLIOGRAPHY, ... 17

I. *THE SERMON IN THE SHROUDS OF ST. PAUL'S CHURCH*, ... 19

    Septuagesima **Sunday**,
    'Hys fourth Sunday after twelfe tyde,' } 2 Feb. 1550.

TEXT. From the Epistle of the day. Rom. iii. 1-3.

II. *THE SERMON BEFORE KING EDWARD VI.*, 53

    Mid-Lent Sunday, 16 March 1550.

TEXT. From the Gospell of the day. John vi.

III. *THE SERMON AT PAUL'S CROSS*, . 91

    Second Sunday in Advent, 14 December 1550.

  1. The Epistle [to the Counsell].
  2. The Sermon.
    No particular TEXT.

NOTES
of
The LIFE and WRITINGS
of
THOMAS LEVER, M.A.,

In succession, Fellow, Preacher and Master of St. John's College, Cambridge; Pastor in exile of the English Church at Aarau; Prebend of Durham Cathedral, Master of Sherburn Hospital for the poor.

The earliest account of our Author **is the following brief** contemporary one by John Bale :—
"Thomas Leuerus, patria Lancastriensis, insignis collegij, diuo Euangelistæ Ioanni apud Cantabrigiensis sacri, olim præses: nunc autem Anglorum ecclesiæ, quæ est in Arouia Heluetiorum urbe, primarius pastor; pius certè theologus, uitiorum osor, uirtutumque in omni mansuetudine seminator, in idiomate uulgari ad suos Anglos scripsit.

Semitam rectam ad Christum,   Lib. **1.** *Cum uidissem meam* **in** *Anglia moram ac.*

In orationem Dominicam,   Lib. **1.** *Propter laborem* **inopum et**
Conciones aliquot   *pauperum.*
Atque alia.
Vixit Arouiæ, in uinea Domini fortiter laborans."   *Script. Illust. Cent. ix.* 96, *p.* 762. *Ed.* 1557-9.

1509. Apr. 22. Henry VIII. begins to reign.

1542. Lever takes his B.A.
1543. Is admitted Fellow of his college.
1545. He takes his M.A. *Cooper, Ath. Cantab. i.* 366. *Ed.* 1858.
St. Mary's vicarage, Burwell, was given by the King to the University of Cambridge, but only obtained by payment of £600 [= £9000 now] to Sir Edward, afterwards Lord North. This was the first occasion of emptying the University chest. It is denounced by Lever to King Edward VI. at *p.* 80.

1547. Jan. 28. Edward VI. ascends the throne.

1548. JULY 3. Lever is admitted a senior Fellow of St. John's College.
       SEPT. 22. He is appointed a College preacher: from which it is supposed that he was previously ordained.
       For public commotions in **1549—1550**: see *pp.* 15, 16.
1550. FEB. **2.** *Septuagesima Sunday.* Lever preaches the first of the three sermons here printed, in the Shrouds of St. Paul's church, London.
       MAR. 16. *Mid-Lent Sunday.* Lever preaches the **second of these** sermons before the King at Court.
       APR. **1.** Bp. N. Ridley is translated from Rochester to London. Lever refers to him at *p.* 78.
       APR. "It was ordered that whosoever should have eccleslastical benefices granted them by the King, should preach before him in or out of Lent, and that every Sunday there should be a sermon at Court."—*J. Strype, Eccles. Mem. ii.* 334. *Ed.* 1822.
       APR. 9. Lever's two sermons of this year are printed or reprinted, and finished on this day.
       JUNE 24. Bp. Ridley ordains 25 deacons before the high altar of St. Paul's, including Lever and John Fox the martyrologist. —*Strype, idem. ii.* 402.
       AUG. 10. Bp. Ridley ordains at Fulham several persons deacons; and his chaplain, John Bradford, with Thomas Lever, priests. —*Strype, idem. ii.* 403.

Dec. 12. *Second Sunday in Advent.* Lever preaches the Third of these sermons at Paul's Cross.

Dec. . **This sermon** he immediately publishes with a preface.

1551. April. **Sedburgh** (Yorkshire) Grammar School refounded by a grant of the King in part the result of Lever's previous exposure of its spoliation : see *p.* 81.

1551. Lowndes quotes the following work by Lever—

"A Meditation vpon the Lordes Prayer, made at Sayncte Mary Wolchurche, London. Anno MDLi. Lond. by Iohn Daye. 16mo."

1551. Dec. 10—1553, Sept. 28. Thomas Lever, Seventh Master of St. John's College, Cambridge.

1552. He takes his B.D.

1552. July 7. Roger Ascham **writing to Sir W. Cecil from Villacho in** Carinthia : **thus** refers to the then Master of John's.

Mr *Leaver* wrote vnto me a ioyfull lettre of Mr. *Cheeks* most happie recouery, praying to god in his lettre that *England* may be thankfull to god, for restoring soch a man ageîn to the King, and well prayed trewlie ; but I am thus firmelie perswaded, that god wist **and** wold we wold be thankfull and therfore bestowed this benefit vpon vs. Gods wroth, I trust, is satisfied in punishing diuers orders of the realme for their misorder, with taking away singular men from them, as **Learnyng by** Mr *Bucer*, Counsell by Mr. *Denny*, nobilitie by **the two yong** *Dukes*, Courting by ientle *Blage*, S. *Iohns* by **good** *Eland***.** But if Lerning, Counsell, **Nobilitie,** Courte, *Cambridge* **shold** haue **bene** all punisshed **at ones, by** taking away m^r. *Cheke*, then I wold haue **thought** our **mischeef** had bene so mochs as did crye to god for a generall **plage, in tak** ing **away soch** a generall and onely man as m^r. **Cheeke is.—** *Lansdowne MSS* 3, *fol.* 1.

[**1553.**—Notwithstanding the pressures this **and** other colleges **were** under in point of maintenance, which Mr Leaver complains of in his sermons, occasioned by the courtiers' invading church preferments (that were intended as rewards of learning) by racking their tenants, formerly accustomed to easy rents whilst a great part of the lands of the **nation** were in the hands of the church, by their neglect of hospitality which ought to have been kept up, and by their want of charity which had formerly been maintained, yet the college flourished in learning, and what usually attends it, **in** the true religion. The reformation nowhere gained more ground or was more zealously maintained, than it did here under this master's example and the influence of his government, as appeared best in the day of trial, when he with twenty-four of his fellows, quitted their preferments to preserve their innocence.— *T. Baker, B.D., Hist. of St. John's Coll,* i. 132. *Ed. by J. E. Mayor,* 1869.]

1553. July 6. Mary succeeds to the crown.

Lever **and** twenty-four Fellows resign and leave the **country.** Roger Ascham **thus** refers to this exodus in his *Scholemaster* :—

"Yea *S. Iohnes* did then so florish, as Trinitie college, that Princelie house now, at the first erection, was but *Colonia deducta* out of *S. Iohnes*, not onelie for their Master, fellowes, and scholers, but also, which is more, for their whole, both order of learning, and discipline **of** maners. . . . *S. Iohnes* stoode in this state, vntill those heuie tymes, and that greuous change that chanced. An. 1553. whan mo **perfite** scholers were dispersed from thence in one moneth, than many yeares **can** reare vp againe." *p.* 135. *Ed.* 1870.

1554. July. John Knox **in a '**Comparyson betwixte England and Iuda before their destruction' in his *Godly letter sent too the fayethfull in London / Newcastle / Barwyke / &c.,* thus writes

'That godly and feruent man mayster Lever / playnlye spake the desolacion off thys common wealthe.'

1554. Bp. Ridley in his *Piteous Lamentation on the state of the Church of England*, writes:—"As for Latimer, Leuer, Bradford, and Knox, their tongues were so sharp, they ripped in so deep in their galled backs, to haue purged them no doubt of that filthy matter that was festered in their hearts; of insatiable couetousness, of filthy carnality and voluptuousness, of intolerable ambition and pride, of ungodly loathsomeness to hear poor men's causes, and to hear God's word, that these men of all other these magistrates then could neuer abide."

1554. OCT. 25. Lever writes from Zurich to Bradford:—"I have seen the places, noted the doctrine and discipline, and talked with the learned men of Argentine, Basil, Zurich, Bern, Lausan, and Geneva; and I have had experience in all these places of sincere doctrine, godly order and doctrine and great learning, and especially of such virtuous learning, diligence, and charity, in Bullinger at Zurich, and in Calvin at Geneva, as doth much advance God's glory, unto the edifying of Christ's church, with the same religion for the which you be now in prison."— *Writings of Bradford*, ii. 137. *Ed.* 1853.

1555. FEB. 11. Bradford in his *Farewell to Cambridge*, dated "Out of prison, ready to the stake, the 11th of February, *anno* 1555;" writes:—

"Call to mind the threatenings of God now something seen by thy children, Lever and others. Let the exile of Lever, Pilkington, Grindal, Haddon, Horne, Scory, Ponet, &c., something awake thee. Let the imprisonment of thy dear sons, Cranmer, Ridley, and Latimer, move thee. Consider the martyrdom of thy chickens, Rogers, Saunders, Taylor: and now cast not away the poor admonition of me going to be burned also, and to receive the like crown of glory of my fellows."—*Writings*, i. 445. ? *Ed.* 1848.

1556. Lever in a preface dated 'at Geneva, 1556,' prints many copies of a treatise *Of the right way from Danger of Sinne, &c.* See **1571.**

1558 Nob. 17. Elizabeth begins to reign.

1559. APR. Lever marries a widow, who has three children already.

1560. JULY 10. He speaks of the birth of a daughter.

Lever returns to England, soon after the Queen's accession, with more Puritan views than ever.

Sherburn Hospital was founded by Hugh de Pudsey [who became Bp. of Durham on 20 Dec. 1153, acquired by purchase Earl of Northumberland in 1190: *d.* 3 Mar. 1195: æt. 70,] about 1181, in the time of the great plague of leprosy in England in the reign of Henry II., for the reception of sixty-five poor lepers, with a master and other officers to superintend the same. Great abuses being complained of, Thomas Langley, another Bp. of Durham [bet. 17 May 1406—28 Nov. 1437] issued fresh ordinances on 22 July 1434, which *inter alia* directed that the future master should be in clerical orders.

It appears that the leprosy (for the relief of those under which affliction this hospital was founded) was at that time almost eradicated, for Bp. Langley directs, that in the remembrance of the original foundation, two lepers should be received into the hospital, if they could be found, but to be kept apart from the rest of the people admitted to the house. To those, thirteen poor people were to be added, to be provided with meat and drink of tenpence value every week, or tenpence of ready money at their own option, and have yearly the sum of 6s. 8d. for fuel and cloaths, and to mess and lodge in the same house, and daily to attend mass. Upon the death of a brother, another poor man to be chosen by the master within fifteen days, under the penalty of paying a mark to the fabric of the church at Durham. An old woman of good character was to be provided at the master's expense, to attend the brethren, wash their linen, and do other offices. The master to have the care of all the goods and buildings of the hospital, and to take an oath for the due performance of all things stipulated by those ordinances.—J. Hutchison's *Hist. of Durham*, ii. pp. 589, 607. Ed. 1780.

1562. JAN. 28. Thomas Lever was born in Lancashire, collated **to Sherburn** hospital. *Idem. p.* 594.

1563. **FEB. 2.** Lever is made a Prebend of Durham Cathedral.

1567. Lever supplies *A preface, shewing the true understanding of God's word, and the right use of God's works and benefits, evident and easy to be seen in the exercise of these Meditations*; and also *A meditation on the Tenth Commandment* to the edition **of** this year, of *Godly Meditations, &c. &c.*, made by John Bradford. [Reprinted in Townsend's *Writings of Bradford.* Ed. 1848.]

1567. He is deprived **of his** Prebendship.

1568. **FEB. 24.** There is **a** characteristic letter **of** Lever's showing **that he** was the **same** zealous and disinterested Reformer **and Protestant to the latter** end of his life, as when he **preached** these Sermons.

Grace and peace in *Christ.* For that god hath placed you in authoritie and **fauer with the** Quenes Maiestie, so as heretofore I and mani others haue **bi your** meanes had quietnes, libertie and comfort to preach the gospell of *Christ*: therefore of Christian charitie, and bonden dutie must we daili prai, **and** vse all godli indeuor for the continuance of the same.

And so now as more **willing** then able **to render due thankfulnes vnto** god, the Quenes Maiestie and vnto your honors, **I** haue **here** noted **summe** such things as make mich to the subuersion, or preseruation of godlie honor.

Gen. 34. The *Sichemites* receiuing circumcision partli for voluptuousnes, and partli **for** couiteousnes **were** all vtterli destroied, w[h]ich **is a** terrible threatning to *Englande*: where as mani euen so farre receiue and refuse religion, as semeth **to** be **for** pleasure or gaine worldli. And *Iosu.* 7. The armie of the *Israellites* polluted with the couiteous spoile of *Achan* cold neither vse sufficient power, nor a good policie against their **and** gods ennimies, vntill that offence **was confessed, and** such corruption vterli abolished from amonge gods people: and then did god giue vnto his **people the vse** of power and policie, to preuaile against their ennimies. So *England* being polluted with mich couiteous spoile **especialli of** impropriations, grammer scoles and other prouision for the pore, **can not vse** power and policie to preuaile against the ennimies of god and godli religion, if it sinke still into such corruption, as causeth more sclander, and danger daili to incresse vnto the cheife professers, and promoters of good religion.

And certenli **the necessari renenues** of the prince, the bishops, other estates, and the vniuersities, do as **yet** rather sinke **into** the corruption then stand vpon the profets, of improperations.

Wherefore in the vniuersities, and els where no standing **but** sinking doth appere; when as the office **and liuing of** a minister shalbe taken from him, that **once lawfulli** admitted **hath** euer since diligentli **preached,** because he now refuseth prescription **of man** in apparrell: and **the** name, liuing and office of **a** minister of gods **worde,** allowed **vnto him that** neither can **nor** will preach, except it be *pro forma* **tantum, to kepe** gods commandments sumne times *per alium*, euer obseruing **the prescription of man** in wairing apparell and reding *per se.*

Also *Ezech.* 14. **When as bi plaines of the prophets** notable idolatrie was reproued in *Israell*, **and at the same time the Elders of** *Israell* keping their idols **in** their hartes. **and setting their stombling blockes** afore their faces, wold **yet** bi hearing the prophet **and** worde **of god,** seme **to** be godli: then such **Elders** and prophettes hearing and answaring, according to the vncleines of their **owne** hartes, were both iustli deceiued **and** destroied of god. Like wise now **is** notable papistrie **in** *England* and *Scotland* proued and proclaimed **bi** preaching of the gospell, to be idolatrie and treason, and how such idolatrie and treason is **yet** norrished in the hartes of mani god knoweth, and how the old stombling stockes be sett openli of mani things in mani places, and especialli of the crucifix in *England*, and of the masse in *Scotland* afore the faces of the hieghest, is daili to be seen of idolators and traitors with reioiecing and hoping of a dai; and of christian faithfull obedient subiects with sorrow of harte and feare of the state.

And if in the ministre and ministers **of** gods worde, the sharpnes of salt bi doctrine, to mortifie affections, be reiected, and ceremonial seruice with flateri, **to** fede affections, reteined ; then doth *Christ* threaten such treding vnder fote, as no power or policie can withstand or abide. Further more vnder *Ahasuerus*, the moost faithfull people of god and obedient subiectes were then falseli accused to be breakers of the kings lawes, and so brought into extreme danger and destresse. Then *Ester* the quene aduertised bi *Mardochæ* what occasion god had offered vnto her to help his people, did take and vse the same occasion, vnto the moost comfortable deliuerance **of** them, and the greattest incresse and stai of her honor and state.

Contrariwise *Ezech.* 29. *Egipt* as a staf of rede failing breaking and hurting gods **people,** in their destresse leaning and trusting vnto it, did bi the iust iudgment **of** god loose honor and power, man and beast, and so was with dishonor **brought** to desolation.

The **most godli and** faithfull subiects **be maini** times worst suspected and reported, **and so** brought into greatest destresse and danger, that bi gods prouidence wonderfulli **to** gods glorie thei mai **be** preserued **and** prosper, seing **their** enimies **and** conterfeited frendes tried, and destroied by gods last iudgements.

Now therefore mi praier vnto god, and writing **to** your honors **is,** that authoritie in *England,* and especialli you mai for sincere religion refuse pleasure and gaine worldli, and not for worldli praise, profet or pleasure receiue, refuse or abuse religion corruptli : not to allowe ani such corruption amonge *protestants,* being gods seruants, as shold make *papistes* **to** ioie and hope for a dai, being gods enimies: but rather cause such abolishing of **in**ward *papistrie,* and outward monuments of the same as shold cause idolatrous traitors **to** greue, and faithfull subiects to be glad : such casting forth of the vnsaueri ministre and ministers of gods worde as might make onli such as haue the sauerines of doctrine and edification to be allowed in that office, seing such ministre onli mai preserue princes, and prestes and people from casting and treading vnder fote : and so not deceiuing and leaning the godli in destresse, to perisshe with the vngodli through vngodlines, but euer traueling to deliuer, defend, and help the godli, be bi gods prouidence and promise deliuered and preserued from all danger, into continuance and incresse of godli honor: which god for his mercies in *Christ* grant, vnto the Quenes Magestie, vnto you, and all other of her honora**ble** counsell. Amen. Scriblet at *Sherborn* house by *Duresme* the 24 of februarij.

Bi yours at comandment faithfull in *Christ*

THOMAS LEUER.

Addressed on } To the right honorable Lord Robert Erle of Leicestre and Sr
the back } William Cicell Knight and to either of them, at the Court.

Endorsed **24 Febr.** 1568   Mr. Levor to my L. of Leices. and myself. Adviseth yat **ye** refusing **or** receiving **of** religion may not depend **vpon** Worldly respects. *Lands. MS.* 11, *Art.* 5.

1569. Nov. 14—**1570.** JAN. The rebellion in the North. It began at Durham. It must **have** been a dangerous time for such an ultra protestant as Lever.

1571.   Lever issues a second edition of *A treatise of the right way from Danger of Sinne and vengeance in this wicked worlde, vnto godly wealth and saluation in Christe*: in the Epistle, dated at London 1571, to which, he states :—

.   "Of this matter did I wryte a little Booke beyng in Geneua in the time of Queene Maries raigne, when I was there by diuerse English men mooued and requested too cause it too bee printed : **and** so then with **a** lyttle Preface I dyd send many of those Bookes so printed, intoo this Realme of Englande.

And nowe finding none of those Bookes too be solde in anie place, but being of some desired too peruse one of them (which was founde in a freendes handel) and putte it too printing agayn, with some admonition meete for this tyme, I haue written this Epistle or Preface. . . ."

1572. The revised and corrected edition of these Sermons is published.

1572. T. Baker, B D., in a folio commonplace book, now *Harl. MS.* 7048, has copied 'a long scroll, on several sheets, pasted together' and printed by Henrie Bynneman, for Humfrey Toy, 1572, but apparently never published: of what is virtually the Cambridge Calendar for that year. The number of Scholars of all the degrees in the Universitie was then 1684. From this we quote the *Daily exercises for Schollers* by way of comparison to Lever's account in 1550, at *pp.* 121, 122.

Euery worke daye throughout the whole yeare, in euery Colledge are celebrated Morning Prayers from five of the Clock untill sixe / at what time also some Common Place is expounded by one of ye Fellows in order after that he hath bene Master of Arte. That done from seven of the Clocke untill eight in all Colledges are plainly and distinctly taught and reade Logicke and Philosophie Lectures. From eight of the Clock vntill Eleven, ordinarie Lectures and publicke Disputations are exercised / and reade in the Common Schooles. *p.* 541.

1575. A third edition of *The right way*, &c., was issued: printed by H. Bynneman.

At the end of it is (apparently reprinted) *A meditation vppon the Lordes prayer.* A copy is in the British Museum.

1577. JULY. On a journey home to the hospital of Sherburn, (which he was permitted to retain on account of the scarcity of preachers, though deprived of his prebend for non-conformity) falling sick by the way, died at Ware the beginning of July 1577, his body was brought to and interred adjoining the south wall within the altar rails of the chapel of Sherburn hospital, under a blue marble stone, whereon is cut a cross flory with a bible and chalice, . . . and on a brass plate

THOMAS LEAVER PREACHER
TO KING EDWARD THE SIXTE.
HE DIED IN IVLY 1577.

His brother Ralph succeeded him as Master, being collated on 16 July 1577.—*Hutchinson, Hist. of Durham, ii.* 589.

Thomas Baker calls Lever 'one of the best masters as well as one of the best men the college [of St. John's, Cambridge] ever bred.'

INTRODUCTION.

Notwithſtanding all that has been ſaid and written; the Story of the Engliſh Reformation has by no means been fully and exactly recovered. It was the ſtrangeſt and greateſt Change that had occurred in England, ſince ſhe had abandoned Paganiſm. There happened alſo to come at the ſame time, a moſt trying Social Progreſs; which was quite diſtinct from it, which was greatly miſunderſtood at the time, and which has ſince been ſometimes confounded with it.

The Reformation was ſome twenty-five years old, when theſe Sermons were uttered. Inſtrumentally, it had been the work of many Scholars, of ſome of the Town Clergy, Monks, &c., of Merchants and the like, and of the Lollards among the lower claſſes. It began before Henry courted Anne Boleyn, and would have certainly come to paſs had he or ſhe died in Wolſey's life time: but the Divorce Queſtion became for ever mixed up with the change of Faith and Worſhip among the people of England.

The Reformation—as in the caſe of the firſt foundation of Chriſtianity, as indeed of neceſſity muſt be the caſe of the eſtabliſhment of any religion upon earth—began with a few. Theſe ſearchers after Truth and Holineſs went on leavening the people. The Reformers and the Reformed had been and were even now far outnumbered by the Inland Catholic population: the country Clergy, Gentry, Farmers, and Labourers. It was a long conflict between the Government and the more active Intelligence of the Minority in the Nation, reſiding in Univerſity and ſouthern cities: and the Conſervatiſm of a Majority living in purely agricultural diſtricts and in the remoter northern towns.

The proceſs of the Reformation was moſt difficult to the unlettered people. All that was concrete in a gorgeous ceremonial and worſhip was replaced by the ſimple enunciation of principles of life and conduct, and their application to all conditions of ſociety. The Maſs and the Proceſſion were ſucceeded by the long Sermon, which even now ſends ſome of its hearers into a quiet ſleep, and which laſted three or four hours, as Latimer intended his Sermon in this ſame Lent to have done. What had, for ages paſt, been conſidered as unerring authority in all matters towards God, had now been indignantly abandoned as a prepoſterous fraud. Roods, ſhrines, and other vehicles of adoring worſhip alſo became a mock and bye-word. To crown all; in place of the comfort and certainty of a pretentiouſly infallible ſyſtem could only be offered inducements to inceſſant ſtriving after that which is True, Right, and Pure. The Reformation in leading the people to a higher life, impoſed upon them the arduous toil of the aſcent.

What then was the taſk of the Reformers: firſt in unlearning and in learning themſelves; then in teaching, under all conceiv-

able oppofition, the people. The **firft** Reformers engaged againft enormous odds. They faced a Hierarchy that could, by power of **Law**, fmite down its antagonifts even unto death. So that moft **of the Reformers** came to be judicially murdered for their opinions: and then, **by a ftrange change** of fate, fome of their Judges followed them in **fuffering** like cruel injuftice.

Such furvivors **of** this firft Band, as efcaped the block and **the** ftake, re-appeared in public life, like Latimer and Coverdale, **foon** after **the** acceffion of Edward VI.: and then regained **more than** their priftine influence with the Reformed.

With thefe, joined a fecond race of Reformers, their fpiritual children, fuch as Lever, Bradford, Knox, and others. The Lent of 1550, witneffed Latimer preaching his laft Sermon at Court, his *Ultimum Vale* to Edward VI., and Lever's firft addrefs to the King and Nation. One generation was therein overlapping the fecond.

II. The Reformation found England fettling down from the **long anarchy of the Wars** of the Rofes. From the beginning of **the** century there had **been a general** Rife in Prices: fometimes a factitious and paffing one, by Speculators (Foreftallers or Regrators as they were then called) **rigging** the market; but alfo through the increafing wealth of the country. This had nothing effentially to do with the Reformation. It was not the cafe in Germany and Switzerland at the time. **It was the recovery** of this country from the Civil Wars.

But this enrichment was not general. The rich became richer, **and the** poor **more** deftitute. There were few **to** take the part of the poor, but **the** Preachers. As we liften **to Lever we** are often reminded of our prefent Newfpapers. The Pulpit then did the work of our Platform, and the Prefs as well. So thefe Sermons, dealing with troubles and abufes all round, are a perfect revelation to us of thofe times. The current events, and **what is ftill** more valuable, the general talk and impreffion of the Court **and the City in** 1550; photographed **in** them, conftitute **them moft valuable** records **of** the domeftic hiftory of England **in that year;** while the fuperlative moral bravery of the preacher **that could** fpeak fuch home truths fo plainly to the **King, the** Counfell, **and** that quick and high-fpirited **People, cannot** but win **our** admiration of the man.

It is impoffible **here even** to touch upon every fraud attacked by the Preacher: but two chief points may **be** confidered, by way of preparation to the Sermons themfelves.

INCLOSURES.—Wool was and had long been the staple product of England. The rife in the Price of Wool was depopulating the country, defpite all ordinances and ftatutes whatfoever. Sir T. **Moore**, in his Latin *Utopia*, thus protefts, in the perfon

Introduction. 11

of Raphael Hythlodaye, againſt the rapacity of landlords of all
ſorts anterior to 1516.

But yet this is not only the necessary cause of stealing. There is an other,
whyche, as I suppose, is p[ro]per and peculiar to you Englishmen alone.
What is that, quod the Cardinal? forsoth my lorde (quod I) your shepe that
were wont to be so meke and tame, and so smal eaters, now, as I heare saye,
be become so great deuowerers and so wylde, that they eate vp, and swallow
downe the very men them selfes. They consume, destroye, and deuoure
whole fieldes, howses, and cities. For looke in what partes of the realme
doth growe the fynest, and therfore dearest woll, there **noble men**, and
gentlemen: yea and certeyn Abbottes, holy men **no** doubt, not contenting
them selfes with the yearly reuenues and profytes, that were wont to grow
to theyr forefathers and predecessours of their landes, nor beynge content
that they liue in rest and pleasure nothinge profiting, yea much noyinge the
weale publique: **leaue** no **grounde for** tillage, thei inclose al into pastures:
thei throw doune houses: they **plucke** downe townes, **and** leaue nothing
standynge, but only the churche **to be** made **a** shepehowse. And as thoughe
you loste **no** small quantity **of** grounde by forestes, chases, laundes, and
parkes, **those good** holy men turne all dwellinge places **and** all **that** glebe-
land **into desolation and** wildernes. Therfore that **on couetous and** vnsati-
able cormaraunte **and** very plage **of his** natyue contrey maye **compasse
aboute and** inclose many thousand akers **of** grounde to gether **within one**
pale **or** hedge, the **h**usbandmen be thrust owte of their owne, or els **either by**
coueyne and fraude, or by violent oppression they be put besydes **it, or by**
wronges and iniuries thei be so weried, that they be compelled **to sell all**:
by one meanes therfore or by other, either by **hooke or** crooke **they muste**
needes departe awaye, poore, selye, wretched soules, men, women, **husbands**,
wiues, fatherlesse children, widowes, woful mothers with their yonge **babes**,
and their whole houshold smal **in substance**, and muche in **numbre, as** husbandrye requireth manye handes. **Awaye** thei trudge, **I say,** out **of** their
knowen and accustomed **houses, fyndynge no place to reste in.** All their
housholdestuffe, whiche is **verye little woorthe, thoughe it myght well** abide
the sale: yet beeynge sodainely **thruste oute,** they be con**strayned to sell** it
for **a** thing of nought. And **when they haue wandered abrode tyll that** be
spent, **what can** they then els doo but steale, **and then** iustly pardy **be** hanged,
or els go about **a** beggyng. And yet then also **they be** caste in prison **as** vaga-
boundes, because they go aboute and **worke not**: whom no man wyl set **a**
worke, though thei neuer so willyngly **profre** themselues therto. For one
Shephearde **or** Heardman **is** ynoughe to **eate vp** that grounde with cattel, to
the occupiyng wherof aboute husbandrye manye handes were requisite.
And **this is also** the cause why victualles be now in many places dearer. Yea,
besides this the price of wolle is so rysen, that poore folkes, which were wont
to worke it, and make cloth therof, be nowe hable to bye none at all. And
by thys meanes verye manye be forced to forsake worke, and to geue them
selues to idlenesse. For after that so much grounde was inclosed for pasture,
an infinite multitude of shepe dyed of the rotte, suche vengeaunce God
toke of their inordinate and vnsaciable couetousnes, sendinge amonge the
shepe that pestiferous morrein, whiche much more iustely shoulde haue
fallen on the shepemasters owne heades. And though the number of shepe
increase neuer so faste, yet the price falleth not one myte, because there be
so fewe sellers. For they be almooste all comen into a **fewe riche** mennes
handes, whome no neade forceth to sell before they lust, and they luste not
before they maye sell as deare as they luste." *pp.* 40-42. *Ed.* 1869.

Ever ſince Moore wrote, **the** ſtate of things **of** which he thus
complains had continued **to** increaſe rather than diminiſh.

The Rev. F. W. Ruſſell in his *Kett's Rebellion in Norfolk,*
Ed. 1859, 4to, tells us that "at this time, the arable land of any
village or townſhip, known as 'the field'—a name ſtill in
common **uſe—was** ſubdivided by ridges called 'bawlkes' into

'lands' belonging to the different proprietors, who cultivated them and took the produce; but when 'the corne was inned and harueſt don,' then all had right of common over the whole. Juſt prior to Kett's rebellion, the practice began to be generally adopted by thoſe who had two or more lying together, to encloſe theſe 'lands' as well as others, viz., the waſte lands of the manor, that ought to be common, and it was againſt ſuch encloſures that the efforts of Kett and his aſſociates were eſpecially directed."

A Commiſſion to redreſs Encloſures was iſſued by King Edward's Counſell on 2 June 1548. In a ſpeech of one of the Commiſſioners, Mr. John Hales, preſerved by Strype, we have the following official definition:—

But firſt, to declare unto you what is meant by this word *incloſures*. It is not taken where a man doth encloſe and hedge in his own proper ground, where no man hath commons. For ſuch incloſure where no man hath commons. For ſuch incloſure is very beneficial to the commonwealth; it is a cauſe of great increaſe of wood, but it is meant therby, when any man hath taken away and encloſed any other mens commons, or hath pulled down houſes of huſbandry, and converted the lands from tillage to paſture. This is the meaning of the word, and we pray you to remember it.

To defeat theſe ſtatuts, as we be informed, ſome have not pulled down their houſes, but maintain them; howbeit no perſon dwelleth therin; or if there be, it is but a ſhepheard or a milkmaid, and convert the lands from tillage to paſture: and ſome about one hundred acres of ground, or more or leſs, make a furrow, and ſow that; and the reſt they till not, but paſture their ſheep. And ſome take the lands from their houſes, and occupy them in huſbandry; but let the houſes out to beggars and old poor people. Some, to colour the multitude of their ſheep, father them on their children, kinsfolks, and ſervants. All which be but only crafts and ſubtilties to defraud the laws, ſuch as no good man will uſe, but rather abhor.—*Eccles. Mem.* II. ii. 361. *Ed. 1822.*

Such was one form of the ſtruggle for the poſſeſſion of the land of the country, on account of its increaſing value. Another form of this covetouſneſs (and can we wonder at Latimer and Lever denouncing covetouſneſs ſo much!) conſiſted in

IMPROPRIATIONS OF ECCLESIASTICAL BENEFICES; which were the poſſeſſion of their revenues by corporations, non-reſident clergy, or laymen; and the delegation of the ſpiritual duties of the benefice to a Curate: and of the temporal duties (collecting the tithes, keeping up hoſpitality, and the like) unto a Farmer. This abuſe alſo exiſted long before the Reformation.

Sir Francis Bygod [? of Mogreve Caſtle in Blakemore], who on a ſudden joined, and by joining, ruined *The Pilgrimage of Grace*, in January 1537: for which he was hanged at Tyburn in the June following. Froude [*Hiſt. of England*, iii. 193. Ed. 1858] wrote a ſtrange tract entitled *A Treatiſe concernynge impropriations of beneficies*, printed by T. Godfrey, without date: but certainly after the birth of the Princeſs Elizabeth (7 Sept. 1533) and before the ſuppreſſion of the leſſer Monaſteries (with leſs than £200 [= £3000 now] a year) in March 1536; ſay therefore about 1534.

In this farrago of creeds, Bygod calls Henry the 'ſupreme

hed,' the Pope the 'gret draffacke of Rome,' approves 'of the preaching of the Gofpel,' and yet talks of the 'bleffed Mafs.' Notwithftanding all this, Bygod—apparently then a 'Six Articles' man—could write to good purpofe on his grievance.

But me thynketh I here you whysper that ye be no murtherers / theues / pykers / sacrylegans / nor yet none of all this geare / No ar nat? Well / than I se well we must haue more to do with you. For as moche as ye denye the cryme layde vnto your charge. You shall vnderstande that good and vertuouse men before our dayes / whiche loued the wyll of god / whiche loued his holy pleasure / whiche regarded his commaundement / whose medytatyons and studye both day and nighte was / to set forth his glorie / to auaunce his blessed worde / and to mayteine the ministers of the same / dyd (no dout of it) with the consent of higher powers of kynges and of princes / and of their most honourable counsels / folowynge (in this behalfe) the olde lawe / for the most easyest waye and spedyest prouisyon / appoynt / assygne and ordeyne (for the same ministers to be mayteyned) decymations or tythes / wyllynge and myndynge by this good prouisyon / that within euery congregation or parysshe / the minister of goddes worde there / shulde be sure at all tymes of a lyuynge raysed and gathered of these sayde decymations / and therein to haue added a certayne name / callynge it a benefyce / personage or vycarage / and lyke wyse turnynge the name of a minister or curate / to the name of a persone or vycare. Furthermore orderynge that one man shall haue authoritie / as patrone / to name this parsone / and so to giue this same benefyce : albe[i]t / peraduenture that other in the same paryshe gyue as moche to the annuall lyuynge of the parsone as the patrone doth. Besydes this / they ordeyned him a mantion to dwel in among them / to th[e]entente that for his dilygente administration / he shulde haue euery thinge necessarye for him within his owne gouernance : yea / and haue it brought euen home vnto him / to dyspose at his pleasure / as it shall be most expedyent and necessary for him / that the more quyetly he mighte studye and apply him selfe to minister vnto them the pure worde of god / and to be euer redy at hande to enstructe them of all thinges necessarye for ye helth of their soules / and to be their trewe watchman and shepherde to take them from the rauysshynge wolfe / and lyke a good trew herdesman / a pastoure to go afore them in spirytuall and vertuouse conuersation : and euer whan they be scabbed to anoynte them gentely with the softe and swete salue of goddes worde / all rancoure and stryfe layde a parte. Nowe my maisters impropriated or improper maisters howe saye ye by youre fathers / haue nat you with your crafty collusyon / almooste throughe Englande / dystroyed these holy and godly prouysons / made for the mayntenance of goddes holy word / and for th[e]administratyon of this most blessed sacramentes / for the helth / welth / and saluatyon of mans soule / for the vpholdynge of the trewe and catholyque fayth / for the supportacyon of vertue / and dystruction of vyce. Haue nat you (I saye) by the glykynge and gleynyng / snatchynge and scratchinge / tatchynge and patchynge / serapinge and rakynge togyther of almost all the fatte benefyces within this realme and impropriatynge them vnto youre selues / distroyed this most godlye and holy prouision / bereyned the peple of ye worde of god / of ye trew knowlege of ye blessed sacramentes / of their trew beleue and faith in god the father / and the blode of Iesu Christ. For howe can the people haue any faith in god withoute preachinge? Howe shulde they haue any preachynge whan ye haue robbed them of their ministers? How shulde the ministers serue them whan ye haue robbed them of theire lyuynge? If the peple haue no faith how can they haue charyte? If they haue no charytie / what merueyle is it / if they ronne hedlonge and be caryed from one vyce to another / from one mischefe to another? Be nat ye th[e] occasion of all this? Who is elles I praye you? Haue nat ye the impropriations? Be the impropriacyons any thinge els sauynge benefyces as parsonages / and such lyke? Do we not say such an abbot is parsone here / suche a priour is parsone here? yea / suche a prioresse is parsone here?

After dealing with the objection 'We haue teachinge inough / and that there is neuer the lesse preachynge for you;' Bygod thus goes on.

But nowe ye wyll obiecte that no ordynaunce of god is broken / hindered / or prohibyted on your behalfe in this mater. For thoughe the benefyce be impropriate to a monster / I wolde saye to a monasterye / yet th[e]abbot or prioure appoynteth a monke or chanon to be the minister / and to preche the worde of god to the parysshe / who shall tarye and abyde amonge his parysshoners / and haue oute of the same benefyce a suffycyente lyuynge / and the reste thereof to come home to th[e]abbot and his bretherne: and this is no breakynge of goddes ordynaunce / but rather a turnynge of it to a better vse. Wherevnto I answere / that where any such vicare or minyster is instytuted of his abbot or prioure / and trewly laboureth in th[e]administration of goddes worde / it is nat onely well done to gyue him a suffycyent lyuynge out of the same benefyce / but also he were wel worthy to haue it eueryywhitte / and as for the rest that haboundeth / let him kepe hospytalyte / as Paule commaundeth / or of necessytie wylleth him to do / and I saye / there shall but lytell remayne to sende home to th[e]abbot / and if he do nat kepe hospytdlyte of the rest / then is he a thefe and th[e]abbot another / for the rest is the poore indygentes. But howe faythfull and dilygent suche men be so instytuted by abbotes and priours to preache the worde of god / and howe sore they be therwith charged by their heedes. I thynke though I wolde cloke it / yet th[e]effecte wyl nat suffre it. Yet / I beleue rather that they ben the stronge persecutors of goddes worde / rather than the furtherers therof. . . .

But nowe these men beynge neuer without excuses / may peraduenture thinke this to be a good answere for me. We praye for the soules of them that haue improperated such benefyces vnto vs / and synge masse and diryge for them / and set vp tapers for them to burne both daye and night. Wherevnto fyrst I say / that if a man demaunded of you an accompte to be gyuen of youre so doynge / askynge you who taught you to apply ye blessed masse that waye / with the psalmes and lessons in the diryge conteyned / and desyred you to shew scripture for it. I thynke peraduenture that ye might come short home of a wyse answere / which if ye can make / I thinke ther is no man but he wyl be wel content ther with. . . .

Some men that fauoure these newe founde sectes / wyll peraduenture say: Well / yet it is better these monkes / chanons / and suche lyke haue the impropriatyons (whiche though they preche nat / yet they kepe some hospitalyte) rather than the seculer priestes shulde haue them / as they haue had before / which kepe no hospitalytie nor preche nother. To this it is easy to answere: That it is not mete that any man what soeuer he be / shuld receyue the benefyte or frute of a precher / onles he do his duty therfore. . . .

Is it nat great pitye to se a man to haue thre or foure benefyces: yea peraduenture halfe a score or a dosyn / which he neuer cometh at / but setteth in euery one of them a syr[1] Iohn lacke laten / that can scarce rede his porteus / orels suche a rauenynge wolfe as canne do nothynge but denoure the sely shepe with his false doctryne / and sucke their substaunce from them. Lorde / if it be thy pleasure / ones haue mercye vpon vs / and gyue grace that we may haue some remedye founde for thys myschiefe / bothe of impropriatyons / and also of them that minister not the worde of god faythfully vpon their benefyces: as they ought to do: for I haue knowen suche / that whan they hauen rydden by a benefyce wherof they haue ben persone / they coulde natte tell that it was their benefyce. This is a wonderfull blyndnesse.

We have not space here to illustrate the great *fiasco* of the Suppression of the Monasteries, the decay of the Universities, the uprising of the lower classes against the Nobility and Gentry, the utter destitution of the poor, the pluralities of benefices, the general covetousness, and the other crying abuses denounced in these Sermons. Most of the complaints of that time have been ably collected by Mr. F. J. Furnivall, in his *Ballads from MSS.* Vol. I. Ed. 1868, to which we must refer our readers.

[1] The customary title of respect at this time for priests, as Esquire is now for the laity.

The best setting we can put to these discourses are the following brief extracts from Stowe, of the commotions of the two years 1549 and 1550—

1549. MAY. By meanes of a proclamation for inclosures, the commons of Somersetshire and Lincolnshire made a commotion, and brake vp certain parks of Sir *W. Herberts*, and Lord *Sturtons*, but sir *W. Herbert* slewe and executed many of those rebels.

JULY. The commons of Essex and Kent, Suffolk and Norfolk, rose against inclosures, and pulled down diuers parks and houses.

Also the commons of Cornewall and Deuonshire rose against the nobles and gentlemen, and required not onely that the inclosures might bee disparked, but also to haue their old religion, and act of sixe articles restored: these besieged the citie of Excester, which was valiantlie defended. Against these rebels was sent *John* L[ord]. *Russell* Lord priuy seale, with a number of souldiers, who entered the city of Excester the 5 of AUGUST, where they slew and took prisoners of the rebels more than 4000, and after hanged diuers of them in the towne and country about. The L[ord]. *Gray* was also sent with a number of strangers, Almaine and Germaine horsemen, who in diuers conflicts slewe manie people, and spoiled the country.

31 JULY. *William*, L[ord]. marques of Northampton, entred the city of Norwich, and on the next morning, the rebels also entred the towne, burned parte thereof, put the L[ord] marques to flight, and slew the L[ord] Sheffield.

22 JULY In this meane time diuers persons were apprehended as aiders of of the foresaid rebels or reporters of their doinges, of the which one was the Bailife of Romford in Essex, hanged within Aldgate, and an other of Kent, at the bridge foot toward Southwark, both on *Mary Magdalens* day by martiall law.

8 AUG. The French Ambassador did in name of his maister the F[rench] King, made defiance vnto the King of England, and so the war began.

In the beginning of AUGUST the French [suddenly attempted Guernsey and Jersey, but were repulsed with the loss of a thousand men.]

The 16 of AUG., a man was hanged without Bishopsgate of London, and one other without Aldgate, the third at Totenham, the fourth at Waltham, and so forth in diuers other places, all by martiall law.

The rebels in Norfolke and Suffolke encamped themselues at mount Surrey, in a wood called S. *Nicholas* wood, neere vnto Norwich, against whom sir *Iohn Dudley* earle of Warwike went with an army, where bothe he and a great number of gentlemen meeting with the rebels were in such daunger, as they had thought all to haue died in that place, but God that confoundeth the purpose of all rebels, brought it so to passe, that aswel there as in all other places, they were partly by power constrained, partly by promise of their pardon, perswaded to submit themselues to their prince: the earle of Warwike entred the city of Norwich the 27 of AUGUST, when he had slaine aboue 5000. of the rebels, and taken their chief captaine *Robert Ket* of Windham [Wymondham] tanner, which might dispend in lands fifty pound [=£750 now] by yeere, and was worth in moueables aboue a thousand markes, [£666—say £10,000 now]. When he had put to execution diuers of the rebells in diuers places about Norwich, he returned.

The 28 of AUG. tidings was brought to K[ing] *Edward* and the lord protector, that the French men had taken Blacknes, Hamiltew and Newhauen by Boleine, and had slaine all the Englishmen, and taken the kings ordinance and victuals.

About this time also, a commotion began at Semer in the north-riding of Yorke-shire, and continued in the east-riding, and there ended; the principall raysers whereof were *William Ombler* of east Hesterton yeomen, *Thomas Dale* parish clearke off Semer, and *Stevenson* of Semer: being preuented by the lord president from rising at Wintringham, they drew to a place at Semer by the sea coast, and there by night rode to the beacon at Staxton, and set it on fire, and so gathered a rude route; then they went to master

Whites house, and tooke him, and *Clopton* his wiues brother, *Sauage* a merchant of Yorke, and *Bery* seruant to sir *Walter Mildmay*, which foure they murthered a mile from Semer and there lefte them naked: their number increased to 3000.

On 21 AUG. the kings pardon was offered, which *Ombler* and other refused, who were shortly after taken, and brought to York, where *Thomas Dale* and other were executed the 21 of SEPTEMBER.

[6-14 Oct. The *coup d'état* of the Earl of Warwick aided by some of the counsell and the Londoners; ending in the deposition of the Duke of Somerset as Lord Protector.]

14 OCT. The Duke of Somerset brought from Windsor and put in the Tower.

29 Nov. *Robert Ket* was hanged in chaines on the top of Norwich castle, and *William Ket* likewise hanged on the top of Windham [Wymondham] steeple.

NOV.-DEC. The Scots tooke Burticrage in Scotland, and other holds then possessed by Englishmen, where the Scots slue man, woman, and childe, except Sir *John Lutterell* the captaine, whome they took prisoner.

1550. 27 JAN. *Humfrey Arundell* esquire, *Thomas Holmes, Winslowe* and *Bery*, captaines of the rebels in Deuonshire, were hanged and quartered at Tyborne.

2 FEB. Candlemas Day; also Septuagesima Sunday.
  (1) 𝕿homas 𝕷eber's 𝕾ermon in the 𝕾hrouds of 𝕾t. 𝕻aul's.
  (2) The Duke of Somerset makes his Submission in the Tower.
  (3) The Lords of the Counsell are changed, Warwick's faction coming into office

6 FEB. The Duke of Somerset delivered out of the Tower.

10 FEB. One *Bel* a Suffolke man, was hanged and quartered at Tyborne, for mouing a new rebellion in Suffolk and Essex.

16 MAR. Mid-Lent Sunday. 𝕿homas 𝕷eber's 𝕾ermon before the 𝕶ing.

31 MAR. Peace proclaimed between England and France.

8 APR. The Duke of Somerset came to court at Grenewich and was sworn of the Privy Counsell.

2 MAY. Joan of Kent was brent in Smithfield for heresie.

14 MAY. *Ric. Lion, Goddard Gorran*, and *Ric. Ireland* were executed for attempting a newe rebellion in Kent.

Trinity Terme (11 JUNE—2 JULY) was adiorned till Michaelmas, for that the gentlemen should keepe the commons from commotion.

11 JUNE. At night the high Altar in Paules Church was pulled down, and a Table set where the altar stoode, with a Vayle drawne beneath the Steppes, and on the Sundaie next [15 June] a Communion was sung at the same Table, and shortly after all the altars in London were taken downe, and Tables placed in their room.

14 DEC. Second Sunday after Advent. 𝕿homas 𝕷eber's 𝕾ermon at 𝕻auls 𝕮ross.

All thefe evils were by many charged **to the Change of** Faith. Hence **the energy** of the Preachers to rebut the flander, by expofing their **true and many** caufes. The political economy of that time—faulty as we **now fee** it **to** be—was bafed upon the principle of difinterefted fervice for the common good. Men were urged not by their felf-interefl, but by the dread and love of **God**, to do their duty to each other and the State. Among all thofe preachers none more bravely **fought the battle** of the loyal **poor**; none more vigoroufly, **even to** perfonal hazard and **danger**, expofed the cruelty, covetoufnefs, and craft of the **rich and the** clergy than Thomas Lever, the Cambridge **Fellow, and the** Boanerges of the Reformation.

BIBLIOGRAPHY.

Lever's printed Sermons were very popular when first published. No less than five editions of the three discourses were published in 1550: viz., two of the Sermon in the Shrouds, two of that before the King, and one of that at Paul's Cross.

Twenty-two years later, they were revised by Lever, and published together, under a fresh title. Since then, they have not been printed until the present edition.

One reason for this has been the excessive scarcity of copies of all these first Editions. They were soon thumbed out of existence, like the Author's *Right way from the daunger of sinne, &c.* printed at Geneva in 1556, which had all but perished by 1571: and after his death they were virtually lost in oblivion.

It may be useful therefore to quote their titles and colophons: and to distinguish the present possessors of copies, so far as I know.

ISSUES IN THE AUTHOR'S LIFETIME.

I.—As separate publications.

Sermon in the Shrouds of St. Paul's.

Septuagesima Sunday, 2 Feb. 1550.

∴ *A dated and an undated edition.*

1. TITLE. A fruitfull Sermon made in Poules churche at London in the Shroudes, the seconde daye of Febuari by Thomas Leuer. Anno M. D. and fiftie.
   COL. ☙ Imprinted at London by Iohn Daie, dwelling ouer Aldersgate, and William Seres, dwelling in Peter Colledge (∴) *Cum priuilegio ad imprimendum solum.* H. PYNE.

2. 1550. APR. 9. TITLE: as at *p.* 19.
   COL. as at *p.* 52. H. PYNE (wants title); BODLEIAN.

Sermon before King Edward VI.

Mid-Lent Sunday, 16 March 1550.

∴ *A dated and an undated edition.*

3. 1550. APR. 9. TITLE, as at *p.* 53.
   COL.: as at *p.* 90. H. PYNE (T. Baker's copy): BODLEIAN.

4. 1550. TITLE. A Sermon preached the thyrd Sondaye in Lente before the Kynges Maiestie, and his honorable Counsell, by Thomas Leauer. Anno Domini. M.ccccc.l. ∴
   COL. ☙ Impryted at London by Ihon Day dwellinge ouer Aldersgate, beneth saint Martyns. And are to be sold at his shop by the litle conduit in Chepesyde at the sygne of the Resurrection. *Cum priuilegio ad imprimendum solum.* Per septennium. H. PYNE.

There is a misprint in most of the title-pages. These copies have 'the thyrd Sonday in Lent,' but the text is the same. Lever took his text from 'the gospell of this day, written in the. vi. of Iohan,' see *p.* 58. This fixes the particular Sunday with absolute certainty, for in Edward VI.'s first Prayer-Book, which came into use on the Feast of Pentecost (9 June) 1549, as in our present version of it, the Miracle of Feeding the Five Thousand is the Gospell for the fourth Sunday in Lent, which fell in 1550, on 16th of March. Lever also puts the true date in the revised edition of 1572. See below.

∴ There is no authority for the above order, as regards the undated impressions. It will be seen that **1, 2** and **3** are printed by Day and Seres jointly: and **4** by Day alone.

Sermon at Paul's Cross.

Second Sunday in Advent, 14 December 1550.

5. 1550. TITLE, as at *p*. 91.
COL., as at *p*. 144. BODLEIAN.

II.—*Collected together.*

6. 1572. FIRST TITLE. ¶ Three fruitfull Sermons, made by Thomas Leuer. Anno domini. **1550.** ¶ And now newlie perused by the aucthour. London. *Imprinted by I. Kyngston, for Henry Kirckham,* 1572.

TITLE TO SECOND SERMON. A Sermon preached the iiii. Sondaie in Lente, before the kynges Maiestie and his honorable Counsaile, by Thomas Leuer. Anno Domini. 1550.

TITLE TO THIRD SERMON. A Sermon preached at Paules **crosse** the xiiii. daie of December, by Thomas Leuer Anno **Domini** 1550.

COL., as at *p*. 144.
LAMBETH LIBRARY: ST. JOHN'S **COLLEGE, CAMBRIDGE,** (See Rev. C. H. Hartshorne's *Book Rarities of the University of Cambridge, p.* 443. Ed. 1829.)

∴ The principal variations of this edition are shown within [ ], words omitted in it that are in the earlier impressions are asterisked *. One characteristic of the revision is the prefix of *Saint* to the Apostles' names.

ISSUES SINCE THE AUTHOR'S DEATH.

I.—*Collected together.*

1870. Nov. 15. 8vo. *English **Reprints*** : see title at *p.* 1.

∴ Cordial thanks are due to Mr Pyne, (who first pointed out to me the importance of these Sermons,) for the loan,—out of his splendid collection of English Books, before 1600 A.D.,—of his copies of them; and to the Hon. Librarian of **Lambeth** Library, for permission to collate the 1572 edition.

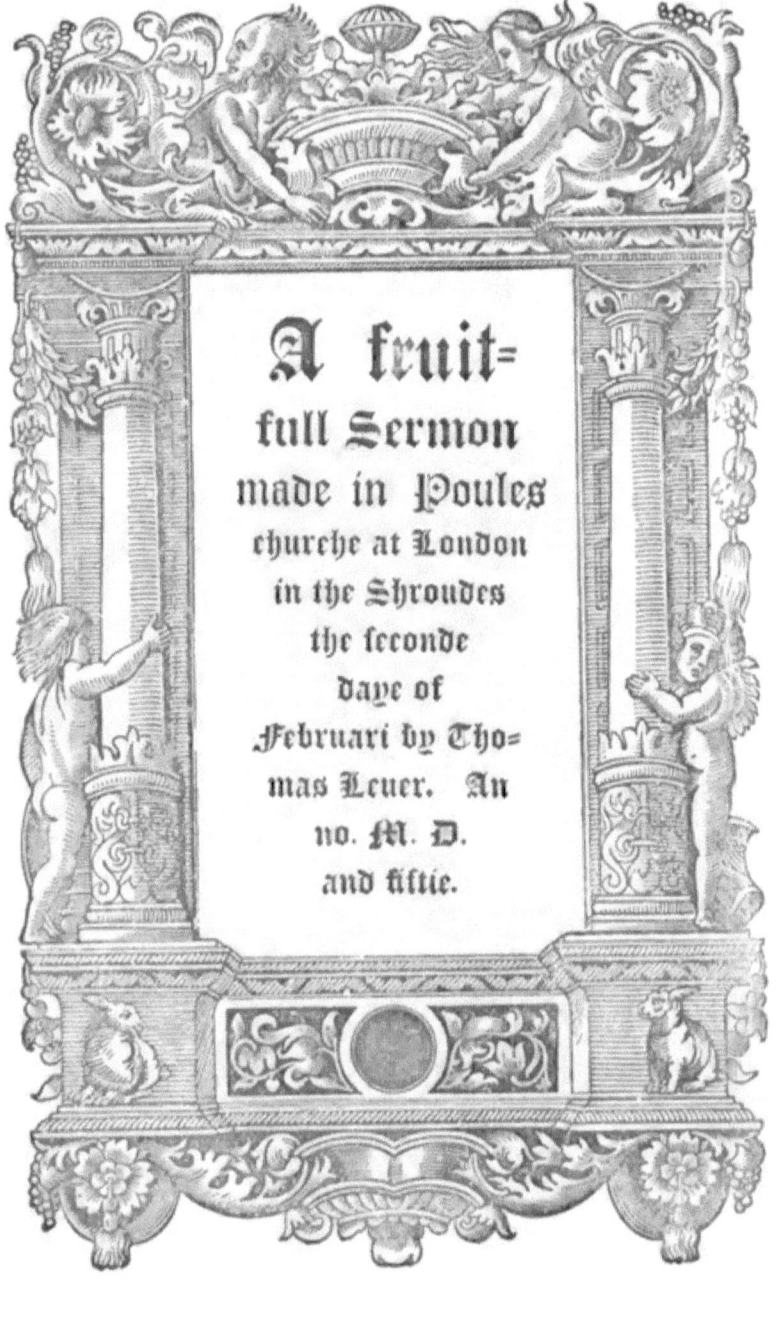

A fruit-
full Sermon
made in Poules
churche at London
in the Shroudes
the seconde
daye of
Februari by Tho-
mas Leuer. An
no. M. D.
and fiftie.

God be merciful unto vs.
Good Chriften people Chrifte Iefu the fonne of God, the wyfedome of the father, the fauiour of the worlde, whyche hath redemed vs with his precious bloud moft pitifully lamentyng our myferies, and earneftlye threateninge our wylfull blyndnes, cryeth oute by the voyce of the wyfe king Salomon, faying: *Quia uocaui, et renuiftis. et cete. Proue. i.*[2] Becaufe I haue called (fayeth the wyfedome of God) and ye haue denyed, I haue ftretched forth my hand, and there was none that woulde beholde: yea ye haue difpifed all my councels, and [al] my rebukes haue ye not regarded, I therfore fhall laugh at your deftruccion, and I fhal mocke, when it is come vpon you whiche ye haue feared. Affuredlye good people, God, *Qui mortem non fecit, nec lætatur in perdicione uirorum*,[3] God whiche (as the boke of wifedome fayth) made not death, ne dothe not delyghte in the perdicion of manne, cannot be of fuche affeccion, as to delyghte in laughynge or mockyng our miferies: but euen as that man whyche dothe delyghte to laughe at other mens griefes, is a man moft farre of from lamentynge and pytyinge them to do them good: fo is God fo fore offended and dyfpleafed wyth them that difpyfe hys counfelles, threatning or promifes, while they might haue mercy, that he wyll as it were rather of mockyng, laughe and fkorne, then of pitye lamente and help their miferable wretched griefes, when as they would haue conforte. Se therfore howe mercyfully God hath called by the fayinges and wrytinges of Moyfes, the Prophetes, and the Apoftles, and howe fewe haue

---

[1] in the Shroudes in London. 1572.   [2] Prov. *i*. 24.
[3] Wis. of Solomon, *i*. 13.

harkened to beleue. Se how wonderfully God hath ftretched forth hys hande, in creatynge heauen and earthe, and all thynges in them conteyned, to the vfe, commoditie, and conforte to man: and how fewe do dayly behold thefe creatures, to be thankefull vnto the creatoure. Se howe muche good counfell and earnefte threatenynge God hath geuen of late vnto Englande, by fettynge forth of his worde in the englyfhe tonge, caufynge it to be read dayly in ye churches, to be preached purely in the pulpites, and to be rehearfed euery where in communicacion, and how many continuing, yea increafynge their wycked lyues, regarde not gods worde, dyfpife his threateninges, defyre not his mercye, feare not his vengeance.

Wythoute doute good people verye manye haue deferued the vengeaunce of God, and yet by repentaunce founde plentye of mercye: but neuer none that euer refufed the mercye of God hath efcaped the vengeaunce of God in the time of hys wrathe, and furye.

Yea but what mercyes of God haue we refufed, or what threatenynge of God haue we here in England not regarded: whyche haue forfaken the Pope, abolyfhed idolatrye and fuperfticion, receyued goddes worde fo gladly, reformed all thynges accordinglye therto fo fpedily, and haue all thinges moft nere the order of the primitiue churche vniuerfallye? Alas good brethren, as trulye as al is not golde that glyftereth, fo is it not vertue and honefty, but very vice and hipocrifie, wherof England at this day dothe mofte glorye. Wherfore the worde is playne, and the fayinges be terryble, by the whyche at thys tyme God threateneth to punyfhe, to plage, and to deftroy England. It is a wonderous playne worde to faye that Englande fhall be deftroyed: and vpon thys worde enfuinge, it fhould be a terrible fight to fe hundred thoufandes of Scottes, Frenche menne, Papifts, and Turkes, entryng in on euery fyde, to murther, fpoyle, and to deftroye. Thys playne worde of a credyble perfon fpoken, wyth thys terrible feyng afore our eyes in fight [our iyes in prefence,] wold make oure corage to fall, and oure hertes to ryue in peces, for wofull forowe, feare, and heauineſſe.

Alas England, God, whom thou mayeſt beleue for his truthe, hathe fayd playnly thou ſhalt be deſtroyed, and all thyne ennemyes, bothe Scots, Frenchmen, Papiſtes, and Turkes, I **do not** meane the men in whome is ſome mercye, but the moſt cruell vices **of** theſe thy enemyes beynge wythout all pitie, as the couetouſenes of Scotland, the pryde of Fraunce, the hipocryſy of Rome, and the Idolatrye of the Turkes. A hundred thouſande of **theſe** enemies are landed **at** thy hauens, haue entred thy **fortes, and do** procede to ſpoyle, murther, and vtterly deſtroy: and yet for all this thou wretched Englande beleueſt not gods worde, regardeſt not hys threatninge, calleſt not for mercye, ne feareſte not gods vengeaunce. Wherfore God beinge true of hys word, and righteous in hys dedes, thou Englande whyche wylt haue no mercye, ſhalt haue vengeaunce, whyche wylte not be ſaued, ſhalte be deſtroyed. For God hath ſpoken, and it is wrytten.

Omne regnum in ſeduiſum deſolabitur.[1] Euerye kyngdome that is deuyded in it ſelfe, ſhall be deſolate, and deſtroyed. And Salomon ſayeth: Becauſe they haue hated learnyng and not receiued the feare of God, deſtruccion commeth ſodaynlye: Yea trulye, and bryngeth Idolaters vnto miſery, and proude men vnto ſhame. Ye all here fele, ſee, knowe, and haue experience, howe that this Realme is deuyded in it ſelfe by opynyons in relygyon, **by** rebellious ſedicion, yea and by couetouſe ambicion, euerye manne pullynge and halynge towardes them ſelues, one from another.

It is not onelye diuyded, but alſo rente, torne, and plucked cleane in pieces. Yea and euerye couetouſe manne is an Idolater, ſettynge that mynd and loue vpon ryches, whyche oughte to be geuen vnto God onely.

Euery couetouſe man hateth learnynge, and receyueth not the feare of God, for the gredy deſire that he hathe to the lucre of thys worlde. Euerye couetouſe man is proude, thynkynge hymſelfe more worthy a

---

[1] Matt. xii. 25.

pounde, then a nother man a penye, more fitte to haue
chaunge of fylkes and veluettes, then other to haue
bare frife cloth, and more conueniente for hym to haue
aboundaunce of diuerfe dilicates for hys daintye toth,
then for other to haue plenty of biefes and muttons for
theyr hongry bellyes: and finnally that he is more
worthye to haue gorgeoufe houfes to take his pleafure
in, in bankettynge, then laborynge men to haue poore
cotages to take reft in, in flepynge. Vndoubtedlye
God wyll make all thofe to fall wyth fhame, which fet
them felues vp in pryde fo hygh, that they can not fee
other men to be chyldren of the fame heauenlye father,
heires of the fame kingdome, and bought wyth the
fame pryce of Chriftes bloude, that they take them
felues to be. That realme, that realme that is full of
couetoufnes, is full of diuifion, is full of contempt of
goddes mercye, yea and fclaunder of hys worde, is full
of Idolatry and is full of pryde. Diuifion is a figne of
deftruccion, contemning of goddes mercye caufeth his
vengeaunce to come fodeynly: Idolatrye euer endeth
in mifery, and pryde neuer efcapeth fhame. Then if
you fele, knowe, and haue experyence, that Englande
by reafon of couetoufnes is full of diuifion, is full of
contempte of goddes mercye, is full of Idolatrye, is
full of pryde, Flatter not your felues in youre owne
phan[ta]fies, but beleue the word of God, whiche telleth
you truelye that Englande fhall be deftroyed fodainly,
miferably, and fhamefullye. The fame deftruccion
was tolde to the Sodomites, was tolde to the Niniuites: was deferued of the Sodomites, and was deferued of the Niniuites: but came vpon the Sodomites,
and was tourned from the Niniuytes. And why? For
becaufe the Sodomytes regarded not goddes threaten-
ynges and were plaged wyth gods vengeaunce, the
Niniuytes regarded goddes threatnynges, and efcaped
gods vengeaunce.

Now all you Englyfhe men at the reuerence of God,
for the tender mercyes of Iefu Chrift, for the reuerent
loue to youre moft gentle and gracious kynge, for the

fauegarde of your cuntry, and for tender pyty of your
owne wiues, your children, and your felues, caufe not
Englande to bee deftroyed wyth gods vengeaunce, as
was the Cytie of the Sodomites: but repent, lament and
amend your liues, as did the good Niniuites. For if ye
fpedely repent, and myferably [and pitifully] lamente, and
be afhamed of your vainglory, couetoufnes, and ambicion,
ye fhal caufe couetous, fedicious, proude, and vicious
Englande, fodenly, miferablye yea and fhamefully in the
fyghte and iudgement of the world, to vanyfh away.
And fo finne and abhominacion deftroyed by the repentaunce of man, this pleafaunte place of Englande,
and good people fhall be preferued and faued by thy
[the] mercy of God. For els if man wil not forfake his
fynne, God wyll not fpare to deftroye both the man
and hys place with his fynne.

Wherefore the Epyftle by the order nowe taken, appoynted for thys fourth Sunday after twelfe tyde, is a
leffon moft mete to teache you to knowe and lamente
youre greuous finnes of late committed, whyche as
yet be in fuche cafe, that man wythout
greate repentaunce cannot fone amende
them, nor god of hys ryghteoufnes
much longer fuffer them. It is
written in the beginning
of the.[x]iii. Chap. of
Paul to the Rom.
on this wyfe.

Verye foule be fubiecte vnto the hygher
powers, for there is no power but of God.
Thofe powers whych be, are ordeyned of
God. Wherefore he that refyfteth power,
refyfteth the ordinaunce of God, but they
whyche doo refifte, fhall receyue to themfelues iudgement. For Rulers are not to be feared for good
doinges, but for euil. Wouldeft thou not feare the
power? do that whiche is good, and thou fhalt haue

praife of it. But if thou do euyil, feare: for he beareth not the fweard wythout a caufe, for he is the **minifter of God to** auenge in wrath, hym that doeth euyl.

Wherefore ye muft nedes be fubiecte, not only for wrathe, but alfo for confcience fake. For thys do ye paye tribute: For they **are** the minifters of God attendyng to thys fame thynge. Geue therefore vnto **euery one** dueties: tribute to whome trybute is due, cuftome to whome cuftum **is** due, feare to whom feare is due, honoure to whom honoure is due.

Thus **haue** ye heard howe that euery one oughte to be vnder obedience, and geue vnto other that whych is due. Howbeit experience declareth howe that here in Englande pore men haue been rebels, and ryche men haue not done **their duetie.** Bothe haue done euyll to **prouoke** goddes vengeance, **neyther** doth repente to procure gods mercye.

Nowe for the better vnderftandyng of thys matter, here in thys texte, fyrft is to be noted, how that *Anima*, the foule, for as muche as it is the chiefe parte of man, is taken for the whole man: as we in oure englyfhe **tonge,** take the bodye beynge the worfe part for **the whole. As if I** faye, euery bodye here, **I meane euerye man or** woman here. **So in** the fourthe of **Leuiti.** *Anima quæ peccauerit, ipfa morietur.*[1] The foule that finneth, it fhall dye: meanyng the **man** or woman **that fynneth.** And euen fo here Paule **by the** Ebrue phrafe and maner of fpeche, commaundeth **euery foule, whych is by the englifhe** phrafe euery bodye, **that is to** faye, euerye **perfon, man,** woman, **and** child to be fubiect. As **thou art in** dede, fo acknowledge thy felfe in thine **own mynde** *Hypotaffeftho* [ὑποτασσέσθαι], yat is to faye, fet **or** placed vnder the hygher powers, yea and that by God. For as there is no power of authorithy but of god, fo is there none put in fubieccion vnder theym but by **God.** Thofe powers whiche be are ordeyned of God. **As** is the power of the father euer hys chyldren of the hufband ouer hys wyfe, of the mafter ouer hys feruauntes, and of the kynge ouer hys

---

1 Ezek. *xviii.* 4.

lande and fubiectes: wyth all kynde of magiftrates in their offices ouer their charge.

Nowe to proue that thefe bee the ordinaunces of God, we haue **by** goddes word bothe in the olde teftamente and in the newe, their names rehearfed, theyr offices dyfcribed, and theyr duties [duetie] commaunded. Yet that* notwythftandynge fome there be that labour by wreftynge of the fcripture to pulle them felues from vnder due obedience: faiynge that it appeareth in the actes of the Apoftles **how** that they hadde all thynges commen, and therfore **none** more goodes **or** ryches, power or aucthoritie, then other, but all alyke.

Truthe it is, that the Apoftles had all thynges comen, yea **and that** chriften men, in that they are chriften men rather then couetous men, haue all thynges comen, euen vnto thys day. How be it ther can be nothyng more contrarye or further difagreyng from that phantaftical commenneffe, or **rather** from that diuelyfhe diforder, and vnrighteoufe robry [robberie], where as Idle lubbers myghte lyue of honefte mennes **laboures**, then to haue all thynges comen as the Apoftles hadde, **as** chriften men haue, and as I do meane. **And thys** is theyr vfage, and my meanynge: that ryche menne fhoulde kepe to theym felues no more then they nede, and geue vnto the poore fo muche as they nede. For fo Paule wryteth to the Corinthes. I meane not (faythe Paull, fpeakynge **to the ryche) to** haue other fo eafed, that you therby fhoulde be brought **in** trouble of nede, but after an indif[fe]renc[i]e, that at this tyme **your** abundaunce, myght helpe their nede.

And fo dyd the Apoftles take order as appeareth in **the** fourth of the actes. *Quotquot habebant agros et poffeffiones. etc.*[1] As many **as** hadde landes and poffeffions dyd **fell** them, and broughte the prices vnto the feete of the Apoftles, and diuifion **was** made vnto euerye **one** accordinge vnto euerye mannes neede. So they whyche myght fpare dydde frelye geue, and they whiche hadde nede dyd thankefully receyue.

For fo is it [it is] mete, that chriften mens goodes fhuld

---

[1] **Acts** *iv.* 34.

be comen vnto euery mans nede, and priuate to no mans
lufte. And thofe [thefe] comune goodes to bee difpofed
by liberall geuers, and not fpoyled by gredy catchers.
So that euery man may haue accordyng to hys nede
fufficient, and not accordynge to hys fpoyle fo muche
as he can catche, no nor accordyng to the value of the
thyng, euerye man a penye, a grote, or a fhyllyng.
For they that Imagyne, couet, or wyfhe to haue all
thynges comune, in fuche forte that euerye man myght
take what hym lufte, wolde haue all thynges comen
and open vnto euerye mans lufte, and nothynge referued or kept for any mans nede. And they that
wolde haue like quantitie of euery thyng to be geuen
to euerye man, entendyng therby to make all alyke,
do vtterly deftroy the congregacyon, the mifticall bodye
of Chryft, wheras there muft nedes be dyuers members in
diuerfe places, hauynge diuerfe duetyes. For as [fainct]
Paul fayth : yf all the bodye be an eye, where is then
hearyng? or yf all be an eare, where is then fmellyng?
meanyng therby, that yf all be of one forte, eftate,
and roume in the comen wealth, how can then dyuerfe
duetyes of diuerfe neceffarye offices be done?

So that the fre herte, and liberall gyfte of the ryche,
muft make all that he may fpare, comen to releue the
nede of the poore : yea yf there be great neceffitye, he
muft fell both landes and goodes, to maynteyne charitie:
And thus to haue all thinges comen, doth derogate or
take away nothynge from the authoritye of rulers.
But to wyll to haue all thynges comen, in fuche forte
that idle lubbers (as I fayde) myghte take and wafte
the geines of laborers wythout reftraint of authoritie,
or to haue lyke quantitye of euerye thynge to be geuen
to euery man, is vnder a pretence to mende al, purpofely to marre all. For thofe fame men pretendinge to
hate [haue] couetoufnes, wold be as rych as the rycheft :
and fayinge that they hate pryde, wold be as hyghly
taken as the beft, and femynge to abhorre enuye, can
not be content[ed] to fe any other rycher or better then
they them felues be. Now I heare fome faye that

thys errour is the fruyte of the fcripture in englyfhe.
No, neyther thys, nor no other erroure commeth becaufe the fcripture is fet forth in the englyfhe tonge, but
becaufe the rude people lackynge the counfell of learned
menne to teache theim the trewe meanynge when they
reade it, or heare it, mufte nedes folowe theyr owne
Imaginacion in takynge of it. And the chiefeft caufe
that maketh them to imagine thys abhominable errour,
that there fhuld **be** no ryche menne nor rulers, cum-
meth becaufe fome ryche men and rulers (marke that I
faye fome, for all bee not fuche) but I faye fome ryche
men, and rulers by the abufe of their ryches and aucthoritye, dothe more harme then good vnto the comen
wealth, and more griefe then confort vnto the people.
For nowe a dayes ryche menne and rulers do catche,
purcheffe, and procure vnto them felues great commodities from many men, and do fewe and fmall pleafures vnto any men.

As for example of ryche men, loke at the **mer-**
chauntes of London, and ye fhall fe, when as by their
honeft vocacion, and trade of marchandife god hath
endowed them with great abundaunce of ryches, then
can they not be content with the profperous welth
of that vocacion to fatiffye theym felues, and to helpe
other, but their riches mufte abrode in the countrey
to bie fermes out of the handes of worfhypfull gentlemen, honefte yeomen, and pore laborynge hufbandes.
Yea nowe alfo **to** bye perfonages, and benefices, where
as they do not onelye bye landes and goodes, but alfo
lyues and foules of men, from God and the comen
wealth, vnto the deuyll and theim felues. A myf-
cheuoufe marte of merchandrie is this, and yet nowe fo
comenly vfed, that therby fhepeheardes be turned to
theues, dogges into wolues, and the poore flocke of
Chrift, redemed wyth his precious bloud, mofte miferablye pylled, and fpoyled, yea cruelly deuoured. Be
thou marchaunt of the citye, or be thou gentleman in
the contrey, be thou lawer, be you courtear, or what
maner of man foeuer thou be, that can not, **yea** yf

thou be mafter doctor of diuinitie, that wyl not do thy
duety, it is not lawfull for the to haue perfonage,
benefice, or any fuche liuyng, excepte thou do fede the
flocke fpiritually wyth goddes worde, and bodelye wyth
honefte hofpitalitye. I wyll touch diuerfe kyndes **of**
ryche men and rulers, that **ye maye fe what harme**
fome of theim do wyth theyr ryches and authoritye.
And efpeciallye I wyll begynne **wyth theym** that be
beft learned, for they feme belyke to do mofte good
wyth ryches and authoritie vnto theim committed. If
I therefore beynge a yonge fimple fcholer myghte be
fo bolde, **I wolde** afke an auncient, wyfe, **and** well
learned doctor of diuinitie, whych cometh not at **hys**
benefice, **whether** he were bounde to fede hys flocke
in teachynge **of** goddes worde, **and kepyng** hofpitalitie
or no? He wold anfwere and **faye:** fyr my curate
fupplieth my roume in teachynge, **and** my farmer in
kepynge **of houfe. Yea but** mafter doctor by **your**
leaue, both thefe more for your vauntage then for **the**
paryfhe conforte: and therfore the mo fuche feruauntes
that ye kepe there, the more harme is it for your
paryfhe, and the more fynne and fhame for you. **Ye**
may thynke that I am fumwhat faucye to laye fynne
and fhame to a doctor **of** diuinitie in thys folemne
audience, for fome of theim vfe to excufe the matter,
and faye: Thofe whych I leaue in myne abfence do
farre better then I fhoulde do, yf I taryed there my
felfe.

Nowe good mafter doctor ye faye the verye truthe,
and therfore be **they** more worthye to haue the benefice then you **your felfe,** and yet neyther of you bothe
fufficient mete, or able: they for lacke of habilitye, and
you for lacke of good wyll. Good wyll quod he?
Naye I wolde wyth all my harte, **but** I am called to
ferue the kynge **in other** places, **and** to take other
offices in the comen wealthe. Heare then what I
fhall aunfwere yet once agayne: There is lyuynges
and rewardes due and belongyng to theim that labour
in thofe offyces, and **fo** oughte you to be contente

wyth the lyuyng and reward of that office onelye, and take no more, the duetye of the whyche office by your labour and diligence ye can difcharge onlye, and do no more. And fo Paule wryteth vnto the Corrinth. fayinge: The Lord hathe ordeyned that they whyche preache the Gofpell, fhulde lyue vpon the Gofpell.[1] And vnto the T[h]effalonians. He that dothe not labour fhulde not eate.[2]

By thefe textes well fet together, you may conclude and learne, that there as you beftowe your labour, there maye ye take a lyuynge, and ther as ye beftowe no labour, there ought ye to take no liuyng. Well let vs procede further vnto other nowe, for I perceyue that **all that** which I haue fpoken againft them that take greate geynes of theyr benefices, and do lytle good to theyr benefice, maye feme to be fpoken agaynft the vniuerfityes, yea and againft the kynges mayeftye : whyche now by reafon of improperacions haue no lytle geynes of benefices, and yet beftowe no great laboure nor almes vpon the paryfhioners of thofe benefices. Surely, for as muche as I feare the vengeaunce of God more yf I fhoulde not fpeake the truthe, then the difpleafure of man yf he be offended in hearynge of the truth, trulye I wyll tell you. Seyng that improperacions beynge fo euyll that no man can alowe theym, be nowe fo employed vnto the vniuerfities, yea and vnto the yerelye reuenues of the kynges maieftye, that **fewe** dare fpeake agaynft them, ye maye fe that fome men, not onelye by the abufe of ryches and authoritie, but alfo by the abufe of wyfedom and pollicie do much harme, and fpecially thofe, by whofe meanes thys realme **is** nowe brought into fuch cafe that eyther learnyng in the vniuerfitie, and neceffarye reuenues belongynge to the mofte hygh authoritye is lyke to decaye, or elles improperacions to be mayntened, whyche bothe be fo deuyllyfhe and abhominable that yf eyther of them come to effecte, it wyll caufe the vengeaunce of God vtterly to deftroy this realme. Do not thynke that I meane

---
[1] 1 Cor. ix. 14. [2] 2 Thess. iii. 10.

any thyng agaynft that whyche the kynges mayeftye by acte of Parliament hathe done : no nor that I wyll couer in fcilence, or alowe by flatterie that whyche couetoufe officers (fome as I fuppofe nowe beyng prefente) contrarye to goddes lawes, the kynges honour, and the comen wealth vfe **to do.** For in fuppreffinge of Abbeyes, Cloyfters, Colleges, and Chauntries, the **entente of** the **kynges** maieftie that **dead is,** was, and of this our kynge now, is verye godlye, and the purpofe or els the pretence of other, wonderoufe goodlye: that therby fuche abundaunce of goodes as was **fuper-**fticioufly fpente vpon vayne ceremonies, or voluptuoufly vpon idle bellies, myght come to the kynges handes to beare hys great charges, neceffarilie beftowed in the comen wealthe, or partly vnto other mennes **handes,** for the better **releue** of the pore, the mayntenaunce **of** learning, **and the** fettinge forth of goddes **worde.** Howe be it couetoufe officers haue fo vfed thys matter, that euen thofe goodes whyche dyd ferue to the releue of the poore, the mayntenaunce of learnyng, and to confortable neceffary hofpitalitie in ye comen wealth, be now turned to maynteyne worldly, wycked couetoufe ambicion.

I tell you, at the **fyrfte the** intente was verie **godly,** the pretence wonderoufe goodly, but nowe **the vfe** or rather the abufe and myforder of thefe thynges is worldlye, **is** wycked, is deuilyfhe, is abhominable.

The kynge maye haue, and wolde to God he hadde in hys handes **to** beftowe better, all that was euell* mifpente vpon fuperfticious Ceremonies, and voluptuous Idle bellyes.

But you whych haue gotten thefe goodes into your **own*** handes, to turne them from euyll to worfe, and other goodes mo frome good vnto euyll, be ye fure it **is euen you** that haue offended God, begyled the kynge, robbed **the** ryche, fpoyled the pore, and brought a comen wealth into a comen miferye. It is euen you, that muft eyther be plaged with gods vengeaunce as

wer the Sodomytes, or amende by repentaunce as did
the Nineuites. Euen you it is that muſt eyther make
reſtitucion and amendes ſpedely, or elles fele the
vengeaunce of God greuouſly. Do not thynke that
by reſtitucion and amendes makyng I **meane** the
buyldynge agayne of abbeyes or cloyſters, no I do
not: For yf charitable almes, honeſte hoſpitalitie, **and**
neceſſary ſcholes, for the bryngynge **vp** of yougth had
ben indifferently maynteyned and not cleane taken
away in ſome places, I woulde not at this **time** haue
ſpoken of reſtitucion. **Howe** be it ſure I am, that if at*
the orderinge of theſe thynges there had been **in** the
officers **as much** godlines as there was couetouſnes,
ſuperſticious men had not bene put from their liuinges
to their penſions out of thoſe houſes, wher they myght
haue had ſchole maſters to haue taught them to be
good, and for leſſe wages: or for the reſeruacion of
their penſions, receyued into cures, and perſonages,
where as they can do no good, and wyll do muche
harme. Here as concerninge theſe thinges I ſaye, if
man do not make reſtitucion, God wyll take vengeaunce. For the people that by thys meanes contynue
in deuelyſhe ſuperſticion, and begyn vngracious rebellion, do dye, and are damned in their owne ſynnes,
but the bloud of their bodyes and ſoules ſhall be required at youre handes. Yea and the abhominable
errour of thoſe **that would haue no** rulers in authoritie,
cometh partelye by your occaſion, whyche vnto your
owne vayne glorye, and pryuate commoditie [priuate
authoritie], do abuſe the power and authoritie ordeyned
of God to hys glorye, and to the commen wealthe.
Thus **ye** perceyue howe that ſome ryche menne and
rulers abuſynge their ryches and authoritie, do make
ſome eyther to iudge that it ſhoulde be farre better
then it is, if there were neyther riche men nor rulers:
Howbeit thoſe men are farre deceyued. And Paule
telleth the truth, ſayinge that thoſe which be, are ordeyned of God.

Then ſome wyll aſke thys queſtyon: Seynge there is

no euyll of God, howe can euyll rulers or officers be of God? You honeſte men that be here, and dwell in the countrey, heare this leſſon, and marke it, and take it home wyth you, for your ſelues, and your neyghbour. It is God, *Qui facit hypocrita regnare propter peccata populi.* It is God, as the ſcripture in the xxxiiii. of Iob doth teſtifye, whych maketh an hypocritie to be a ruler for the ſynnes of the people. Nowe the people of the countrey vſe to ſaye, that their gentlemen and officers were neuer ſo full of fayre woordes and euyll dedes (whych is hypocriſy) as they nowe be. For a gentleman wyl ſaye that he loueth his tenaunt as well as hys father dyd, but he kepeth not ſo good a houſe to make them chere as hys father dyd, and yet he taketh mo fynes, and greater rentes to make them neadye, then hys father hadde.

Another wyll ſay that he would bye a Lordſhyppe of the kyng, for the loue that he hath to the tenauntes thereof, but aſſone as he hathe boughte it, by takynge of fynes, heyghnyng of rentes, and ſellyng away of commodities, he maketh the ſame tenantes pay for it. Another ſayth that he would haue an office to do good in hys contrey, but as ſone as he hath authoritie to take the fee to hym ſelfe, he ſetteth hys ſeruaunte to do hys duetye, and in ſtede of wages he geueth them authoritie to lyue of pyllage, brybry and extorcion in the countrey.

Now you of the countrey, marke your leſſon I ſaye, and take it home wyth you. It is God that maketh theſe euyl men to be gentlemen rulers, and officers in the countrey: it is the ſinnes of the people that cauſeth God to make theſe men youre rulers. The man is ſometymes euyll, but the authoritie from God is alwayes good, and God geueth good authoritye vnto euyll men, to punyſhe the ſynnes of the euyll people. It is not therefore repynyng, rebellyng, or reſiſtyng gods ordinance, that wyll amende euyll rulers. For [ſainct] Paule ſayeth, that all powers be of goddes ordinaunce. And in Iob it is playne, that euyll menne bee made rulers

by God: So that who foeuer refyfteth the offycers, be
the menne neuer fo euyll that be in office, he refifteth
the ordinaunce of God, he can **not** preuayle againfte
God, **but** furely he fhall be plaged of God. And as
the people can haue no remedye againft **euyll rulers
by rebellyon**, fo **can the** rulers haue **no redreffe of rebellious** people by oppreffyon. Example of bothe we
haue in the thyrd **booke of** Kynges, where as it appeareth **that** Roboam leauyng good **counfell to vfe** the
people wyth gentlenes and folowyng euyll **counfell to**
kepe them vnder by extremytye, dyd **fo exafperate and
ftyrre vp** the hertes of the people againft him beyng
their kyng, that ten partes of them dyd by fedicious
rebellion, burfte oute from hym, and were neuer after
fubiecte vnto hym, nor to none of his pofteritie. And
thofe rebellious people by Ieroboam whom they them
felues chofe to be their kynge, or rather the captayne
of theyr rebellyon, were brought into farre worfe cafe
and more myferye then euer they were afore, compelled to forfake God, **and to** vfe Idolatrye, and **were**
euer after plaged wyth fodeyne **deathe**, honger, dearthe,
warres, captyuytie, and all kynde of myferye.

Learne therefore ye people if ye inforce to eafe your
felues, wheras ye imagine that ye be **euyll** entreated of
men, be ye fure that ye fhall fele in deede that ye fhall
be more greuouflye afflycted by the ordynaunce of God.
And learne ye rulers if ye intende by onely fuppreffion to kepe vnder rebellion, be ye fure if ye thrufte
it downe in one place **it** wyll brafte out wyth **more**
vyolence and greater daunger in ten other places, to
the further dyfquietynge of you **beynge** rulars, and
to the vtter deftruccyon of all youre people beynge
rebelles.

Heare **ye** people what God fayeth by thofe people
that wyll **not** be in fubieccion, becaufe they thynke the
men to be euyl whiche be in authoritye. Yea harke
what the Lord fayeth as concernynge the proude, am-
bycyoufe, and vncyrcumcyfed Kynge Nabugodonozer
whyche was an euyll manne in dede, in the twentie

and feuen Chapter of Hieremye. *Gens et regnum. et cetera.*¹

That people and realme that doth not ferue Nabugodonezer ye kinge of Babilon, and whofoeuer putteth not his necke vnder the yocke of Nabugodnozer the kynge of Babilon, I (fayeth the Lorde) wyl vifet vpon that people in fweard, honger, and in peftylence. And in the xxvii. of the fame Prophete. *Catenas ligneas contriuifti, et facies pro eis* [*catenas*] *ferreas.*² Thou haft broken the fetters of wood, and fhalt make for them fetters of yron. By the whiche he declareth yat as a pryfoner in ye kepynge of a gayler, if he breake hys fetters of wood, fhall not therefore by the gayler be fet at lybertye, but rather cheyned wyth more ftronge fetters of yron: Euen fo, people beynge in the kepyng of God, if they by rebellyon breake their yocke of fubieccion, whych they nowe haue, fhall not therfore by God be putte at libertie, but rather be thrufte into a more ftraite, greuous, and ftronger yocke, where they fhall be fure neuer to haue libertie nor eafe.

Wherfore ye people, if ye fele your burden is heauye, and your yocke greuoufe, pacyently fuffer, and call vnto the Lorde: for then he wyll heare thee, and he wyl relieue thee, and he wyll delyuer thee.

And you rulers, becaufe ye knowe that the people oughte not to forfake or refufe what burden or yoke fo euer ye charge them wyth all, fee that ye charge them with no more then they maye beare and fuffer. For if they cry vnto you for reliefe and eafemente, and you wyll not regarde theyr forowes, but imagynynge that they be to wealthy, ye wyll encreafe their miferye, and decay their wealthe, as Pharao, and Roboam dyd: Well then, if the examples of Pharao and Roboam wyll not fuffyce you, marcke what God, by the prophet Ezechi. fayth (I pray you) in the. xxxiiii. of Ezechiel, *Audite paftores. &c.*³ Do not thynke that for becaufe paftors be named there, yat therfore it is al fpoken onely vnto the clargye, but for afmuche as all officers and rulers ought rather to be feders then fpoilers, it is

---

¹ Jer. *xxvii.* 8.　² Jer. *xxviii.* 13.　³ Ezek. *xxxiv.* 8.

spoken vnto you officers, which do not enter in by ye dore
of loue, as the fhephearde to feede, but clime ouer another
awaye [an other waie] thorowe couetoufnes as a thiefe,
to robbe and fpoyle the flocke of Chrift in your office.
Here what the Lorde fayeth vnto you officers yat fede
youre felues by feking of gaines, and not your flocke
by doing your dutie. Thus fayth the Lord: I my felfe
wyl vp on thefe paftors, and I wil require my fhepe at
their handes, and wyll make them to ceafe from fedyng
of my flocke, yea the paftors fhal fede them felues no
more, for I wyll delyuer my flocke out of their handes,
and they fhall be no longer a praye **for** them to fede
vpon. Vndoubtedly if ye fhuld entende by your authority **rather** your felues to liue in riote, then to kepe **ye**
people in quietnes, your rulynge fhulde not longe continue. Surely ther is none other remedy for ryche or
poore, high or low, gentleman or yeoman, to helpe **to**
amende the difquietnes in thys realme, but to pulle
and rote that* out of youre hertes, which is roted **in**
euery one of your hertes, the rote of all euyll, whyche
is couetoufnes. For euen you hufbandmen whyche
crye out vpon the couetoufnes of gentlemen and
officers, it is euen couetoufnes in you, yat caufeth,
and ingendreth couetoufnes in them. For, for to **get**
your neyghbours ferme, ye wyll offer and difire them
to take bribes, fynes, and rentes more then they loke
for, or then you your felues be **wel** able to pay. It
is a wonderous thing **to fe** gentlemen take fo great
rentes, fynes, and ingreffaunce for couetoufnes to aduaunce theyr owne landes: Howebeit it is a farre more
wonderfull thyng to fee hufbande men offer and geue
fo greate fynes, rentes, incomes, yea and bribes for
couetoufnes to gette other mennes fermes. It femeth
to come of great couetoufnes for riche men, to make
ftrayte iawes to faue their owne goodes: Howebeit it
is in deede a farre more couetoufnes for poore men by
rebellion to robbe, and fpoile other mens goodes. And
this dare I faye, takyng all you to beare recorde, that
the foreft lawes that euer any tyraunt made in **any**

lande, if they fhuld continue many yeares coulde not caufe fuch and fo great murther, myfchiefe, and wretchednes as ye perceyue and know that thys rebellyon in England contynuynge but a fewe monethes, hath caufed: by the which ye may learne that althoughe lawers be comenly called moſt couetous, yet compare them with rebels, and as pickinge theft, is leffe then murtheryng robrye [robberie]: fo is the couetoufnes of gredy lawers which begyle craftely, farleffe then the couetoufnes of rebelles, whych fpoyle cruelly. Lette vs therefore euerye one acknoweledgynge our owne fautes, where as moſt euyll fpryngeth, there laboure fyrſte wyth moſte diligence to plucke vp the roote of that euil, whyche is couetoufnes: that God ingraftynge grace in vs, maye geue occafyon vnto oure Rulars rather to bee occupyed in rewardynge of vertue, then in punyſheyng of vyce: Yea that God be not prouoked by our finnes to fende euyll rulers to punyſhe euyll men, but rather moued by oure repentaunce, to preferue thefe good rulers whiche be fente alreadye to the greate comfort of all good men: efpecially the kinges maieſty, whofe godlynes, vertue, and grace, is lyke to make this realme to floryſhe, if oure fynnes do not caufe God to thinke our realme vnworthy to enioye the treafure of fo precyous a Iewell. Manye other noble men therebe as I truſte, fome that I do certaynlye knowe, whofe tender heartes do muche lamente youre griefes, and whofe godlye prouifion wyll be muche vnto youre comforte, if your vnpaciente ſtubburnes do not difapoynte their good purpofe. If euer at any tyme God did fend vnto any afflycted people releyfe, comforte, and profperytye, it came alwayes by good rulers, at fuch tyme as the people beeynge in afflyccyon, dyd humble them felues in pacyence, and cryed vnto the Lorde wyth prayer, as is apparente in the houndreth and feuen Pfalme. *Clamauerunt ad dominum cum tribularentur, et de neceſſitatibus eorum liberauit eos.*[1] When they were in trouble they called vnto thee [the] Lorde, and he de-

---

[1] Ps. *cvii.* 13.

liuered them forth of their troublousefome gryefes. And in the bookes of the iudges and of the kynges, ye maye reade how that God, to delyuer his people forth of miserye, and to profper them in wealth, dyd reyfe vp good rulers as Gedeon, Barac, Iepthe, Sampfon, Dauid, Samuel, and fuche other. And wythoute doubte euen at this time here in England, God hathe rayfed vp a gracyous kynge, and fome fuche noble men as be neyther cruell nor couetous. If ther be therfore in vs pacience, humility, thankfulnes, and prayer, furelye we fhall foone feele relyefe, conforte and profperitie.

Thei therfore yat as yet feele them felues greued, let them cal vnto ye lord, lokinge for his helpe in paciente fuffering, not prouoking his vengeaunce by vngracious rebellinge agaynfte hys officers, vnhappye refifting hys ordinaunce: vnhappy refiftyng may I well call it, for vnhappye are all they that vfe it, purchafing thereby to them felues iudgement, vengeaunce, and damnacyon. O howe vnhappye haue they been here in England, whiche haue not quietlye fuffered a confortable reformacion of their greateft griefes and harmes, to procede from god to them by his ordinaunce, but vnpacientlye grudginge haue offended god, difquieted this realm, and vndone them felues, by refyftynge goddes ordynaunce. For the greateft griefe that hathe been vnto the people in thys realme, hath bene the inclofing of comens, as concernyng the whyche the powers ordeyned of GOD for that purpofe, made an acte of parlyamente, forbiddynge anye man to enclofe vnto hys pryuate vfe, that whyche of long tyme had bene taken, and vfed as common. And afterwardes, the fame powers dyd fende forthe proclamacions, warnynge theym whyche contrarye to thys acte of parliament had inclofed groundes, offendynge the people, that they accordynge to thefe Proclamacions fhoulde laye the fame inclofed landes abroade agayne, to fatyffye the acte of parliamente, and to releue the people. And for becaufe neyther of thefe wayes toke effecte, there was immediatly further commiffions dyrected to put fuche men in authoryty, as could eafelye, and woulde gladly, and were **pur**pofed fpedely to haue layed vnlawfull inclofed landes abrode agayne, in fuch quiet forte as fhoulde haue bene moft **to the** kynges honour, to ye **wealth** of thys realme, and to **the** greateft comforte of **thofe** whyche were moft greued. Now howe the people dyd take or rather how they dyd refyfte and wythftand **thys, ye know.**

And I fhall rehearfe whan as I haue telled **you of** one other thyng whyche beynge of longer contynuance in Englande, hath done ferre more harme, and yet the gryef therof fer leffe, yea nothynge at all felt. For the deadely wound therof dyd brynge the people paft all felynge of gryefe. And the venomous poyfen broughte **the people** in fuche **a Maze, that they** dyd not fele and perceyue them felues to be in moft horryble myferable wretchednes, whan as the worde of GOD, the breade of lyfe, the **fauyng** health in Chrift Iefu, was taken a way, and in a ftraunge language fhut, and clofed **vp** from theym, fo that they wythout felyng were **led from** God by mannes tradicions **vnto** vayne ceremonis, to be moft venemoufly poyfoned wyth dyuelifhe fuperfti**cion.** Therefore whan **as** the mercyfull goodnes of God beholdyng the miferies of the people, by the prouydence **of** the kynges maieftye, and his counfell, purpofely **ordeined of** God to conforte, **healpe,** and amend the people of thys realme, by the reftoryng of goddes worde, and fettynge it playnelye forthe in the Englyfh tong, with the ryght vfe and dew adminiftra**cion of** hys facramentes to be imprynted, and con**fyrmed** in our hartes : **Whan as** I faye, by thefe gracyous meanes, **and** godlye **order,** God hym felfe dyd offer vnto the people, relyefe, comforte, and profperitye : Then the vngodlye, vngracious and vnhappye people, beynge moofte vnkynde, where as they fhoulde haue bene moofte thankefull, dyftrufted GOD, dyfpifed hys ordinaunce, and prefumed of theyr owne wylfulnes so farre as they coulde or myghte, to wythstand the ordynaunce of God, refused the grace of God, and procured to theym selues the vengeaunce of God. Wherfore we hauynge thys terrible example in fresh memorye, and seynge a gracyous Kyng, and Godly rulars ordeyned of GOD, to amende oure gryefes, althoughe all that cannot be amended in one day, whyche hath bene appayryng manye yeres, yet let **vs** pacientlye suffer for a tyme, not doubtynge but that that reliefe, comforte, and wealth, whyche God hathe promysed vnto Englande by hys word, offered of hys goodnes, and begon by his ordinaunce, shalbe brought vnto passe, by hys wysdome and myghte: in suche wyse as shall **be** moste for hys glorye, the kynges honoure, the **wealth of the** realme, and most to the conforte of theym that mooste pacyentlye in hope, truste to [in] goddes goodnes. These examples haue I rehearsed to teach you as it were by experience, howe true this saying of [saincte] Paul is: They whyche wythstande or resyste the powers ordeyned of God, receyue vnto them selues Iudgemente: whyche is vengeaunce, and damnacion. Let vs therfore amend our lyues, and be good men, and we shall not nede to hate and feare, but haue greate occasion to loue, and truste those whyche be nowe our chyefe rulars. For they be as [S.] Paule sayeth, made rulars, not to put theym in feare that do good, but theym whyche do euyll: so that none nedeth **to** feare these rulars, but euell doers. Whyche in euyll doynge haue deserued of the rulars to be punyshed, and in resystynge theyr power ordeyned of GOD, do hasten, and aggrauate towardes theym selues, **the** fore vengeaunce of GOD. It foloweth: Wouldest thou be wythout feare of power, do that whyche is good, and thou shalte haue prayse of it: for he is the mynyster of God to do the[e] good, but yf thou do euyl, feare. For he beareth not the swearde wythout a cause, but is the mynister of GOD to aduenge in wrath hym that doeth euyll.

All these wordes [sainct] Peter concludeth bryefelye in

the second of hys fyrſt Epiſtle, ſaying that thoſe that haue rule and authorytye, be ſente *ad vindictam malorum, laudem vero bonorum*.[1] That is to ſaye: to take vengeaunce of euell doers, and to commende the good.

Whoſoeuer thou arte therefore and of whatſoeuer degree or ſorte thou bee, yf thou bee a Subiecte thou muſte remember, and conſyder howe that powers be ordayned of God for the, yf thou be euyll to make the good by dewe correccyon: yf thou be good to make the[e] better, by the encoragemente of commendacyon, prayſe, and mayntenaunce. Looke therefore all you that haue power, and authorytye of GOD, that ye vſe it, as ye are commaunded by God: to correcte and punyſhe the euyll doer, and to encorage, rewarde, and mayntaine the good.

Se that for ſo ferre as your power extendeth, there be no euyll vnpunyſhed, nor no good vnrewarded. But harcke a lytle, and I ſhal tell you of an ab[h]omynable robbery done in the Citye, knowen to the officers of the city, and as yet not punyſhed, but rather mayntayned in the city. There is a greate ſumme of monye ſente from an honorable Lord by hys ſeruaunte vnto thoſe whome he is indetted vnto in the cityе. The officers knowynge that they to whom thys monye is ſente haue great nede of it, knowe alſo in what places, at what tymes theſe vnthryftye ſeruauntes by whome it is ſente, at gamnynge, banckettyng, and riot, do ſpende it. If thys be an euell dede, why is it not punyſhed? Bycauſe it is not knowen ſome ſaye. But whyther they meane that it is not knowen to be done, or not knowen to be euyll I doubte. And therefore here now wyll I make it openlye knowen boeth to be done, and alſo to be euell done, and worſe ſuffered. But doeth not manye of you knowe? ſure I am that all you that be officers oughte to know that all that ryches and treaſures whyche rych men, and rufflers, waſte at gredye gamning, glotonous banckettinge, and ſuche riote, is not theyr owne, but ſente by theym from the honorable Lord of heauen, vnto other that be honeſt, pore,

---

[1] 1 Peter *ii*. 14.

and nedye: vnto whome God by hys promyfe is indetted. Ye knowe, that *Domini eſt terra et plenitudo eius.*[1] The yearthe is the Lordes, and the plenty therof. **So** that no man hath any thyng of hys owne: But hath receyued all of the Lorde. For, *Quid habes quod non accepiſti ?*[2] **What** haſte thou that thou haſt **not** receyued: **Yea thou as** a feruaunte haſte receyued of thy Lord, whych gyueth vnto hys feruauntes the Talentes of hys treaſures. **And** to knowe for what purpoſe he gyueth theym vnto you, reade Eſaye, the xviii [.lviij.]. *Frange eſurienti panem tuum. etc.*[3] Breacke thy breade vnto the hungrye, and the nedye: and the wanderyng leade into thy houſe: whan thou **feeſt one** naked cloth hym, and do not dyſpyſe thyne **owne fleſhe.** Heare you feruauntes of the Lorde, whyche haue receyued the treaſures of the lord, vnto whom the lorde by you hath ſente them: vnto the houngrye, the nedye, the naked, and thoſe that be of the ſame fleſhe and bloude that you youre ſelues be. Nowe you offycers knowynge that greate ryches, and treaſures ſente from the honorable lord of heauen, vnto his welbeloued people, the nedy members of Chriſtes bodye, by theſe vnthriſtye feruauntes is ſpente at gamnynge, and riote, within your offyces, ye muſte nedes knowe that an euyll dede is done. Let vs therfore I praye you, knowe howe it is punyſhed. Peraduenture ye wyll ſaye: ther is no lawe in England that appoynteth any punyſhmente for gamners. If therefore euyll dedes maye be done in Englande wythout feare, than **is** the ſweard of authoritye borne **in** Englande, wythout **a** cauſe. But I wyll tell the that **art an** offycer in England or in what Chryſten lande ſo euer it be: whereas there is no certayne punyſhment for any euyl dede by mans law, there the offycer may and ought to vſe any kind **of** puniſhment to amende **or** reſtreyne the euyll doer, by goddes lawe. But without doubte yf thoſe ſame men ſhould ſpende in the ſame ſorte of ryot, ſo great treaſures ſente from the Kynges Maieſtye vnto the Aldermenne

---

[1] **Pſa.** *xxiv.* 1.   [2] 1 Cor. *iv.* 7.   [3] **Iſa.** *lviii.* 7.

of thys Cytye, there fhoulde be punyfhmente, correccyon, and reamedye founde for theym quyckely.

And of very confcience is not god as much to be feared as the kynge, and the poore, and nedye as well to be pytied and prouyded for as the rych and wealthy?

Well, gamners, ryotters, and all euell doers, yf they do not repente, fhalbe damned in theyr owne fynnes: but the bloude of theyr foules fhalbe requyred at the handes of the officers, whyche by feare fhoulde haue caufed theim to leaue fynne. Yea but what fhall me [we] than faye by vfurye, whyche is nowe made fo lawefull that an offycer yf he would, can not punyfh, to make men to leaue it? As concernynge thys matter we haue playne commaundemente in the fiftene of Deutro[nomie]. And in the fyfte of Math. To lend to hym that nedeth, and wold borowe. And in the fyxte of Luke it is playne. *Date mutuo, nihil inde fperantes.*[1] **Lende** fayeth Chrifte, trufting to haue **no** gayn therby. **Here** we haue two commaundementes, the one is to lende, and the other not to lende for lukar [lucre]: nowe he that breaketh goddes commaundement muft nedes go to the deuyll. So that in breakynge thefe two commaundementes, here is two wayes for you ryche men to go **to the** dyuyll: Eyther in lendynge **for luker** [lucre], or **els in not** lendynge anye thynge at all. Manye of **you there be,** that whofoeuer fayeth nay, wyll nedes the **one of thefe** two wayes. For yf mans lawe do ftop vp vfurye, fo yat by lendyng thou canft haue no gaynes, than wylte thou the other waye apace, and lend nothyng **at all.** So fhalte thou be fuer to come ther away to the **deuyll.** For than fhall no man in no cafe haue anye **vfe of thy** goodes. Therefore neyther **the** lawe, nor the officer in fufferynge a lytle vfurye, **and** commaundinge none, doth mayntayne or allow vfurye. But for becaufe you [thou] beynge an vfurer wylte nedes to **the** dyuell, they fuffer the to goo fuch awaye as fome commodytye myght come to other by fome vfe of thy goodes, rather than by ftoppynge vp that

[1] Luke *vi.* 35.

waye, to dryue the there awaye as no man coulde haue
any vſe of anye of thy goodes. For where as God
commaundeth, and thy nedy neyghbour deſyreth the
to lende, and thou neyther at the reuerence of God,
nor for pitye of thy neyghboure wylte lende of loue
frelye: but contrarye to goddes commaundemente
wyth out pytye of the poore, thou wylte not ſtycke to
lende for gredyneſſe of luker couetouſlye: thy owne
dedes declare the to be ſo voyde of all godly charity,
and ſo ful of diuilyſh couetouſnes, that thou art fer paſt
all mans cure, and helpe, either by law or puniſhmente.
So wyl I leue the, and ſpeake of thoſe that myght, and
oughte to be healed by men beynge in authorytye, and
yet **wyll not.**

For ther be ſum ſuche ioyly felowes that they wylbe
ſubiect to no powers, which by fear myght cauſe them
to forbeare theyr vayne pleaſures in euil: vnto thoſe
now conſequentlye doth [ſaincte] Paule ſpeake, ſayinge:
ye muſt nedes be ſubiecte, not onely for wrathe, but alſo
for conſcience ſake. If ye be ſuche ioyly felowes that
ye feare not the wrath e or dyſpleaſure of officers, whan
as ye do euyll, yet grope youre owne conſcience, that
ye may fele what a greuous ſynne it is to wythſtande
the powers ordayned of GOD to miniſter dewe correccyon vnto euyll doers. For not onely thy conſcyence,
but alſo thyne owne deede in that thou doeſte paye
tribute for thys thynge, ſhall teſtifye agaynſt the: that
thou knoweſt theym to be the myniſters of GOD, at-
tendynge to thys ſame thynge, to thys bryngynge euell·
doers in feare. It is therefore a matter of conſcience
for the[e] ſo to withſtande the powers ordayned of God,
that thei take no place in the, but that thou wylt do
euell wythout feare, and maintaine that whych is euell
done, by worſe preſumpcion. I do not ſaye that whatſoeuer the magyſtrates commaunde is a matter of conſcience, but what ſoeuer is euell, is a matter of conſcyence. And to refyſte ryghte by myghte, ſo that
thou wylte not be ſubiecte in humylitye, vnto thoſe
powers whyche God by hys righte hath ſet ouer the[e] in

authoritye is a greate euell, and therefore a greate
matter of confcience. Manye examples we haue
whyche doeth proue that euerye commaundement of
magiſtrates be not matters in confcience, and yet
euery refiſting or rebelling againſt their autority is a
matter in confcience. The Iewes had a cuſtume
confirmed by their elders whiche were magiſtrates,
that no man ſhould eate wyth vnwaſhen handes:
Chriſte Iefu leafte thys cuſtome, brake thys tradicion
wythout any grudge of confcience.

Dauid knowynge Saule the kyng to be a wycked
man and hys deadly enemy, and hauyng Saule in a
denne, where as if he would, he myghte haue kylled
hym: this Dauid hadde a good confcience not to
touche the lordes anointed, to fuffer Saule to be
kynge and to fubmitte hym felfe. Daniel was commaunded not to praye to God: the Apoſtles were
commaunded not to preache gods worde. Thefe dyd
not rebell againſt the higher powers, no nor yet for
confcience obey men, but rather they obeyed God.
For Daniell did praye, and the Apoſtles dyd preache.
So ryfe not, rebell not, refiſte not, what foeuer the
rulers them felues do: And be ye not fo fcrupulous
as to thynke the bond in confcience vnto euerye
thing that a man beyng a ruler commaundeth the to
do it efpeciallye, if God commaund the contrary.
Nowe it foloweth, geue vnto euerye one that which
is due: Euery dutye belonging to euery body, can not
here be declared, no nor at this tyme rehearfed, I
wyll therefore fpeake briefely of one thynge whych
ſhall be a generall example for all duties. Pau. i. vnto
the Cor. xi. *Vnus panis vnum corpus multi fumus:*[1]
One bred fayeth he one body we are that be many: by
the whiche he declareth that as of diuers cornes of
wheate by the liquor of water knoden into dough is
made one loafe of breade: fo we being diuerfe men,
by loue and charitie, whyche is the liquor of lyfe,
ioyned into one congregacion, be made as dyuers
members of one miſticall body of Chriſte, where by I

---

[1] 1 Cor. x. 17.

say, as by one example in the stede of many, learne that the more gorgeous you youre selues bee in silkesand veluettes, the more shame is it for you to see other poore and neady, beyng members of the same bodye, in ragges and clothe, yea bare and **naked**.

Doest thou not thynke them to be members of the **same** bodye that thou arte? Then arte not thou a member of Christe, then arte not thou a chylde of God, then art not thou a christen man. One member oughte as well to be prouided for, as a nother: I do not say that one oughte to haue as costely prouision as a nother.

But **as** there be dyuers members in dyuers places, hauyng dyuers duties, so to haue dyuers prouision in feedyng and clothyng.

And as they be all in one body, so none to be without that feedynge and clothyng, whych for that part of the bodye is meete and necessarye. **Euen as** ye do prouide indifferentlye for euery parte of youre naturall bodye, by reason of the which, ye are bounde, and subiecte to corruption : **So** let no parte or member of your Christen bodye be vnprouyded for: By reason of the whyche bodye, ye be heyres of the heauenly kyngdome. And this one example generally shall teache you to gyue that whych is due vnto euery one seuerally. Nowe here soloweth euen. iiii. [fower] wordes: Tribute, custume, fere, honor. Of these. iiii. [sower] wordes wil I conclude almost in **iiii.** [sower] wordes. Ye must **gyue** trybute, to whome trybute is due : custome, to whome custome is due : feare, to whome feare is due : **honour**, to whome honoure is due. Vnder trybute be conteined taxes, fiftenth, subsides, and suche as be payed **at** sometymes to the Rulers, and be not continuall. Customes **be** tythes, tolles, rentes, and such as the people paye vnto the officers continually. For payinge of trybute besydes thys commaundemente of Paule, we haue example of Christes mother, whych beyng at the houre of her trauell went out of Galyle vnto Bethlem, a toune in Iewry, there to be taxed, and pay trybute vnto Cefar.

As concernyng cuſtome, Chriſt hymſelfe commaunded Peter to pay for them **both**, leſt that they ſhulde offend: that is, leſt that they, in not paying, ſhuld geue euyll example **vnto the people.** So Chriſten men muſt nedes paye both trybute **and** cuſtome. What trybute and cuſtome good men may **take**, it appereth in that that goeth afore: ſurelye euen ſo muche and no more as ſhall ſufficientlye diſcharge their **coſtes**, neceſſaryly beſtowed in correctynge of euyll, and **rewardyng** good. Marke that I ſay they may or **oughte** to take no more: **for here** I tell them their duty. **For** truly if they do requyre more of you that be their ſubiectes, then is it youre duty **to** pay that whiche they **aſke**, and not **to** be curyous to know for what cauſe **it is** aſked, but this onlye to take hede that with due **reuerence** ye pay it, as Paule **commaundeth, and as** Chriſte and hys mother haue geuen **you example.** Feare and honoure belonge chieflye, yea in a manner onely vnto God. For God onely for hym ſelfe is to be feared and honoured.

All other for gods cauſe, are ſo to be feared and honoured: as that feare and honoure which is geuen vnto them, may procede and come finally vnto God. For, *dominum deum tuum adorabis et illum ſolum coles.*[1] Thou **ſhalte honoure** the Lorde thy God, and hym only **ſhalt** thou reuerentlye ſerue. As **for the** Deuyll, feare **hym** not, for he wyll doo no leſſe harme vnto thee then he canne: he canne do no more then **God** wyll ſuffer hym. Feare therfore leſte that thou offende God, and **he** ſufferre the Deuyll to vtter hys malyce, and myſchyefe towardes thee.

That feare, honoure, or ſeruice whyche accordynge **to** goddes commaundemente is done vnto thoſe perſonnes whom God hath authoryſed to receyue it in hys name, is done vnto God.

As that money whych by thy commaundemente is payde to thy ſeruaunt in thy name, is paid vnto the[e].

[1] Matt. *iv.* 10.

Therefore Chrifte rulynge in magiftrates by authorytye, and beynge houngrye and coulde in the poore by pytye, doeth commaunde vs to geue, and promyfeth that he hym felfe wyll receyue and rewarde that **honoure of** reuerence, feruyce and obedyence doone to the hygher powers, as to hys ordinaunce in the common wealth: and alfo that honour of charitable almes [almofe], relyefe, and conforte, whych is beftowed **vpon the** poore and neady, as vpon the lyuely members of his owne **body**. As for that whych wythout goddes commaundement, of mans phantafticall imaginacion is doone vnto Images, muft nedes be hyghe dyfhonoure, and greuous difpleafure vnto God, when as the lyuely ymage **of** God created wyth hys owne hande in flefhe and **bloud, doth** honor, reuerence, and homage vnto a dead picture of man, grauen in ftocke or ftone, wyth a workemans tooles.

God is alfo honoured in all hys creatures, when as they be taken wyth thankes, and vfed as he hath commaunded: and therfore, when as they be vnthankfully taken, or wyckedly abufed, then is he difhonoured, and difpleafed.

Nowe, heare a fhort conclufion, *Qui ex deo eft, uerbum dei audit.* He that is of God, heareth the worde of God. All you I faye that be Chriften men, Gods chyldren, and indued wyth Goddes fpiryte, wyll heare the worde of Gods threatenyng, **and** fearyng his vengeaunce, repent, wyll heare the woorde of gods commaundement, and folowyng his counfels amende youre lyues, wyl heare the worde of Gods promyfe, and paciently fufferynge, truft to hys goodnes. As for you that wyll not heare and regarde goddes worde, ye declare your felues not to be of God. But for becaufe ye haue the deuyl to your father, ye wyll fulfyll the luftes and defyres of the Deuyll, whyche is your father. And the lufte and defire of the Deuyll is, to hynder the worcke and pleafure of God: and thys is the worke and wyll of God, that we fhould repofe oure faythe and trufte in Chrifte Iefu, and beftowe oure laboure and diligence in our owne vocacyon.

'herefore the **deuyll** poyfonynge all hys wyth greadye couetoufenes, wyll caufe them euer to truft **to their owne prouifion, and neuer to be** content wyth their owne vocacion, but beynge called of God to be marchaunt, gentleman, lawer, or courtear, yet to be readye at a becke of their father the **deuyl**, befydes this their godly vocacion, deuyllyfhelye to proule for, feke, and purchafe farmes, perfonages, **and benefices, to** difcourage houfbandemenne from tyllynge **of the** grounde, **and** minifters from preachynge of Goddes woorde: **that** therby maye come a greuoufe honger, dearth, **and lacke** both of naturall fubftaunce for the bodye, and alfo of heauenly foode for the foule And then thofe in the countrey that be not gods chyldren, but **deuyllyfhe vipers,** will hyffe, whifper, and fwell **wyth venemous** prefumpcion, **and their** fting of rebellion to deftroy both them felues, and al the cuntry. But they of ye cuntry or els wher, that be the chyldren of God **in** dede, knowynge **couetous riche men and** officers **to be** fparpled **abrod in the cuntry as the** fcourges of god, to beat them **for their fynnes, lyke** gentle chyldren, **wyl** acknowledge their **owne** fautes, **and** paciently fuffryng correccion, pitifullye crye vnto **their** heauenly father for mercy, forgeueneffe, and conforte. So all **you in** England, that haue any godly knowledge, grace, and charitie, wyll fay with the prophet Dauid : *Virga tua, et baculus tuus, ipfa me confolata funt* :[1] **Thy** rod, O Lorde and thy ftaffe, they it be whyche haue conforted **me.** Thy rodde of correccion, whych is thefe couetous ryche **men,** and officers, and thy ftaffe of conforte, whyche **is** the kynges maieftie, whom thou haft **endowed** wyth **a** gracious gentle nature, godly educacion, wonderful wyt, and great learnyng : yea, and thofe noble men whom thou haft called **from** their vayne plefures, to take great paynes, of a reuerent loue towardes the kyng, and of a chari-

[1] Ps. *xxiii.* 4.

table pitie towardes vs, **to** beſtowe their landes and goodes, tyme, and ſtudye, and all that **euer they** haue, **to** proſper the Kynge, **to** prouide for hys realme, **and to** cheriſh vs his people **therof.** Thus thy rodde of **correccion,** O Lorde, **hath taught vs to be** ſubiecte in humilitie vnto all **hygher** powers, **as** to thy ordinaunce: and this thy ſtaffe **of** conforte o **Lorde,** doth encorage **vs to** loue and truſt them, eſpecially **vnto whome** thou haſt geuen **hyeſt** power and authoritie. So that we can nowe wyllynglye geue vnto **euerye one** that whyche **is due:** vnto **ye** higher powers, reuerence, feruyce, and obedience, **vnto** all in general faythfull dealynge, **and** vnto the poore and needye, charitable almes [almoſe], releeſe and conforte.

Giue therfore vnto **vs, o** Lord, mercye and grace, that we maye render **vnto** thee thankes and prayſe for euer. **Amen.**

¶ Imprinted at London by John Daie, dwellinge ouer Aldersgate, and Wylliam Seres dwelling in Peter Colledge. The yeare of our Lorde God M. D. L. the nynth daye of Apryll.

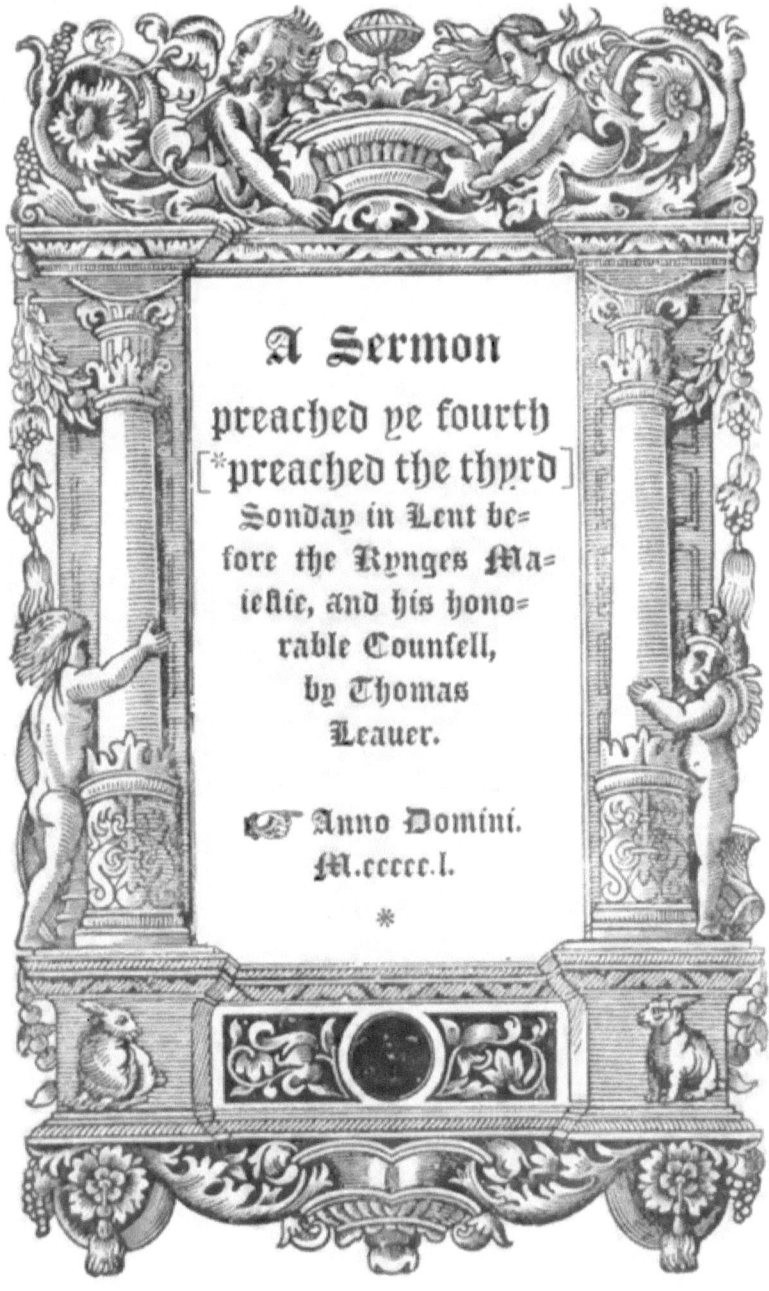

A Sermon
preached ye fourth
[*preached the thyrd]
Sonday in Lent be=
fore the Kynges Ma=
iestie, and his hono=
rable Counsell,
by Thomas
Leauer.

☞ Anno Domini.
M.ccccc.l.

*

☞ *Cum priuilegio imprimendum folum.*

* As incorrectly printed on some title pages to this sermon.

In nomine Iesu Christi.

OD be mercifull vnto vs : For the tyme is euen nowe comynge, when as God muſte needes either of his mercye here in Englande, worke ſuche a wonderfull miracle vnto our conforte, as farre paſſeth mans expectacion : orels of his righteouſnes take ſuch vengeance of this lande to th[e]example of all other landes, as ſhall be to our vtter diſtruccion.

Ye know, that immediatly after the preachynge of Noe, came the great floud that drouned ye world. After the warnyng of Loth, came fyre, brymſtone vpon the Sodomites and Gomorrians. When Moiſes had declared Gods thretnynges in Egipte, kyng Pharao and his people were plaged vpon the lande, and drouned in the red ſea.

Suche plages came euer where Gods worde truly preached, is not beleued, receaued, and folowed. But at the preachyng of Ionas, the Niniuites repented wonderfully. When the boke of the law was reade vnto Ioſias the kyng, he, with all his people ſpedely repentyng, found exceadyng mercy, bleſſyng, and grace : as lykewyſe all other ſhalbe ſure to find, which heare the worde of God and keepe it.

For when Chriſt and his Apoſtles had preached the Goſpel vnto the Iewes, thoſe that beleued were delyuered frome the curſe of the law, vnto the bleſſing of grace, out of worldly miſery, to be inheriters of the heuenly kyngdome : and thoſe that did not beleue, were caſt from God, oppreſſed of men, ouercome, ſpoyled, murthered, and diſtroyed of their enemyes.

Wherfore Englande, whiche at this preſent tyme, by

reafon of the worde of God fetfurth, reade, preached, and comuned, dothe in euerye place heare the counfell of Noe, the warnynge of Loth, the law of Moyfes, the threatnynges of the Prophetes, and the grace of the Gofpell, as it was declared and taught by Chrift and his Apoftles: Thys Englande mufte nedes, either by beleuynge of thefe thynges, obteyne of God wonderfull grace of amendement, orels by neglecting them, prouoke the vengeance of God, as a dewe plage and punyfhment.

Take heede therfore England, for if thou by **vnbelefe**, let and ftop God from workynge of miracles to thy confort, then furely dooeft thou prouoke God to powre doun vengeaunce vpon the, to thy vtter diftruccion: But if thou doo regarde, receaue, and **beleue Gods worde**, he wyll worke wonderfull miracles to thy conforte, wealthe, and profperitie. Yea, let **euerye** man, of what eftate or degree foeuer he be, grope his owne confcience: for if he **dooe not there** feele that the worde of God dothe take place to moue hym to repentaunce and amendment of lyfe, then fhall he be fure fone to **haue experience**, that the vengeaunce of God, by a **fhamefull fhorte** ende of his wretched lyfe, wyll bryng him vnto an euerlaftynge dampnable deathe. For all thofe that wyll not creepe vnder the merciful wings of god, as the chikynnes of Chrift, fhalbe **caught and** deuoured of puttockes, haukes, and kytes, as **a pray for the deuyll**. The wynges of God be ftretched abrode here in Englande, by the kynges gracious maieftye and his honorable counfell, of mighty **power**, with ready wyll **to fhadowe**, defende, and faue all thofe that with reuerent loue, **come** humbly creepyng vnder their ordinaunce, rule, and gouernaunce, whiche is the power, the **wynges**, and the honour [the order] of God.

The filthye gredye **puttockes**, wylde **haukes, and** rauenyng kytes be fuperfticious papiftes, carnall gofpellers, and fedicious rebelles, which as ye haue feene, by **late** experience, haue moft cruelly caught, fpoyled, and deuoured the lambes, the chekynnes, the chyldren of God, redemed and boughte with Chriſtes bloude. Wherfore as Chriſt in his owne perſone dyd once lament and bewayle Ieruſalem, ſo dothe he nowe many tymes in the perſons of his propheticall Preachers, lament and bewayl Englande, ſaying: O England, howe ofte wolde I haue gathered thy chyldren, as a hen gathereth her chikens vnder her wynges, and thou woldeſt not. Euen with the ſame affeccion that the ſhepherde cryeth, ſeeyng the wolfe le[e]ryng towardes the ſhepe, and with the ſame affeccion that the hen clock⸗ eth and calleth, ſpyeng the kyte houeryng ouer her chekyns: with the ſame affeccion it behoueth the miniſter and preacher of God, ſeeyng vntollerable vengeaunce hangynge ouer Englande, to crye, to call, and to geue warnyng vnto the people, ſaying as [it] is written in the firſt of Eſay: If ye willyngly wyl heare and obeye, ye ſhall eate the good conſortable frutes of the earthe: but if ye wyll not, and prouoke me vnto angre, the ſwoorde ſhall deuoure you: *Quia os Domini locutum eſt.*[1] For it is the mouth of the lord that hath ſpoken.

Now your reuerende maieſtie, moſt gracious kyng, and you honourable wyſe godly counſellers, you are the chiefe ſhepherdes, you are the moſt reuerende fathers in Chriſte, hauynge the wynges of power and authoritie, to ſhadow, ſaue, and keepe theſe lambes of god, theſe [the] chekens of Chriſt, and theſe chyldren of the heauenly father, redemed with Chriſtes bloude, and committed vnto your handes, to be ſaued, kepte, and prouyded for.

God be prayſed, with thankful obedience, and lou⸗ ynge reuerence dewe to your gracious maieſtye and honorable counſell, whiche haue ſurely wyſely pro⸗ uyded for, diligently kept, and charitably ſaued this realme, by driuyng away the wylde [wilie] foxe of papiſticall ſuperſticion, and by caſtynge out the vn⸗ cleane ſpirit of ignorance, to gods glorye, your honour, and our conſort.

[1] Is. i. xx.

But alas moſt gracious Kyng and godly gouernors, for the tender mercyes of God, in our Sauiour **Ieſu** Chriſt, take **good** and diligent heede when ye be chafyng the wylde [wilie] fox of papiſticall ſuperſticion, **that** the greedye wolfe of **couetous** ambicion, do not **creepe in** at your backes : For ſurely he wyll doo more harme in a weeke, then the foxe dyd **in a yere.**

Take heede, that **the vncleane ſpirite of** ignoraunce, returnynge with. **vii.** other worſe then himſelf, ſynde no place vnwarded, where he may **creepe in** agayne. For if he returnyng with his felowes, enter **in agayne,** then wyll he make the ende of this generacion to bee worſe then the begynnyng.

Then ſhall you leeſe the rewarde of your former diligence, and be dam[p]ned for your later negligence. Then **ſhall** the **welſpryng of** mercye, which of long tyme hath watered thys Realme with **the** grace of God be cloſed vp, and the blodye flouds of vengeance guſhing out from the wrath and indignacion of God, ouerflowe all togyther. Then wyll not God, by workyng of miracles declare mercy, **but** by takynge of vengeaunce, execute rightouſnes.

But God beyng as mercyfull yet, as euer he **was, if** you contynewe as faythfull, wyſe, and dilygent as ye haue ben, to handle the wolfe, as you haue doone the foxe, to keepe out the deuyll, as to caſt out the deuyll: **then ſhall** the people of this lande feede in quyetnes, without feare of euyl : then ſhal you contınuyng to the[e]nde, be ſure of an hunderdfold reward in this lyfe, and afterwards, euerlaſting lyfe, ioye and glorye. Then ſhall God **doo** wonderfull miracles in Englande, to declare **howe mercy** ſhall triumphe ouer rightouſnes.

And that wee maye **all** dyſpoſe our ſelfes the more conuenientlye for God to worke ſuche a miracle amonge **vs, wee** haue appoynted for the goſpell of this day, **writen in the. vi.** of **Iohan, a** wonderfull miracle of. **v.** thouſande men, fed and ſatisfyed with. **v.** loaues and **ii.** fyſhes, **wheras euery man** may and ought to learne

his owne **dutye, whiche shall** cleare[ly] appeare too a
kyng in Christ, to head gouerners vnder the kynge, in
the Apostles, beyng most neare about Christ, and to all
other men, in that multitude of the people, whiche
folowynge Christ, **were** obedient **to syt** doune at the
commaundment of his Disciples, **not** knowyng, **nor**
enquiring why **they were** so **commaunded.**

And as surely **as this wonderfull miracle was done
to** the great confort of them in **Christes tyme:** so
truly is it left in writyng for to learne **vs by pacience**
and confort of the Scriptures, **to haue good hope** at
this tyme.

And as Christe, hauynge alwayes speciall respecte
vnto hys audience, dyd teache the fyshers by talkyng
of nettes, preachynge vnto the Iewes by dyuers
parables, and called the Gentyles by the eloquence
of Paule: so I, in handlyng of this miracle, hauing
respect vnto thys audience, wyll applye the wonderfull great charitable prouision **of** Christe, **vnto** the
Kynges Maiestye: the faythfull diligence **of the**
Apostles, **vnto** the nobilitie: and **the** dewe **obedience** and hertye thankfulnes **of the** multitude, **vnto
all** other **of** the communaltye. **Not doubtyng but**
that charitable prouision of liberall **benefites, wyll be**
a thyng most plesaunt and honorable for **the** Kynges
Gracious Maiestye, **and** faythfull diligence in dispos-
yng great benefites **most conuenient,** and commendable for all that **be in** high **authoritie:** and **finally,**
humble obedience, **and** vnfayned thankfulnes **to be**
most necessary, requisite, **and looked** for **at this** tyme,
in all inferiours and **commune sorte** of people in Englande.

Marke a litle after the begynnyng of the syxt Chap.
of Iohan, **and** ye shall heare, when as much people
[commyng vnto Iesus, hauyng nothyng to] eate, what
Iesus dyd. I wyll passe the discripcion of the wylder-
nes, with the causes and the maner of the peoples
goyng togither, and begynne at that whiche Christ
dyd, when they were cummyng towardes hym.

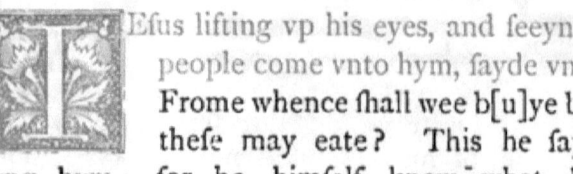Iesus lifting vp his eyes, and seeynge muche people come vnto hym, sayde vnto Philip: Frome whence shall wee b[u]ye bread, that these may eate? This he sayd temptyng hym: for he himself knew what he wolde do. Philippe answered vnto hym: Two hundreth penye worth of breade wyll not be sufficient vnto these so that euerye one myght take a lytell. One of hys disciples Andrew, Symon Peters brother, sayth vnto hym: There is one boye here, whych hath .v. barley loaues and .ii. fyshes, but what ar those amongest so many? Iesus said: Make the men to syt doun. There was muche grasse in the place. The men therefore sat doune, about the numbre of .v. thousands. Iesus tooke the breade, and after thankes geuynge, dyd diuide it vnto his disciples, and the disciples to them that were sette: And lykewyse of the fyshes, so muche as they woulde. And when they were filled, he sayde vnto his disciples: Gather vp the broken meates remaynyng, that nothynge bee lost. They gathered therfore, and fylled .xii. baskets full of those meats which remayned, after that thei hadde eaten. The men therfore seeynge what a sygne Iesus hadde done, sayde that this is trulye the Prophet whiche cummeth vnto the worlde.

O Mercifull Lorde, what a greef is it to see those which a man loueth hertely, with suche diseases infected, that euery thing ministred by the Phisicion to doo them good, by their owne vnquietnes and misusynge of the same, doth encrease their greuous daungerous syckenes. For these [people in the wildernesse, destitute of all prouision, and in great lacke and neede of bodily sustenaunce, were then by a wonderfull miracle, plentifully fedde of Chrift, occafionyng then by the yearthly and bodily foode, to defire and feeke the bread of life, defcendyng from heauen: but then tooke, **and** turned that occafion cleane contrary, imaginyng to make Chrifte an yearthly Kyng, and were **fo** greedie to feede their bodies, that thei had no defire nor taft of the foode of the foule. **And now** England hauyng occafion, by the abolifhyng of Papiftrie, to embrace fincere Chriftianitie, tourned that occafion, to take the fpoyle of Papiftrie, whiche **is** the caufe that many neglecte, **and fclaunder fincere** Chriftianitie. And fo haue, and **doe tourne all** occafions of godly charitable reformation, into worldly couetous **corru**ption. **And the**] people [**of this audience**], hauyng **great** occafion of confort, bi reafon that in [t]his place, through the true preachyng of gods word, all fynne is plainly and freely rebuked: and thofe fynnes efpeciallye **which** dooe appertayne vnto magiftrates, wherby any man of indifferent iudgement, may thynke that thefe magiftrates beeyng prefent, and willingly hearynge, bee purpofed to amende: Thefe people I faye, that thus haue **a** great **occafion of** conforte offered vnto them, by their owne miftakyng of it, dooe tourne all to their further griefe and daunger. For they fpeake vnreuerently, and **vntruly** flaunder the magiftrats, **not** only with the faultes that bee here named, but alfo with rebukyng, imprifonyng, and forbiddyng of the Preachers. And when as by **the** fame **mouth** of the **true** preacher, their venemous tongues be rebuked, then thei fpare not to fay, that the Preacher hath learned his leffon in Iacke an apes court: doyng as much **as lieth** in them, to make other men, neither to **reuerence** the magiftrates, nor beleue the Preacher. What thei them felfes mean therebye, peraduenture by reafon of blyndneffe, they wot not. But we knowyng the craft of the deuyl, **as Paul** writeth. ii. Cor. ii. perceiue yat he wold haue nothing in this place layde to the Rulers charge: Not fearyng how muche be fpoken to thofe of the people, which be paft any amendment by wordes: But all that the deuyll feareth, is, left that the Rulers be put in remembraunce of the great daunger that they be in, for fufferynge fo great enormityes vnpunyfhed amongeft the people.

I therfore truftyng to do moft good in that whiche the deuyll laboureth the moft to hyndre, wyll laye great and many fautes vnto them that haue moft power and authoritie. For fure I am, that rulers ordeyned by God to fee the ignoraunt inftructed, and the euyll punyfhed, be in great daunger of Gods vengeaunce, for the great and manifolde enormities whiche do grow and fpring of ignoraunce, for lacke of knowledge, and of diffolutenes for lacke of due correccion.

And you people be ye fure that the more their daunger is, for lacke of prouifion and punyfhment for other mens faultes, the greater is the damnacion of them that commit and doo thefe fautes.

Nowe I truftyng to God, and not fearyng the deuyll, wyll proceede to declare and applye this parte of fcripture vnto this Audience, fo that for no man I wyll cloke or flatter anye vyce.

Iefus lyftyng vp his eyes, and feeynge muche people cummynge vnto hym, &c.

Here note two thynges: in the people note coming vnto Chrift, and in Chrift, note charitable prouifion for the people. For in this people dothe Chrift declare by example, and proue in experience his doctrine to be true, whiche he had afore taught, faying: Fyrft feeke for the kyngdome of God and the rightoufnes, therof, and all thefe other, meanyng neceffaryes, fhal bee miniftred vnto you. For here they folowyng Chrift, to feke the kyngdome of God, had not onlye this kingdome of God, this bread of lyfe, this woorde of faluacion preached vnto them, but alfo, all their difeafes healed, and their hungrye belyes withe good meates plentifully fylled.

Yea, the plentye of thefe people hauyng enough,

euen fo much as they woulde, was farre more then the plenty of crafty Lawers, difceitful Merchauntes, couetous greedyguttes, and ambicious prollers, whiche canne neuer haue ynough: but alwayes contynew in vnfaciable hunger, and neede of couetoufnes. As [in] the. [xx]xiiii. Pfal. declareth: *Diuites eguerunt*:[1] The ryche haue felt neede and hunger: but they whiche feeke the Lorde, lacke no goodneffe [gooddes].

He that feeketh to be ryche, be he neuer fo poore a flaue, or fo mightye a Lorde, **he** falleth into dyuers temptacions and fnares of **the deuyll**: but they that feeke the **Lorde**, fhall lacke no goodnes. Seke for **to be ryche, and thou** fhalt fynd forow, miferye, and mifcheif: Seeke for to be godlye, and thou fhalt fynd **confort,** welth and profperitie, with al maner of felicitie. If thou wylt be godly, thou muft folowe Chrift: thou muft not folow the fteppes of his feete, which be taken vp into heauen oute of thy fyght, but thou oughteft to folowe the doctrine of his worde, which is lefte here [here left] vpon earth, to guyde the fteppes of thy lyfe, in the way of peace. And whyther wyll **Gods** worde guide the in the tyme of thy trouble and neceffitie? Surely vnto the Lorde, whyche fayth: *Propter miferiam inopum, &c.*[2] For the miferyes fakes of the confortleffe, and fyghynges of the poore, now wyll I ryfe, fayth the Lorde.

O Lorde, feeynge thou hafte manye people in Englande, that as yet be in miferies without confort, and in pouertie, and lacke helpe, how dooeft thou aryfe vnto them? **Vnto** this the Lorde anfwereth, in the. xxxiiii. of Ezechiel: *Sufcitabo fuper eos paftorem vnum,*[3] *&c.* I wyll fet **vp** ouer theim one paftor, euen my feruaunt Dauid, he fhall feede theym, and he fhall be their paftor, and I the Lord, wyl be their God. This prophecye was written longe after Dauids tyme. Wherfore by Dauid here named, is fignified and meante fuche a Kyng as fhalbe as faythfull and diligent to keepe, feede, and cheryfh his fubiectes within hys owne Realme, as was Dauid to his people within Ifraell [, that fame is Chrift in his Kyngdome, in his aucthoritie?]

[1] Psa. *xxxiv*. 10 (Latin). [2] Psa. *xii*. 5. [3] Ezek. *xxiv*. 23.

[And] We hope truste and beleue, that oure gracious Kyng, indued with the faythfull diligence of Dauid, is ordeyned of God, to gouerne, cherish and feede vs the people of this his Realme. Wherfore accordynge to the[e]xample of Christe Iesu, most Christen and Gracious Kyng, for the reuerence of God, which hath set you vpon the high hyll of honor and authoritie, lyft vp your gracious eyes of charitable pitie, and behold much people throughoute all Englande, comyng to seeke releefe, ease, and conforte, sente from God vnto them, by your excellent Maiestye. For althoughe there hathe ben to much mercy shewed vpon the generacion of vypers, the vngracious rebels: Yet is there manye poore people, whiche lyke symple sheepe, shorne to the bare skynne, haue as yet little prouision and great neede: euen as .v. thousandes in wildernes folowed Christ and his Apostles, so many thousandes in Englande, past all other hope and refuge, folow your gracious maiestye and honorable Counsell. For their persons [parsones], which shoulde lyke shepheardes feede them, doo lyke thieues robbe, murther and spoile them. And their landlords, which shuld defend them, be most heauye maisters vnto them: Yea, all maner of officers doo not their duties to kepe the people in good ordre, but rather take such fees as maketh the people veraye poore. Who so hathe eyes, and wyll see, mai easely perceiue that those personages, which be most in nombre, and greatest in value. Throughout all England be no shepherds houses to laye vp fodder to feede the poore sheepe of the parish, but theeuysh dennes, to conuey away great spoyle from all the ryche men of the parish. I say ther is no person there to releeue the poore and nedy, with natural sustinaunce in keepyng of house, and to feede all in generally with the heuenly foode of Gods woorde by preachynge: But there is a persons deputie or fermer, which hauyng neither habilitie, power, nor aucthoritie to doo the persons dutye in feedynge and teachyng the parysh, is able, sufficient, and stout ynough to chalenge and take for his mayfters dutie, the tenth parte of all the parifh. Likewife other officers take many fees, and do few dutyes: And efpecially landlordes take exceedynge fynes and rentes of theire tenauntes, and **doo no good** vnto their tenauntes.

Now my Lordes, bothe **of the laitie and of the** clergye, in the name **of God, I aduertyfe you to take** heede: for **when the Lorde of all** Lords fhal fee his flock fcatered, fpylte, and lofte, if **he folowe** the trace of the bloude, it wyll leade him **euen ftreyght** waye vnto **this** court, and vnto your houfes, where as thefe great theues **which murther,** fpoyle, and **diftroye the** flockes **of** Chrift, **be** receaued, kepte, and mainteyned.

For you mainteyne your chapleynes to take Pluralities, and your other feruauntes mo offyces then they can or wyll difcharge.

Fye for fynne and fhame, eyther gyue **your feruauntes** wages, or els let them go and ferue thofe which do **gyue** them wages. For nowe your chapleynes, your feruauntes, and you* your felues haue the perfons, the fhepherdes, and the offycers wages, and neither you nor they, nor no other dooeth the perfons, the fhepherdes or the offycers dutye, except peraduenture ye imagen that there is a paryfhe priefte, curate, whiche dooeth the perfons duty. But although ye do fo ymagen, **yet the people** do feele and perceyue that he doeth **meane no other** thing **but** pai your duty, paye your dutye. Yes forfoth, **he** miniftreth Gods facramentes, he fayeth **his feruyce,** and he readeth the homilies, as you fyne flatring cowrtiers, which fpeake by imaginacion, tearme it: But the rude lobbes of the countrey, whiche be to fymple to paynte a lye, fpeake foule and **truly** as they fynde it, and faye: He minifheth **Gods** facraments, **he** flubbers vp his feruice, and he can not reade the humbles. Yet is there fome that can reade very well: but how many of thofe be not either fuperfticious papyftes, orels carnall gofpellers, whiche by their euyll example of lyuyng, and worfe

E

doctrine, do farre more harme then they do good by their fayr reading and faiyng of feruyce. But put the cafe, as it maye be, that there bee at a benefyce in fome place at fomtime, fome good curate: all thofe fummes wyll make but a fewe in nombre, and yet ye fee many perfons in many places abfente from their benefices, whiche if they be feldome abfent, may be good, but if they be continually or for the moft part abfent, then can they be neither good, honeft nor godly. For if their duytie be vndone, then can no man excufe them: if it be doone, then is it by other, and not by them: and then why dooe they lyue of other mens labours? He that preacheth the gofpell, fhulde lyue vpon the gofpell, as God hath ordeyned: As for thofe, *Qui mollibus veftiuntur, in domibus Regum*,[1] whiche go gaye in Kynges houfes, and either mofell the labouring oxe, orels fpoyle the poore parifh in the countrey, be of the deuyls ordinaunce. As there is in all offyces, fome putte in by Chrift, fome by the deuyl: fo is there in perfonages [Parfonages], fome fente from Chrift as fhepherds to fede, and fome from the deuyll, as theues to deuoure. Yea, amongeft all kyndes of offycers, fome bee true Prophettes and fhepheardes in dede, and fome haue fhepe fkyns, and be rauenyng wolfes in deede. The one taketh paynes in doyng of his dutye, and the other feketh gaynes in profeffyng of his duty. Take heede of thofe, for they are erraunt theeues.

Alas, if all thofe whiche take the names and profeffyons of offycers, for defyre of luker and honor, and do not execute the duties belongynge to their offyces with paynful diligence, be errant theues, as they be in deede, then is there manye a ftronge erraunt theefe amongeft them that be called honeft, worfhipfull, and honorable men.

For they haue the names, the authorities and vauntages of thofe offyces giuen and payed vnto them, the dutyes of thé whiche be veray flenderly or nothynge at al executed amongeft the people.

[1] Matt. *xi.* 8.

If I were in anye other place in all Englande, I could and wolde vfe an other trade of preachynge afore an other audience: but beyng called of God by your appoyntement vnto this place at this tyme, my confcience doth compell me to vfe this trade and no other, afore this folemne audience. Wherfore with dreede and feare of God, with charitable pitie of the people, with moft reuerende loue and homage vnto your honors, I muft needes crye with the prophet Efaie: *Principes Sodomæ, populus Gomorræ*:[1] Heare the woorde of the Lorde ye Princes of Sodome, ye people of Gomorra: *Quo mihi multitudo victimarum veftrarum*:[1] What care I for the great nombre of your facrifyces, *Dicit Dominus*, fayth the lord: rebukynge all the facrifices, ceremonies, and feaftes of the Iewes, which he himfelfe had commaunded to be obferued and kepte: by the which thyng left in writynge, he doth teache and commaunde me howe to fpeake of your wel doyng here in England. Heare therfore ye Princes of Sodome, and ye people of Gomor, thus fayth the Lord. What pleafure haue I, yea what care I for al your Englifhe Bibles, Homilies, and all youre other bookes: fet furthe no more godly feruyce to honor me with: I hate them all with my herte, they are greuous vnto me, I am wery of them: Yea, it is a great payne for me to fuffer them. Why, o lord, thefe be good, thefe be godly, and thefe be neceffary thynges.

Truth it is, the faulte is not in the thynges that be fet furthe, but in you that haue fet them furthe. *Manus enim veftræ plenæ funt fanguine*:[2] For your handes are ful of blood.

Your handes, your feruyces [feruice] and your houfes be ful of perfons lyuynges, Preachers liuynges, and offycers liuynges. And by you, the perfone hath his difpenfacion, the preacher is put to fcilence, and the offycer vnpunyfhed, for neclectynge of his dutye. And fo through the negligence of the kepers, [(]good order, which is the pale of the parke of this commune welth dekayed[)], the dere therof, moft dearly bought with

---

[1] **Isa.** *i.* 10, 11. [2] Isa. *i.* 15.

Chriftes bloude, haue ftrayed oute of theire owne feedynge, to diftroy the corne of all mens liuynges : Where as very neceffytie hath compelled you with fuch force to driue them backe, as muft needes diftroye manye of thofe dere. Thofe people I mean, which you haue cheryfhed and kept, and as yet doo loue and pitie aboue all other iewels, commodities and pleafures. Alas, thefe that take the liuynges, and doo not the dutyes of Perfons, Preachers, landlordes, Bailyes, and of other officers: Thefe flatterers, thefe wolfes in lambes fkyns, thefe deuyls in mens vyfers haue caufed you to be thought and taken as cruell oppreffers of thofe [thefe] people, whofe furious wylde rage ye dyd fuppreffe and keepe vnder, of veraye charitable pitie towardes them, and all other, whiche with that rebellious rage, fhulde haue be all togither diftroied, if the help of your power and aucthoritie had ben anye longer differred.

Surely, vntyll that thefe prollers for them felues, thefe children of the deuyll, thefe fowers of fedicion be taken out of the way, either by reformacion, or by diftruction, your charitable pitie and prouifion for the people, and their reuerende loue and obedience towardes you, fhall neuer be feene, felt, and knowen. Nowe, as Helye was gilty of the whordome, extorcion, and abhominacion of his fonnes, fo are your hertes full of crueltye, and your handes full of bloude, not fo muche by doyng, as by fufferyng all thefe euyls. Wherfore *Lauamini, mundi eftote* :[1] Wafh, and make your felfes cleane, with the teares of repentaunce. *Auferte malum cogitationum veftrarum ab oculis meis* :[1] Awai with the euil of your thoughtes from afore my eyes. Open your heartes, that the fworde of Gods word may come to wype awaye couitoufnes, whiche is the roote of all euyll, planted in your hertes. For if that roote continew there, than can no good fpring from you : but euen the moft pure and holfome woorde of God fette furth by you, continuyng in couitoufnes, wyll be abhominable in the fyght of God, offenfiue vnto

[1] Isa. *i.* 16.

the people, and damnable vnto your selues. Wherfore, *Quiescite agere peruerse*:[1] Seace to peruerte, manye thynges from euyll vnto worse. *Discite benefacere*:[1] Learne to do well, in conformyng al thyngs that be amisse, vnto a good ordre. *Quærite iudicium*:[1] Seeke [Searche] for righteous iudgement, which is almost banyshed out of Englande. Alas what a iudgement is this, a supersticious papiste, whiche hathe made the faulte, shall haue a pension out of a Chauntrie, so longe as he lyueth, and a poore paryshe whiche hathe great neede and doone no faulte, shall lose and forsayte many Chauntries vtterly for euer. *Subuenite oppresso*:[1] Helpe the oppressed people that be loaden with heuye burdeyns of paiynge wages to manye offyces, and faynte for lacke of releese, and due seruyce of the offycer. *Iudicate pupillo*:[1] Iudge so to the fatherles chyldrens behose, that wardship mai be a good prouision for fatherles chyldren, and not an vncharitable spoyle of yong mens landes. *Defendite viduam*:[1] Shielde the wydow from all mens iniuryes, and compell them not to marye your vnthrifty seruauntes.

Thus hath God by Esaye in his tyme, and by me at this tyme described Rulers Faultes, with a waye how to amende them. Therfore, *Principes Angliæ*:[1] Ye head rulers and gouernors of England, fyrst see, acknowledge and* amende your owne fautes: And then, perusynge all vnder offycers, consyder, and note how few shepheards and offycers doo feede and keepe, by doyng dutyes, and how many theeues, and wolfes do robbe and spoyle the flockes, by takyng fees here in Englande: and then shall ye perceaue that there must nedes be manye sheepe, that with their hertes, myndes, and expectacion, do folow the Kynges Maiestye, and you of his honorable counsell, so farre paste the houses and cyties of their owne prouision, that yf thei haue not spedy reliefe at your handes, many of them is lyke to feynte and decaye by the way.

Therfore this consydered and knowen, as Christ lyftyng vp his eyes, dyd teache you to see and con-

[1] Isa. *i.* 16, 17.

fyder the people: fo learne by that whiche foloweth in Chriftes dooyng, what fhalbe your dutye after that ye fee and knowe the multitude, the ftate and condicion of the people.

And he fayd vnto Philip: From whence fhall we bye breade, that thefe maye eate? But this he fayde to proue him: for he him felfe knewe what he wolde doo.

Chrift faid to Philip, as euery Chriften King ought to fay to his Counfell: From whence fhal we that be gouernors, kepers and feders, bye and prouide with our own coftes, labor, and diligence, bread, foode and neceffaryes, that thefe may eate and be releued, which be our fubiectes, in obedience, brethern in Chrift, and felow heyres of the heauenly kyngdome.

Pharao with his Counfell in Egipte, confulted howe to bryng the welthy people vnto miferye: fo that he is a very Pharonicall tyrant, which laboreth by oppreffion to thruft down the welthy people: And he is a faythful chriften kyng, that humbleth himfelfe by diligence to releeue, conforte, and fet vp the afflycted people. For the one, by worldiy policy, wolde haue much honor, and the other of godlye charitie wyll do much good. Chrift alfo fayde this, to proue and trye Philip, knowyng him felfe what fhoulde be done. So that here, Kynges and great men may lerne to trye and proue the honeftye, wyt, and fidelitie of their Counfellers in fuch matters as they them felues be fo perfect that they can difcerne with what difcrecion and mynde the Counfeller doth anfwere.

[And in this we maie fe, that God doeth not lacke, or neede any counfaile, or helpe of any manne, to dooe any good thyng, but would haue men to vnderftande how muche and wel that God, and how little or nothing menne can deuife, and dooe when as neede is. So therefore will God vfe, and exercife men, as Chrift here doeth vfe, and exercife Phillip, Andrewe, and the other Difciples, for their owne neceffitie, comforte, and commoditie to receiue, and learne of hym, wherewith they maie dooe good vnto others. And this leſſon had not Phillip yet learned.]

Philip aunſwered, that two hundreth **peny worth of breade** wyll not ſerue vnto theſe, ſo that euerye one myght take a lytell.

In the which anſwere, as concernyng his wytte, he declareth it to be to ſlender to prouyde for ſo great a matter in ſo ſhort **tyme.** And his mynde ſeemed to be ſuch, as wolde not haue Chriſt to trouble him ſelfe with ſo great **cares,** but rather as the other Euangeliſtes do declare, to ſende the people awai, and let them prouide for them ſelfes. The ſame mynde and affection was in Peter, after that Chriſt hadde tolde his Diſciples howe that he muſt go to Ieruſalem to ſuffer ſore paynes and miſerable death. For then Peter tooke him a ſyde and ſayde: Maiſter, fauour your ſelfe, doo **not entre** in to ſuche daunger and ſorowes.

And it is not vnlyke, but if your Mageſtye, with your Counſell, ſpeake vnto your nobles for prouiſion now to be made for the people, ye ſhall fynde ſome that bee Philippians and Peters, whiche by ſettynge afore your eyes the hardnes of the matter, the tendernes of your yeares, and the wonderfull charges that ſhulde be requiſite, wyll moue and counſell you to quiet youre ſelfe, to take your eaſe, yea, to take your paſtyme, in haukyng, huntyng or gamnyng. Vnto whom your Mageſtie may anſwere, as Chriſte dyd vnto Peter: Auoide fro me Sathan, thou hyndreſt me by thy carnall temptacion, to doo that thynge whiche God hath moued me vnto by his gracious inſpiracion. Thou haſt no taſt nor fauour how delicious God is vnto a pure conſcience, in godlye exerſyce of good workes. But all that thou regardeſt and feleſt, is voluptuous pleaſure in worldly vanities. And therfore thou doeſt not perceaue, how that they, which be indued with a ſpeciall grace of God, maye fynde more pleaſure and paſtyme in godly gouernaunce, to keepe togyther, and ſaue ſymple men, then in haukyng and

huntynge, to chafe and kyll wylde beaftes. Yea, a
godly kyng fhall fynde more pleafure in cafting lottes
for Ionas, to try out offenders, whiche trouble the
fhip of this commune wealthe, then in caftyng dice at
hafarde, to alow and maintayne by his example, fuch
thynges as fhulde not be fuffered in a commune wealth.
Yea furely, a good Kynge fhall take farre more delyte
in edifiyng with conforte and deckyng with good order
the Congregacion of his people, the Churche and
Houfe of God, the heauenly Citie of Ierufalem, then
in buildyng fuche houfes as feeme gaye and gorgeous,
and be in deede but vile earthe, ftones, tymber and
claye. Suche lyke anfwere ought your Mageftye, and
all noble men to make, if ye fynde anye of youre
Counfellers more carnall than fpiritual, more worldlye
then godly. Orels turne awai your eares from fuche
Philippians, and heare other, as Chrift dyd.

Then fayde vnto hym one of his Difciples, Andrew,
Symon Peters brother, There is a boy here that hath
fiue barley loaues and two fyfhes, but what auayle thofe
among fo manye?

Note here that this boye was the Apoftles page,
and thefe loaues and fyfhes were their vittayles. For
as appeareth in Marke, when he had made fearche how
many loaues they them felues had, this anfwer was
made, that thei had. v loues and. ii. fifhes: but what
be thei amongeft fo many? As who fhulde fay: although thefe be al that euer we haue, and feeme more
meete to be kepte amongeft a fewe, then to be gyuen
vnto many: yet forbicaufe thei [that] be cum [come],
[whiche beyng] many haue more nede then we: yet
[therefore] ar we willyng to giue them to be difpofed,
and wyffhe that they were of more value to dooe more
good amongeft the people.

Thefe men cared more for the Commune people
then they dyd for them felues, and therfore were very
meete to be Counfellers, and neare about a great Kyng.
[And furely none can continue neare, and deare vnto our

kyng Chrift but fuche, for others that euer prolle for priuate profite, bee hypocrites and flatterers as was Iudas. And] Here wee perceyue what fymple Philip, and **good Andrewe thynke, but here is nothing declared of couetous Iudas** counfell. **No, for Chrift** beyng fully purpofed **to doo a** good deede, **dothe neither afke, nor** heare any counfell of couetous **Iudas: teaching all them** which intende any **goodnes, neuer to** afke **nor admit anye counfell of thofe whom** thei **know to be** couetous. For trulye **the couetous mans** counfell, although **it** feeme **neuer fo good and** honeft, **yet is it** in **deede** nought **and deuelifh. For what could feeme better counfell, then yat a litle ointment, the fwete fmell of the whiche continued but a** whyle among **a few, fhuld haue ben foulde for.** iii. hundreth pence, the great **price of the** whiche, beftowed amongeft manye poore, **fhulde haue done them good for a great ceafon [feafon]?**

The Euangelift dothe **fhewe howe that** Iudas dyd gyue **thys** counfell, not **for** that **he had anye care of the poore,** but becaufe he was a **theefe, and baire the bagges.**

Iudas **pretence** was **wonders goodly, to fell the** oyntment **for a great** fumme **of** money, **to relieue the poore with: but his purpofe was** deuelyfh, **to get the** money **in** his bagges, **and keepe it to** him **felfe.** And thofe in Englande, **which dyd** pretende, that befydes the abolyfhynge **of fuperfticion, with the** landes of Abbeyes, **Coliges [**Colledges**], and Chauntryes, the** Kyng fhuld **be enriched,** learnyng **mainteyned, pouertye relieued,** and **the commune** wealth **eafed, and by this pretence, purpofely haue** enriched **theim** felues, fettyng **abrode incloyftred** papiftes, **to get their** liuyngs by giuyng **them penfions, yea,** and thruftyng them into benefices to poyfon the whole commune welth for the refignacion of thofe pencions, and fo craftly conueying much from the King, **from** lernyng, from pouertie, and **from** all the commune welth, vnto their owne priuate vauntage. Thefe mennes counfell **femed** better then Iudas counfell was: **and** their couetoufnes, by their owne deedes appeareth no leſſe then Iudas couetouſneſſe dyd. Well, beware, for if ye play Iudas part on ſtyll, and make no reſtitucion, vntil ye go to hangyng, ye ar lyke to fynde deſperacion at th[e]ende of your life, bicauſe ye wold not by reſtitucion amende your life. Ye noble men, and eſpecialli you of the kings counſel, for the reuerence of God, pitie of the commen wealth, and ſafegarde of your ſelfes, awaye with theſe Iudaſſes, let them go hang them ſelfes: excepte peraduenture ye thynke yt fytte and neceſſary, that you fyrſt hang them afore they betray you. For vndoubtedly, he that hath the couetouſnes of Iudas in his hert, he wyll playe all the other partes of Iudas, if he euer haue ſuche oportunitie as Iudas had.

Away with Iudas, and learne at Andrew, to ſaye vnto this kynge and his counſell intendyng to relieue the multitude of his people here in Englande, learne ye noble men to ſaye: Here is a boye: Here be feruauntes and retainers of ours, which haue fyue loaues and two fyſhes, many benefyces, ſome prebendes, with dyuers offices: yea, and ſome of vs our ſelues haue mo offyces then we can diſcharge. Pleaſeth it your maieſtie to take theſe into your handes, which haue ben kepte for vs, that they nowe in this greate nede, may be better diſpoſed amongeſt your people. *Quid hoc inter tantos?*[1] Theſe be verye ſmall thynges towardes the amendment of ſo many lackes, in ſo great a multitude. How be it theſe wyll ſerue, ſo that there may be mo good Perſons, good Preachers, and good officers placed abrode in euery countrey, whiche in doing their offices, keping of houſes, and preachyng of gods word, may teache the ignoraunt, relieue the poore, punyſh the fau[l]tye, and cheryſh the honeſt, and ſo repayre the pale of good ordre about this commen welth. For the loue of god gyue your feruauntes wages, and cauſe them to reſtore theſe liuings, which comyng of the ſweate of the labourer, be in dede the reliefe of the poore, ye maintenaunce of honeſty, and the reward of vertue, yea, the very pale,

[1] John *vi.* 9.

wall, and bulwarkes of the commen wealth. The Apoſtles gaue al that thei had of their own, frely vnto other: ſtycke not you to reſtore yat now which ye haue of long time vncharitably kept from other.

Heare what foloweth: whan theſe fiſhes and loaues were brought vnto Ieſus, make (ſayth he) the people to ſyt doune. God alwaies beſtoweth his benefites vpon them that ſyt doune in quietnes, and powreth furth his vengeaunce vpon thoſe that be vnpacient, vnquiet, and full of buſyneſſe. For as appeareth in Geneſis: The people gathered togither in the plain of Sannaer [Sanner], and made a great vprore, buyldyng a towre lyke rebels againſt god, to get them a name. Howbeit god deſtroyed their handywork, confounded their langage, and ſcatred them abrode.

The Scribes and the Phariſeys came vnquietly, tempting Chriſt, and requyred a ſygne from heauen. Chriſt rebuked them ſharply, and ſhewed them no ſygne, but called them a frowarde and aduoutrous generacion. So the people in Englande gathered togyther, thei woulde make maiſteryes, and bee notable felowes, yea, the towre of their preſumpcion ſhuld be buylt vp vnto heauen, in diſpite of gentyl men and nobilitie: they haue partlye felte, and we haue ryghte pitifully ſeene how ſore God was therwith offended. Now I heare ſaye there is as yet remainyng in England ſum ſtiffe necked Iewes, which come preſumptuouſly tem[p]tyng God, and ſay: if theſe our rulers be ſent of God to take better order then other haue done, well then let theym begynne betyme to gyue vs a notable ſygne and token, for els we wyll not bileeue, truſt, nor obey them.

Well, I wyl tell you that thus whyſper: Euen as Chriſte was *Poſitus in reſurrectionem et ruinam multorum in Iſraell*:[1] Set to reſtore and dekay manye in Iſraell: So be Chriſten rulers in euerye commune wealth, ſet and ordeyned of God, to beate doune and kepe vnder theſe ſturdye rebels, whiche be ſo euyll

---

[1] Luke *ii*. 34.

themſelues, that thei can not thynke that any man
doth intende to doo them good, and to reiſe vp, conforte and cheriſh the ſimple pacient people, which be
of a good truſt towards their rulers, knowynge that they
themſelfes haue deſerued no euil: orels if they haue
done euyll, yet by repentaunce and amendment, do not
doute to obteyne mercye at their rulers handes. So God
hath ordeyned rulers to cheryſhe the[e], if thou be made
quiet and pacient, orels to puniſh the if you [thou]
be vnquiet, buſy, and ſtoborne. Learne at [S.] Paul. Ro.
xiii. If you do wel, to truſt wel of thy rulers, and if
thou do euil, not to be without fere of their powers:
for he beareth not ye ſword without a cauſe. Take
hede therfore ye rulers, for gods ſake, and pitie of the
people, ſeyng yat god hath geuen you a ſword, to cut
of rotten cankred membres, for ye ſafegard of ye
hole body, knowing no canker to be ſo dangerus as is
rebellion in a comen welth: If ye finde one perſon infected with that canker, away with him, for ye ſafegard of ye body of yat houſe. If one houſe be infected, away with it, for the ſafegard of yat toune. If
ye toune be infected, awai with it, for ye ſafegard of
the contrey. Yea, if a ſhyre or contrey be al poyſoned,
away with it, for the pitie and ſafegarde of the hole
body of the comen welth. So ye ſe that the ſharper
yat your ſword is, and ye ſoner that ye ſtrike rebellion,
ye more pitie ye ſhew [ſhewe ye] in cutting awai the leſſe,
and ſauing ye more part and porcion of the people,
being al of one body, of one realme and comen welth.
Conſider that Chriſt went from Ieruſalem vnto wildernes, to draw ye gentle people from among ye ſtoborn
ſcribes: and ſo chriſten rulers muſt now nedes defer
ye time to draw ye people yat be good and truſt
well, from among this froward generacion, whiche of
preſumcion loke to haue ordre taken as they require
and appoint ye time, ye place, and ye thing.
Wherfore ye yat be good quiet people beware of
theſe buſi felowes, and as this multitude which ought
to be your example, folowed chriſt into wildernes, ſo

folow you chriſten rulers, gods officers, your chefe gouerners in england. And as thei dyd not murmour, faiing: why ſhal we ſyt doune here in wildernes, being an infinit number wher no meat is, ſeing that in the cities where was more meate, and leſſe gatherynge of the people, we had neuer feaſt gyuen ot hym by his Apoſtles?

So I ſay, do not you grudge and ſaye: why ſhall we quiet our ſelues nowe, truſtynge to releefe, where wce ſee nothyng, and were nothyng at all releeued when there was great plentye of landes, and goodes of Abbeyes, Cole[d]gies, and Chauntries? Do not murmour ſo vngodly, but ſee that there bee no faulte in you, and ye ſhal fynde no lacke in God. Surely, excepte ye do ſytte doune quietly, ye ſhall ſooner prouoke Gods vengeaunce to your damnacion, then deſerue any releeſe of Gods offycers, to your confort. Syt doune and be quiet, for the ſame rulers and miniſters are ordeyned of God, to feede you with plentye: whiche be commaunded of God to make you fyrſt to ſytte doune in ordre and quietnes. Yea, and herke all ye that be godlye Rulers: there was much graſſe in the place. God had prouided much graſſe for theym that loked for no carpets: geuing all godly gouernours example to prouyde thynges neceſſarye for thoſe people that loketh for no ſuperfluities. But alas, here in England, ſuperfluous gorgeous building is ſo much prouided for ryche mens pleaſures, that honeſt houſes do decay, where as labouryng men ought to haue neceſſary lodgyng. It is a commen cuſtome with couetous landlordes, to lette their houſynge ſo decaye, that the fermer ſhalbe ſayne for a ſmall rewarde or none at all, to gyue vp his leaſſe, that they takynge the groundes into their owne handes, may turne all to paſture: ſo now Olde Fathers, poore Wydowes, and yong Chyldren lye beggyng in the myrie ſtretes.

O mercyfull Lorde, what a numbre of Poore, Feble, Haulte, Blynde, Lame, ſycklye, yea, with idle vacaboundes, and diſſemblyng kaityſſes mixt among them, lye and creepe, beggyng in the myrie ftreates of London and Weftminfter?

Nowe fpeakyng in the behalfe of thefe vile beggers, forafmuche as I know that ye vileft perfon vpon erth, is the liuely image of almightye God, I wyl tell the[e] that art a noble man, a worfhipful man, an honeft welthye man, efpecially if thou be Maire, Shirif, Alderman, baily, conftable or any fuch officer, it is to thy great fhame afore the worlde, and to thy vtter damnacion afore god, to fe thefe begging as thei vfe to do in the ftreates. For there is neuer a one of thefe, but he lacketh eyther thy charitable almes [almofe] to relieue his neede, orels thy due correction to punyfh his faute. A great fyn and no leffe fhame is it for him that faith he is a chriften man, to fee chrift lacke things neceffary, and to beftow vpon the deuyl fuperfluofly. It is Chrift Iefu[s] himfelf that in the nedi doth fuffer hunger, thrift and colde. It is the deuil him felfe, that in the wealthye fareth dientily, goeth gorgioufly, and vfeth fuperfluitye. Looke Matthewe the. xxv. and there fhall ye fee playnlye that it is Chrift which lacketh fufficient in the neadye: and therfore the deuyll beyng contrary to Chrift, contrariwife hath to much in the wealthye.

You alfo that do prouide that your cattell dooe not longe tarye pynned in a folde where there is no graffe, whye dooe you fuffer youre owne brethren in Chrift, withoute prouifion to lye in the ftreates, where is muche myer? Thefe fely fols [feelie foules] haue ben neglected throghout al England and efpecially in London and Weftminfter: But now I truft that a good ouerfeer, a godly Byfhop I meane, wyl fee that they in thefe two cyties, fhall haue their neede releeued, and their faultes corrected, to the good enfample of al other tounes and cities.

Take heede that there be much graffe to fytte vpon, there as ye commaund the people to fyt doune, that there be fufficient houfyng, and other prouifion for the people there as ye commaunde them to be quiet. The men fatte doune about fyue thoufandes in number.

If they had not ben obedient to **fyt doune**, Chrift wolde not **haue** ben liberal to haue gyuen theym meate.

Meate was prouided **for the Commens of Englande,** and ready to haue **ben deliuered:** But when **they were** by**dden to** fyt doune **in quietnes, they** rofe vp by re**bellion,** and haue loft **all the chere of that feaft. Yet that** notwithftandyng, **I truft that thofe whiche fat** quietly in dede, fhall **foone be fedde with plentye, if** they fytte **ftyll, vntyll it may conueniently be difpofed. I pray God they may, I truft thei fhall. The Euan-gelift fayth that the men fatte, namyng neither women nor chyldren: how be it there was bothe women and chyldren, as appeareth in the other Euangeliftes. And men be here** named only, **bicaufe all women and** chyldren dyd folowe the example, and **obey the** commaundement of men, chyldren of their[the] fathers, and women **of** their hufbands.

Let not therfore **your wyues and chyldren, when they come abrode, be fo bolde openly, as to fay or do** any **thynges of them felfes, but as they haue example** and commaundement **of you. Nowe the** multitude placed **in quietnes:**

Iefus **toke the** loaues, and when **he had** gyuen thankes, **he diuided** them vnto his Difciples, and the Difciples vnto them that were fet doune: and likewyfe **of** the fyfhes, fo muche **as they wolde.**

Here learne **fyrft of Chrift, to** take nothyng, **be it neuer fo** lytell, **but** with **thankes** rendered therfore **vnto God:** For of God furely thou haft receaued it, by **what** meffenger or **meane fo** euer thou came **vnto** it. **Then** fecondarily, learne **at the** Apoftles to giue vnto other, that which the Lord hath gyuen **vnto** the, that **thou mayft truly** fay with the Apoftle **Paul:** *Quod accepi a domino, hoc tradidi vobis:*[1] That whiche I receaued of the Lorde, haue I geuen vnto you. Beware that **thou playe not** the wycked feruaunt, which kepte his talent **hyd,** and not deliuered vnto any vfe,

---

[1] 1 Cor. xi. 23.

for then it shall be taken from the, and thou shalte be caste into vtter derkenesse.

Now, to applye this miracle vnto this present time, time, the Kyngs Mageſtye may learne at Chriſte, to take of his ſeruantes, Prebendes, Benefices, Improperacions, and all maner of Offyces, that be not preſently occupyed and executed of a faythfull diligent offycer: and after thankes geuen vnto God therfore, to delyuer them vnto his Counſell and Nobilitie, to be diſpoſed amongeſt the people of his Realme, which be in ſuch hungre and lacke of faythfull offycers, and houſekepers, and godly preachers, that thei muſt needes faint, excepte they be ſone prouided for.

And in this diſtribucion of offyces and beneſyces, your Mageſtye with your Counſell had nede to ſtande and beholde the dealyng of your nobles, as Chriſt dyd of his Apoſtles. For it is not vnlike but as there was amongeſt Chriſtes Apoſtles, ſo wyll there be amongeſt euerye Chriſten Kynges Councellers and Nobles, ſome Iudas, whiche is to be truſted no further than he can be ſeene. For in ſyght Iudas dothe as other of his felowes do: but beyng out of ſyght, he ſolde his Maiſter. And ſo the moſte couetous of them all, wyll be a frayde to do any thynge amyſſe, if you loke vpon: but if your backes be turned, then wyll couetous Iudas ſell dearely that which his liberall maiſter gyueth freely. As for example of late dayes, the Kynges Mageſty that dead is, dyd gyue a Benefyce to be appropriate vnto the Vniuerſitie of Cambridge, *In liberam et puram eliemoſynam*: As free and pure almes. How be it, his handes were ſo vnpure, which ſhuld haue deliuered it, that he receaued. vi. hundred poundes of the Vniuerſitye for it. Whether that this. vi.C. pounds were conucied to the kings behoofe priuely for that Almes, which by playne writyng was giuen freely, orels put into ſome Iudas pouch, I wold it wer knowen. For nowe, by ſuche charitable Almes, the kyng is ſlaundered, the paryſh vndone, and the Vniuerſitye in worſe caſe then it was afore.

Pleaſeth it your Mageſtye, with your honorable Counſell, for the reuerence of God, the pitie of the poore, and the godlye zele that ye haue to good lernyng, heare what hath ben done in your tyme.

Your Mageſtie hath had gyuen, and receaued by **Act of** Parliament, Collegies, Chauntries, and guyldes for many good conſideracions, and eſpecially as appeareth in ye **ſame** Act, for erecting **of** Grammer ſcoles, to the educacion of youthe in vertue and godlynes, to the further augmentyng of the vniuerſyties, and better **prouiſion** for the poore **and** needye. But nowe, many **Grammer ſcholes, and** much charitable prouiſion for the **poore, be taken,** folde, and made awaye, to the **great ſlaunder of** you and your lawes, to the vtter diſconforte of the poore, to the greuous offence of the people, to the moſt miſerable drounynge of youthe in ignoraunce, and ſore decaye of the Vniuerſities.

There was in the North countrey, amongeſt the rude people in knowledge (which be moſt readye to ſpende their lyues and goodes, in ſeruyng the Kyng at the burnyng of a Beacon) there was a Grammer ſchole founded, hauyng in the Vniuerſitie of Cambridge, of the ſame foundacion. viii. ſcholerſhips, euer replenyſhed with the ſcholers of that ſchole, which ſcole is now folde, decayed, and **loſte.** Mo there be of lyke ſorte handled: But I recyte thys only, bicauſe I knowe that the ſale of it was once ſtayed of charitie, and yet afterwards broughte to paſſe by bribrye, as I hearde ſay, and beleue it, bicauſe that it is only bribrye, that cuſtomablye ouercometh charitie.

For Gods ſake, you that be in aucthoritie, loke vpon it.

For if ye winke at ſuche matters, God wyl ſcoule [that **is to** ſaie, looke with anger vppon you] vpon you. **Thinke** not that **I** do burden **you** with more than that, which God by his ordynance, not without your willes and conſentes, hath charged you with **all.** For by whoſe fau[l]t[e] or negligence ſo euer it was, that things afore tyme haue ben vncharitablye abuſed, ſurelye it is youre charge, whiche be now in

F

aucthoritie, to fe at this tyme all fuche thynges as yet remain out of ordre, rightoufly, fpedely, and charitably redreffed. And as I do perceiue, that the abufe of thefe thynges afore tyme, hath offended God, troubled the commen wealthe, and brought fome men towardes fhame and confufion : So do I wyfh, pray, and trufte, that now the redreffe of the fame, may be to Gods pleafure, the peoples confort, and to the honor and eftablyfhment of theym that be in moft hygh aucthoritie.

Heare therfore, and I wyll tell you more: There were in fome townes. vi. fome. viii. and fome a dozen kyne, gyuen vnto a ftocke, for the reliefe of the poore, and vfed in fuch wyfe, that the poore cotingers, which coulde make any prouifion for fodder, had ye mylke for a very fmall hyre: and then the number of the ftocke referued, all maner of vailes befydes, bothe the hyre of the mylke, and the pryces of the yonge veales, and olde fat wares, was difpofed to the reliefe of the poore, thefe be alfo folde, taken, and made away. The Kyng beareth the flaunder, the poore feeleth the lacke, but who hath the profit of fuche thynges, I can not tell: but well I wot, and all the worlde fayth, that the Act of Parliament made by the Kynges Mageftye, and his Lords and Commens of the Parliament, for the mayntenaunce of learnyng, and reliefe of the poore, hath ferued fome, as a moft fyt inftrument to robbe learnyng, and to fpoyle the poore. If you that be now in aucthoritie do not loke vpon fuch thynges to redreffe them, God wyl loke vpon you, to reuenge theim. Here haue I reherfed them, that the Kynges Mageftye, with you of his counfell maye learne, not onlye by the doctrine and examples of fcripture, but alfo by experience in his owne lande, to fee and confyder howe his benefytes, put into the handes of his nobles and officers, be difpofed and vfed amongeft his inferioure people.

For if landed men and officers, by keping of houfes, and doing of their dutyes in their countryes, do beftowe amongeft [emong] the people, all that they haue receaued of God, by the kynges gyft, their fathers inheritaunce, or other wayes: then shall God giue such increase, that euery man shall haue inough.

As Salomon, the. xi. of the Prouerbes testifieth:. *Alii diuidunt propria, et ditiores fiunt: alii rapiunt non sua, et semper in egestate sunt*:[1] Some dispose and gyue their owne, and become rycher and rycher: some doo raueyn and spoyle that which is not their owne, and be euer in lacke and neede. **As ye see in** dailye experience, those that do their **owne** dutyes **in** executynge their offyces, and bestowe theire owne goodes in keepyng good houses, haue euer suche plentye, that all other men meruayle from whence God sendeth it. And **those that dooe no** duties, nor keepe no houses, **but** brybe **in** their offyces, and polle their tenauntes, take so much, and haue so lytell, that all men wunder how the deuyl thei wast it.

Nothyng is more true than the gospel: *Date, et dabitur vobis*:[2] Gyue and it shall be gyuen vnto you. Giue plentifully vnto other, and God wyl gyue more plentye vnto you. For God wyll alwayes be afore hande, in giuynge good gyftes. For as appeareth in this gospell, when the Apostles had giuen **vnto** the people so much good meate as they desyred, then **sayeth** the Euangelist:

When thei were filled, Iesus sayeth to his disciples: Gather vp the broken meates that remayn, so that nothynge be lost. They **therfore** gathered, and fylled .xii. baskets ful with **the broken** meates remaining **of** that which they **had eaten**.

Here they gaue **but. v. loaues and .ii. fyshes, and** there **was** gyuen vnto them. **xii.** baskets **ful of meats**.

The Wydowe of Sareptha, gaue but one **handfull** of flowre, **and** a lytle oyle vnto Elias, and **had** gyuen vnto her agayne so muche as serued her and her sonne, al the tyme of **the greate** droughte .iii. Re[gu]. xvii. Learne therfore that couetous bribry and extorcion hath **neuer** ynough: and charitable liberalitie, euer hathe plentye. Here also maye ryche men learne, when and howe to

---

[1] Prov. xi. 24.   [2] Luke vi. 38.

fyll their ftore houfes. Surelye, euen as the Apoftles dyd fyll their bafkettes, when the people haue [had] ynoughe, then by gatheryng vp that which els fhoulde be loft. So dyd Iofephe in Egipt, fuffre no corne to be loft in the yeares of plenty, but ftored it vp in barnes, to relieue the people with, in ye tyme of darth: Not as couitous carles do here in Englande forftall the markettes, and b[u]ye corne at all tymes, to begynne and encreafe a dearth. Bleffed be they that fell, to make good cheape, and curfed be they that b[u]ye, to make it deare. For Salomon fayeth, Prouerb. xi. *Qui abfcondit frumenta, maledicetur in populis: benedictio autem fuper caput vendencium:*[1] He that hydeth vp corne, fhall be curfed amongeft the people: But bleffyng be vpon their heades, that fell.

Nowe, to teache Chriften rulers their dutyes, in the example of Chriftes Apoftles: marke how the Apoftles dyd fyrft minifter vnto the people, and than gathered vp for them felfes: teachyng therby all Chriften minifters, landelordes, offycers, and rulers, fyrfte to minifter vnto the people, euery one the dutye of his owne vocacion, afore they gather of the people, rentes, tythes, or fees, by the name and aucthoritie of that vocacion. *Qui non laborat*, fayth [S] Paul, *non manducet:*[2] He that doth not labour, fhuld not eate. He that doth no worke, fhulde take no wages: he that dothe no dutyes, fhoulde take no fees. Alas, this is Gods woorde, written in his wylle and Teftament, fealed with Chriftes bloude, and yet the cuftomes and lawes of Englande be cleane contrarye. For it hath ben cuftomeably vfed, yea, and by lawes commaunded, to paye wages, tythes, and fees, although no labour, no offyce, no dutye be done. Yea, although he be not a labourer, a paftor, or an offycer in dede, but only by a pretenfed name, vnto whom thefe for the moft parte be payed.

For he that hath the properties, and vfeth the trades of a falfe thefe, and a cruell murtherer, can neuer be a faythful offycer in dede, altho[u]gh he be fo named by

[1] Prov. xi. 28.   [2] 2 Thess. iii. 10

his owne flatery, in the Patrons prefentacion, in the Byfhoppes induction, yea, and in the Kynges Patent, fealed with **the brode** Seale. **I** had nede to take heede howe that I fpeake openly **agaynſt** any **thyng** in any **mans** Patent, fealed with **the kings** greate Seale: Muche more neede had you to take heede, how that **ye** do any thyng expreſſedly **agaynſt Gods wyll and** Teſtament, fealed with Chriſtes precious bloude. It is expreſſedly agaynſte **Gods Teſtament,** to clothe a Wolfe in a Lambes ſkynne: **to call a thefe,** an officer: and a cruel murtherer, a charitable paſtor: to call euyll, by the **name of good:** and good, by **the** name of euyll. Efaye. v. *Væ qui dicitis malum bonum* :[1] Wo be to you that **cal euyl** good. To you I fay, which **not only** by fayings, but alſo in writynges, do name and cal thieues, murtherers, and wolfes that be euyll, by the names of officers, paſtors, and lambes, which be good. I dooe not only meane, Perſones, Prebendaries, **and other** benefifed men, but alſo all maner of* officers, **which** haue wages, fees, or lyuynges, **bicaufe you gyue them** fuche names, and not for that thei **do fuche dutyes.**

Thefe be al Wolfes, and the names and tytles that **you gyue them,** be nothyng **els but ſheepe** ſkynnes. Some faye, they wyll take better heede here after, but that which is now paſt, can not nowe be called backe, and amended. Yea, and it were great pitie, feeyng that they haue payed the fyrſt fruites vnto the **Kynges** Mageſtie, and no ſmall reward **vnto** other men, **per-**chaunce bought their offices dearely, now to put **them** out of thoſe liuyngs, with the loſſe of all thoſe charges, whiche they haue beſtowed in rewardes, as otherwayes, to gette fuche liuynges.

Wo, **wo,** wo vnto you hipocrites that ſtumble at a ſtrawe, and leape ouer a blocke, that ſtrayne out **a** gnat, and fwalowe vp **a** camell, that pitye more the loſſe of mens bribrye, which was geuen to corrupt ſome men, than **the** treding vnder fote of Chriſtes blood, which was ſhead, to faue all men, that dooe imagen it pitie **to** driue the theues, murtherers and

[1] Isa. v. 20.

wolfes from amongeſt the lambes of God, redemed **with** Chriſtes precious blood, and committed **vnto your** gouernaunce and kepynge.

As God ſhal help **me, I** ſpeake with feare, pitie, and reuerence: if you **do not rather** pulle the ſhepes ſkines ouer the wolfes eares, **and hange their** carkaſes **vpon the** pales, than ſuffer **theim to contynewe** ſtyll, **God** wyll plucke **you** doune with **ſome ſodeyn** miſchief, rather than **mainteyn or** ſuffer you **in ſo** hygh aucthoritie, to vſe ſuch vncharitable, vngodly, **and** cruel pitie. You knowe that ſome of them haue bought their benefices, haue bought theire offyces, than muſt **ye nedes** knowe, that eyther Chriſt is **a** lyer, orels that they be entered in as theeues, to ſpoyle, murther, and to deſtroye.

If you **ſuffre** theeues, **murtherers, and** wolfes, to **take** their pleſures amongeſt **Gods lambes, I** tell you playn, God wyll not long ſuffer **you to be** ye hedſhepherds, and gouernors and feders of his lambes.

And **take** hede you people, **that on the other ſyde** ye **runne not into** an vntollerable ſtobornes, deniing your rents, your tithes or other duties: for ye ſcriptur forbiddeth you vtterly, to deny or withdraw any **thing from** them: thou art commaunded if he contend **to take thi** cloke, to giue him alſo thy cote. What ſo euer is aſked, rather gyue more, than by denying of that, **not to** ſhewe thy ſelfe to be an innocent ſheepe that gyueth his fleeſe, but a noyſome Goat, that ſtryketh with **the horne.** You are alwayes bounden to gyue the fleeſe. It is magiſtrates dutyes, to conſyder and note, whether they be theeues, or ſhepheardes, dogges, **or** wolfes that taketh the fleeſe. Medle not with other mens dutyes, for if **ye do,** ſurely ye ſhal fynd no remedy, **but prouoke vncolourable [vntollerable] vengeaunce.**

Now to retourne [turne] to our particular purpoſe, let all theym that do **receaue** offices, landes, power, or aucthoritie from God, by the kyngs gyfte, or **by** other **meanes:** Fyrſt beſtow and diſpoſe the dutyes of thoſe thyngs faythfully amongeſt the people, afore they gather vp to them felues the reuenues amd commodities of the fame from the people. And then, when as no man can come to meat, but by doing of labour, nor none to receauynge of fees, but by doing of duties, furely euery man fhal haue as much as he deferueth, and no man fhall lacke that which he needeth.

For he, that by doyng of great duties deferueth the mofte, by atteinynge the fees and rewardes due for the fame dutyes, fhall haue the beft. And he that is in nede, hauing no truft to get any thyng by idleneffe, craft, or flattery, fhalbe compelled to vfe that labour and honeft exercife, whiche fhall relieue his nede fufficiently. Yea, by this mean no man fhall fpende his tyme in idleneffe, nor vfe no [any] labour or diligence, without due recompence. For nede fhall driue all men from flouthfull idleneffe, vnto labour and diligence: and where as no labour nor diligence lacketh his iuft rewarde, there euery labouryng and diligent man, fhal haue fufficient plenty. So ye fee how this doth confequently enfue, that euery man fhall haue fufficient inough and plentie, where as men do firft difpofe and minifter, and giue according to their duties, and afterwards receiue, kepe and faue that which God doth fende as a rewarde, encreafed and augmented, for doyng of their dutyes.

So dyd the Apoftles, after the faythful diligent difpofyng of the. v. loaues and. ii. fyfhes, receyue and keepe their rewarde wonderfullye augmented, to replenifh and fyl. xii. bafkets. So God graunt, that all officers in Englande, may with fuch faithful diligence do their duties, yat it may pleafe God to giue to all the people fufficient enough, and vnto euery minifter, the bafket of his honeft defire, heped vp by ye brym.

The men therefore feyng what a fygne Iefus had done, fayd that this is ye Prophet, whiche cometh vnto [into] the world. This is euen he whom Moifes, the

law, and the prophetes do teache, to be the fullye and
only fufficient fauiour of ye world. Moifes faiing, in
ye. xviii. of Deut. A Prophet of thy nacion and of thy
brethren, lyke vnto me, fhall the Lorde thy God rayfe
vp vnto the, him fhalt thou heare. The lawe, as a
tutour, leadeth and bryngeth al men to this fauyour,
to receaue of him that perfection, which the law it
felfe lacketh. The Prophetes dyd tel long afore of
this fauiour, which is now comen in our tyme, after
their dayes. This was the peoples confeffion of
Chrift, after that they were by fo great a miracle, fo
plentifully fed. Chrift, ofte afore had wrought wonderfull miracles, difputed learnedly, and preached
plainly : but by all thofe meanes dyd he not fo muche
perfwade the people, and wynne their heartes, as by
this one miracle, in feedyng and cherifhing the people.
Yea, and whofoeuer lifteth to mark thorow out all
England, he fhall fee that a meane learned perfon,
keping an houfe in his paryfh, and kepynge of godly
conuerfacion, fhall perfwade and teach mo of his
parifhioners with communicacion at one meale, than
the beft lerned doctor of diuinitie kepyng no houfe,
can perfwade or teache in his parifh by preaching a
dofen folemne fermons.

Lykewyfe the gentle man that kepeth a good houfe
in his countrey, fhall be in better credit with the
people for his liberalitie, than the beft oratour or
lawyer in England, for all his eloquence. I do not
prayfe thofe men which brybe and polle all the yeare
to kepe riot in their houfes for a fortnyght, a moneth,
or a quarter of a yeare : But thofe I fe be loued,
trufted, and obeyed, that accordynge to their habilitie,
keepe good houfes continually.

And the chiefe caufe why the commens doo not
loue, truft, nor obey the gentle men and officers, is,
bicaufe the gentle men and officers buyld many fayre
houfes, and kepe few good houfes, haue plentye of
eloquence to tell fayre tales, but vfe lytell faythfull

diligence in doyng of their duties. Wherfore, fende forth, and place in euery countrey godly preachers, wel difpofed perfons [Parfones], and faithfull diligent officers, of all fortes. **Yea, but where fhuld we now fynd liuyngs for al thofe.**

For foth I do **tell you :** Out and **away with the wily foxes,** the falfe flatteryng **theeues, and the rauening wolfes,** and than **fee how many loaues, how many** offyces, prebends, **and benefices** ye **finde voyde, how many you haue amongeſt** your felues **that your boye** caryeth, **that your** chapleyns, **your feruauntes, and your houfeholde offycers** haue, **and let all thefe be brought forth : and althoughe at the fyrſt fyght they fhall feeme to lytell, and few to ferue fo great a Realme with fo manye fhyres, beyng all runne nowe out of ciuil** ordre **into rude wildernes. Yet, after equal diuidyng and faithfull diligent miniſtrynge of** thefe [thofe] **loaues and fifhes, of thefe prebends, perfonages, and all kynde of offyce[r]s amongeſt the people, God of his goodneffe fhall** giue fuch encreafe vnto the **people,** hauynge therby fufficient plenty of Chriſtes holy **word, of** good **ciuil ordre, and of** charitable relief, **than there** fhalbe **remainyng fo much** tythes, offryng, **rentes, fees, and rewards, as wyl fyl the** xii. bafkets **of the Apoſtles, I meane the barnes, the** houfes, and purfes **of all fayth- full diligente miniſters** and officers. Then **fhal this one acte perfwade and allure** the **herts of all** Englifh **men more then all that euer was done afore:** For **when they** fhall **fee, that by** this **Kyng and this Coun- fell, the** wilye foxe of fuperſticion **is vtterly banyfhed, the falfe theefe** of flattery apprehended and **taken, and the cruell** wolfe of couetoufneffe flayne, **and hanged vp by the** heeles, fo that the preachers, the perfons, the officers, **and** all maner of **paſtors** reſtored to their places, **doo feede, cherifh, and** kepe their flockes, which **were afore** pilled, **fpoiled** and deuoured : then fhall they of **herty** courage, with **one** mynde, and one voyce confeffe **and** acknowledge, **that** there [this] **is a**

King sent from God, indued with the wysdome of Salomon, and the faythfull diligent stoutnesse of Dauid his father, now guyded by godly counsell, to bring out of miserye, and prosper in welth vs the people of this his* Realme.

Dixit Dominus.
The Lord hath
spoken it.
God graunt you grace to
do it, with thankes and
prayse to hym
for euer.

❡ Imprinted
at London by Jhon
Daie, dwelling ouer Al=
dersgate, and Wyl=
liam Seres dwel=
ling in Peter
Colledge.
The yere of our Lorde God
M. D. L. the nynth
Daye of Apryll.

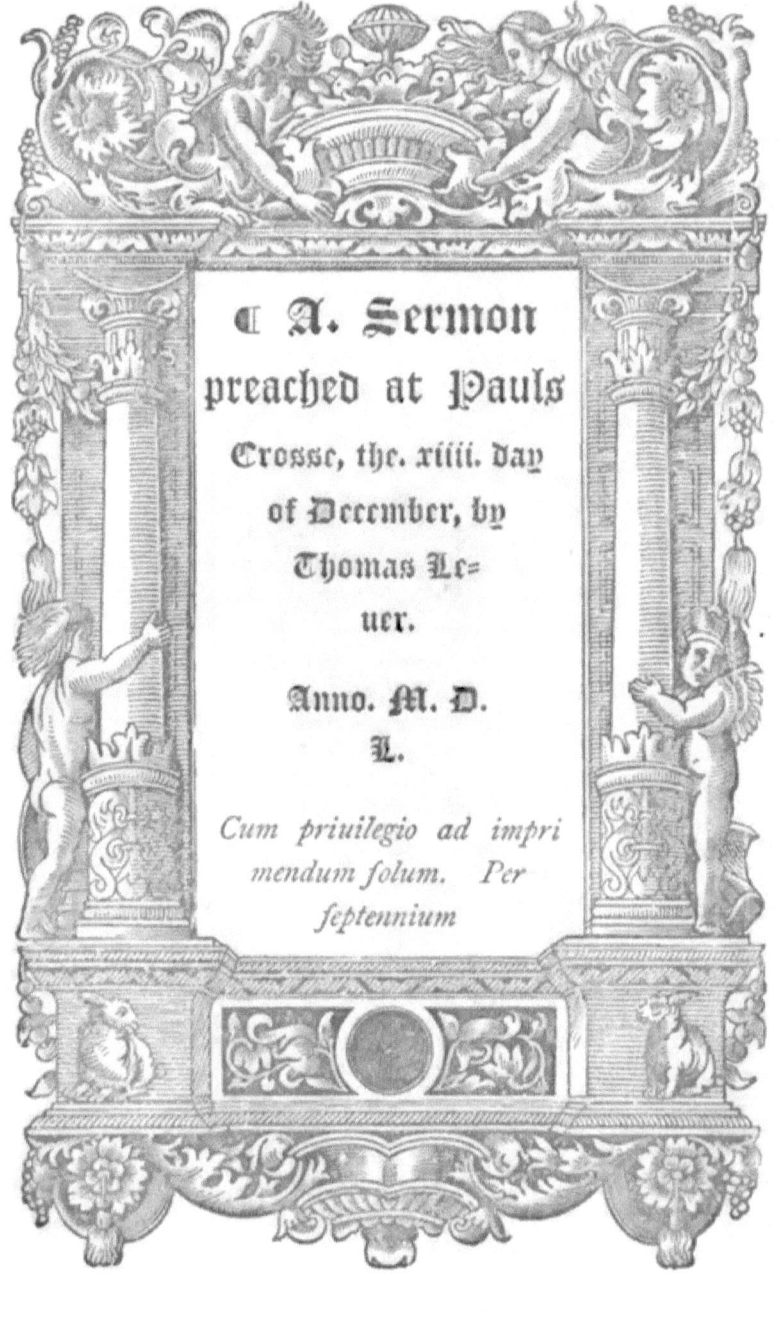

¶ A. Sermon preached at Pauls Crosse, the. xiiii. day of December, by Thomas Leuer.

Anno. M. D. L.

Cum priuilegio ad impri mendum folum. Per septennium

¶ Unto the right honor=
rable Lordes, and others of the
Kynges Magestie hys priuye Coun=
sell, Thomas Leauer wysheth in=
crease of Grace and godly
honoure.

Ercy, grace, and peace from God the father almyghty, vnto your honours, wyth my moste humble and reuerente comendacions.

The enemye of God and man alwayes sekyng lyke a rorynge lion whome he may deuoure, is much at al tymes, but then especially to be taken hede vnto, when as he hym self beyng transformed into the aungell of lyght, doth cloke the ministers of hys myschiefe in a pretensed shew of godlines and vertue, so that therby they be suffered of al men, and maynteined of many men, to worcke and brynge vnto passe a deuillishe dysorder, and shamefull dyshonestye in a Christen commen wealth.

Wherefore, seynge that in thys realme preachers, officers, marchauntes, crafts men, labourers, and such lyke, be displaced of their roumes, and dysapoynted of theyr lyuinges by those whych through a pretensed name, and outward apperance, seme to be necessary and profytable ministers in a common wealthe (howbeit in theyr owne doynges may be euidently tryed and knowen for to be spoylers and disturbers of any common welth) suredly you of the kynges most honourable counsell, beyng the chefe maiestrats and rulers in this realme, had nede to be ware, circumspect and diligent, lest that Sathan banyshyng al faithful Christians, whych should and wold prouyde to helpe one an other, do fyl this realme ful of crafty flatterers, whych can and **wyll** deceyue, begyle, and spoyle one another.

Truly ther be **no** men more againſt Chriſt then thoſe which by profeſſion of Chriſten relygyon, and bearyng **of a** Chriſten name, doo rob Chryſt of hys honor, and Chriſtes miniſters of theyr liuyngs: **nor none** more **parilous** ennemies vnto the kings maieſty, **and vnto** this **realme, then** thoſe whyche haue the names of Engliſhmen, **and the** kyngs ſubiects with **ye condicions** and **maners of** enemies, **and traitors.**

Moſt gracious **good** lordes and maiſters, **for** your reuerent loue towardes God, and the kyng, for your charitable pytye of myſerable ſpoiled people, and for the neceſſary regarde of **your owne** honours, and the ſtate of thys realme, ſe and conſyder how that ambicious **couetous** men, do bye **and ſel**, take and abuſe perſonages, prebendes, offyces, **fees**, marchaundyſe, fermes, landes, and goodes, **ſo** that prowlyng for them ſelues, they be neither afrayde, nor aſhamed **to** ſpoile thys realme of preachyng of Gods goſpel, of iuſtyce and equitie, of cheape and plenty, and of euery **thynge** that ſhould ſaue, kepe, or profytte a commune wealthe.

Wherfore moſt gracious good lordes, and mayſters, **for** the tender mercies of God in our Sauiour **Ieſus** Chriſt, take hede that neyther ſeruaunte, nor frende, re**teyner, nor** youre ſelues do deceyue you wyth flatterye.

For ſeynge that ambicious couetous men do take, kepe, and **enioye** the roumes and lyuynges of euerye mannes vocacion, bothe you and we be in farre more daunger, **then yf** blockehouſes and bulwarkes made and kepte of the kynges faythful ſubiectes for the ſauegarde **of** thys realme, were **taken** and abuſed of ſuche Scottes or Frenchemen, as makyng ſpoyle for theyr owne profit, **would** not ſpare to dyſtroye thys realme.

There is very manye rowmes and lyuynges, belongynge both vnto the eccleſiaſtical myniſterye, and alſo vnto **cyuyll** policye, in the whyche be no fayethful ſubiectes, godlye diligente miniſters and offycers, whiche by doynge of theyr duties, doo ſaue, kepe and comforte the people: but couetous Idolatours, whych neglectyng theyr dutyes, and takynge commodities, doo dyforder, fpoyle and dyftroye the people.

Suerlye if there be any men that goo aboute **to perfwade** the Kynges Mageftye, or you of hys honourable Councell, that thinges in thys realme for the moft parte be honourablye, **godlye**, or charytably reformed, they be but flaterers.

For papiftry **is not** banyfhed **out of** Englande by pure religion, but ouerrunne, fuppreffed and kepte vnder within thys realme by couetous ambicion. Papiftrye abufed many thyngs, couetoufnes hath **diftroyed more: papiftry is fuperfticion, couetoufnes is Idolatry.** Papiftrye **afore** tyme dyd obfcure the Kinges honour, and **abufe** the wealth of this realme, couetoufnes **at thys** tyme doth more abufe and decaye theym bothe, makynge the kynge bare, the people poore, and the realme miferable.

The Kynges procedynges to be **red in** his **lawes,** ftatutes, and Iniunccions be good and godly: **but to be** fene and knowen in the dedes **and practifes of** his officers, feruauntes, and fubiectes, **be vngodly, fhameful, wicked.** For in theyr doynges appeareth no **retournynge** from **euil vnto** good, by **a godly** reformacion: but a procedyng from euyl **vnto worfe, by an** vncharitable fpoyle, **and** deuyllyfhe deftruccion.

Landes and **goodes be** fpoyled: prouyfyon made **for** learning and **pouerty,** is deftroied. Ye knowe in whofe handes thys ryche **fpoyle remaineth,** then can **ye not** be ignoraunt by whofe meanes the wealth of **this realme is fpoyled** and decayed.

If ye wyll haue a godlye reformacion effectuouflye to **procede,** trufte not the feruauntes of Mammon, ennemyes vnto God, and traitoures vnto the kynge, and fpoylers of the people, wyth the fettyng forthe of your godlye lawes, ftatutes and ordynaunces, which be moft contrary vnto theyr couetous myndes, and wycked dedes.

Theyr myndes are alwayes euyll, and theyr dedes be well knowen, when as you geue frelye, or fuffer theym by brybery to by vnto theim felues authorytye: for then, being trufted to make better prouifion for the pore, to erect mo Grammer fchooles, to encreafe and augment the vnyuerfities, and to fe the people taught louyngly, to reuerence, ferue, and obey God, the kyng, and you: they take prouifyon frome the poore, they fell awaye Grammer fcoles, they decai the vniuerfities, and they vfe fuche practifes, as maketh God to be vnknowen, the kynge dyfobeyed, and you fufpected, hated, and enuyed of the people.

Take thefe falfe flatterers whyche haue enryched them felues, makynge the kynge bare, and the people poore, reftore theyr landes and goodes vnto the kynge, theyr rowmes and offyces vnto faythfull and true offycers and minifters: and then fhal the kyng be enryched, the realme vnfpoyled, and the people delyuered from myferable captiuitie vnder cruel extorcioners, vnto an honeft lybertye vnder Godlye gouernoures, whyche fhall fo dyfpofe the hartes and myndes of all people, that they wyllynglye fhall be readye, not onlye to ferue the markettes wyth corne, but alfo to ferue God and the kynge with landes and gooddes, bodyes and lyues, when and where fo euer you fhal commaunde it.

Maruel not thoughe a faythful hearte, wyth humble obedyence and reuerente loue towardes the kynges Maieftye, and you of hys honourable Godly counfel, do barft [burfte] and poure [put] foorthe a lamentable complaynte of greuous forrowe conceyued in feeynge the kyng fhamefully begyled, you fore difhonored, and the wealthe of thys realme vtterly fpoyled.

For menne dooe bye offyces vnto them felues, and landes from the kynge: and by the onlye fpoyle that is made in common offyces and vpon the kynges landes, bothe thefe bargens be payed for, and furthermore all fuch bargeyners wonderfullye enryched.

O mercyfull Lorde, what a griefe is it vnto a faythfull harte, hauinge iuft occafyon to fufpecte, that you lacke faythful counfell to aduertyfe you of the gracious workynge of the Lorde beynge God, and of the freyle fautes of youre felues beynge menne, **in** all youre doynges: for Gods grace woorkynge in you, cauſeth you to dooe honourable and Godlye feruyce to god, the kynge, and the common wealthe, when as ye cauſe an vngodly byſhop to be depoſed. **And yet ſhall** God, **the** king, and the people **be greuouſly** offended, and your honors and fowles **ſo ar indaungered, yf** a biſhops landes or goodes be **deuyded amongſt you** that be godlye magyſetrates **to punyſh euyl doers,** as Chriſtes cote was deuyded amongeſt wycked **foldyers,** which dyd cruelly torment **a** righteous perſon.

Alas moſt gracious **reuerente** Lordes and mayſters, **if ye vſe** the feruyſe, or **hear the aduyſe of falſe** crafty **flatterers, ye** ſhall therewyth **be** ſo blynded that ye **can neyther** perceyue by your felues, **nor** beleue when **as ye** be playnely and faythfully tolde, that manye of your owne doynges, commyng of mans freyltye, do tend muche vnto the diſpleaſure of God, dyſhonour of the kynge, and dyſcredyt of your felues, beyng moſt contrarye to **that** reuerent zele and faythful loue towards God, the kyng, and the commen **wealth, which zele** and loue god of hys goodnes hath graffed in your hartes, **and the** deuyll by **mannes** freyl dedes couered in **fylence or** colored with prayſe **of** flatterers, laboreth to deface, **peruert** and deſtroye.

As God whyche ſearcheth the ſecretes of mans hart, doth **beare me recorde, I** do ſuppoſe, and thynke that you dooe ſo louynglye drede God, reuerence the kyng, and regarde this realme, and your owne honors, that **beyng** charged **wyth** the ouerſight and prouiſion **of caſtels,** holdes, **and fortes, made** and kept for the ſafegarde of thys realme, ye coulde not wyttyngly **be** hyred **to** ſell one of them vnto the kynges ennemyes, for al the treaſures in the world. And yet beyng craftelye deceyued wyth flattery, **ye** vſe a daungerous practyſe in very many of them.

For ther **be** ſome of them ſclenderly aſſauted **at** certayne tymes **of** feble enemyes: and other continuallye beſeged eyther wyth open forſe or craftye con-

G

ueyaunce of fearce, cruel, and perylous enemies. And now crafty flatterers whych haue once serued for theyr wages in **tyme** and place of the fclender aflate, **doo afterwardes requyre and perfwade you** for that bruyfe to geue **them the fpoyle of other** holdes remayning continuallye in more **daunger.** Truly Frenchmen and Scottes be but feble ennemyes, and [yet] at certayne tymes do fclenderly affalt caftels, towers, and fuch maner of holdes. The deuyl feking lyke a roryng Lyon, whom he may deuoure, nyghte and day, wynter and fommer, wyth a wonderful forfe of wycked fpirites, **doth euer** befyege byfhopryckes, fhyres, townes, and parifhes.

Yf thefe **places be** not wel furnifhed with ftout and true **foldiers of bothe the** fortes (I meane both officers in ciuyle polycy, and alfo Prelates in Ecclefiafticall miniftery) **or if thofe fouldyers be** vnprouided of neceffary liuyngs and dewe wages, **then muft the people nedes peryfhe and be** deftroyed **for theyr owne** fynnes, **and the bloud of theyr bodyes and foules requyred at your handes, whyche be charged and trufted of both God, and the king to prouide fouldiers to thofe places, and alfo wages and liuinges to** mayntayne thofe **foldyers continually.**

How be it now* **manye perfonages, benefyces, offyces, and fees** be **fold** vnto **couetous brybers for money, whych feke nothyng** but **the vantage of*** **extorcion, robbry and fpoyle, and** fewe of them **be freely giuen vnto faithful minifters** and officers for their woorthynes, **which could and would by** diligent **doynge of** their dutie, **gouerne, inftruct and cheryfhe goddes** people, the kynges **fubiectes.**

And therefore nowe the moft **part of men lackyng** teachers and **rulers, do without griefe of** confcience, **or feare of** punifhment, **abufe** euery thynge vnto the ruine and deftruccion, whyche **God** hath ordayned **vnto the vpholdyng and increafe of** a chriftian commune **welth.**

As for example, now bying and fellyng **is not vfed as a prouifion for** good cheape and great **plenty, but made the moft occafyon of** dearth **and fcarfitie.**

Wealth and wyt be not ryghtly vsed vnto a common confortable profyt, but shamefully abused vnto a wycked priuate gayne. Many offyces with authoritie be not duely disposed vnto faithful worthy men nor to dooe good vnto other, but vnlawfullye bought and solde amongest couetous, ambicious men, to get gaynes vnto theim selues. So this realme is spoyled, the kynge is made bare, and his faithful true subiectes be many of them very poore: but crafti deceiuers, couetous Extorcioners, brybynge offycers, and suche false flatterers be wonderous rich and welthy.

Thefe Flatterers be wonders perilous felowes, hauynge two faces vnder one hoode. For they beare a face and shew towardes the people, as though by Commyssion and commaundement from you, there must bee more required and taken of the people then euer you dyd meane or thynke: And towardes you thei shewe another face femyng that so much cannot be founde in anye mennes handes as must needes bee procured: but that therefore the kynges landes must nedes be folde, whyche thei are redye to by for their owne auantage, wyth those goodes whyche they them selues haue in theyr owne handes, or rather wyth the spoyle whych they intend to make vpon those landes. These subiects that be not ashamed to procure vnto them selues such riches, that they maye be biers, and vnto their liege Lorde and kyng suche nede, that he muste be a feller of his landes. Thefe be in deede seruauntes vnto Mammon, enemies vnto god, traitores vnto the king, and disturbers of a common welth turning all your godly, wise and charitable deuyces for necessary prouysyon, vnto deuylish deceytes, for to cause and maynteyne vncharitable spoyles. And suredly when as occasions do serue for any men to practise theyr pleasures, manye men of al sortes, and of the lowest sort, the most part do shew them selues the worst infected wyth thys impyety, treason, and rebellyon, the greuousnes and daunger of the whyche wyth occasyons and meanes how to auoyd the same, I preaching at

Paules Croffe the. xiiii. [fowertene] day of December laſt paſt, dyd there openly declare vnto mine audience. And as I did then preach that Sermon as an exhortacion to moue the people, by the acknowledgyng, lamentyng and amendynge theyr owne fautes, to deſerue and receyue the pardon of mercy offered vnto them of both god and the kyng, in thys longe pacient fufferaunce, fo do I nowe here offer vnto your honors, the fame Sermon as an earneſt complaynte, to procure of you that be Gods offycers, fpedyly correccion for them that refuſe to heare, regarde, and obey Gods word.

Be not dyfcouraged in thys matter, wyth your owne freylty beyng greate, or wyth the number of offenders, beyng manye. For it is not your worthynes, but Goddes grace, that hath placed you in hygh authority, and in the fame aucthoritye not your owne powers and polycy, but the myght and wifdome of god, fhal fo ſtrengthen and confyrme you, that yf ye wyll be dylygent, ye fhall be made able to delyuer Gods people, the kynges fubiectes, oute of the handes of fuche as be Gods and the kynges ennemyes.

I befeche the almyghtye God indue you wyth grace, that begynnyng wyth youre felues, ye may fpedely procede vnto the neceſſary and godly correccion of other mens fautes, fo that ye maye be eſtablyfhed in youre rowmes, and increafed in honor, to ferue god and the kynge, prouiding for hys realme in holines and righteoufnes al ye daies of your lyues.

By me humbly subiect and faithful obedient vnto your honors, Thomas Leuer.

Iesus Christus.

⁋ The grace of the holy gost, proceedyng from God the father, by the intercession and meane of Iesu Christ, so prepare your herts, and open my mouth, that I maye declare, and shewe, and that you maye heare, vnderstand, remember, and practise in your liuyng, his liuely word as may be most to his honour and glori and to your soules health and comfort.

Ou Citizins of London, and all other that be here prefent marke, note, and remember what ye heare of me this day: for yf I fhall fay or fpeake any thynge that is euyll, you mufte beare recorde againft me of that euyl. But if I do preache well and truelye, then you fhall vnderftande and knowe your felues to be in great daunger of haynous treafon towards god and the kinges maiefty of this realme, which be by you fpoyled, and robbed: god of his glory, the kyng of hys honoure, and the realme of hys wealth. Howbeit the mercyfull goodnes of bothe god and the kyng hath fent me hyther thys daye, to proclame a generall pardon, intendynge thereby to try out and faue theim that haue offended by fimple ignoraunce, becaufe the force of theyr myghty power is nowe readye and commynge vtterly to deftroye all other that continue in wylfull ftobernes and rebellyous treafon. Wherefore afore the readynge of my commyffion, I wyll declare that piece of fcriptur whyche appoynted to be red in the churche as thys daye, wyll certyfye you that God by his fcriptures hath fhewed the kynge, who be hys fayethfull feruauntes, and who be hys ennemyes. Thys fcripture is wrytten

in ye. iiii. Chapter of the firſte epiſtle of. S. Paule vnto the Corinthians. *Sic nos æſtimet homo ut miniſtros Chriſti, et diſpenſatores miniſtrorum [myſteriorum] dei. etc.*[1]
Filioli mei quos iterum parturio.[2] Albeit I vſe not ſcrupulouſlye the ſame termes, yet conuenyently folowyng the maner and phraſe of ſcrypture, I ſay vnto you as Paule wryteth vnto the Galathyans: My deare chyldren of whom I trauell in byrthe agayne vntyll Chriſte be facyoned in you, I would I now beyng wyth you myght chaunge my voyce, whyche heretofore I haue vſed: declarynge by the worde of God, that you here in England whych wyll receyue no mercye, ſhall feele ſore vengeaunce, which wyll not be ſaued, ſhalbe deſtroyd. Thys voyce vſed here afore of me, nowe wold I fayne chaunge. For nowe ἀποροῦμαι ἐν ὑμῖν I doute I am paſte hope and allmooſte in vtter dyſpayre of you. Tell me you that throughe couetouſnes deſyre the ryches and wealthe of thys world. Haue ye not heard how that he whych wold be a frend vnto the world is made an enemy vnto God, doethe not Paule teache that couetouſnes is the roote of all euyl? Is it not wrytten that couetouſnes is Idolatry? Haue ye not red in the prophet Ezechiel howe that he whyche kepeth his Idolles, meanyng couetouſneſſe in hys hert, and commeth to hear gods word, doth therby prouoke gods vengeaunce to hys vtter deſtruccion. Paule ſayth and teſtifyeth that euery man whiche is circumcyſed, hath not profyt by Chriſte, is gone quite from Chriſt, is fallen from grace. I ſaye and teſtyfye vnto you in the word of the Lorde, yat ſo many of you as be couetous, haue no profit by the preachyng of gods word, the myniſtracion of hys ſacraments and the ſettyng forth of pure religion wythin the realme: no ye be clene from God framyng your ſelues vnto the faſſion of thys worlde, ye can brynge forth no good frutes of charitable workes nouriſhyng the rote of all euyll in youre hartes, ye muſt nedes prouoke the wrath and indignacion of god to your vtter deſtrucion, when as ye kepe the ydoll of couetouſnes ſtyll in youre myndes to

[1] 1 Cor. iv. 1.   [2] Gal. iv. 19.

be honoured and ferued in all your doinges, and yet pretend a zele and loue vnto the religion of Chryſt in your workes and fayinges. I woulde fayne haue had iuſt occaſion to haue ſpoken at thys tyme ſuche thynges as myght haue bene confortable and pleaſaunt for you to heare.

But I muſte needes ſhewe the cauſes of gods wrath and indignacion kyndled agaynſte vs, leaſt that thoſe plages ſhould be aſcribed vnto the word and religion of Chryſt ſet foorthe amongeſt vs, whyche be procured by the wickednes of theym that feruyng couetous Mammon, haue forſaken, offended, and ſlaundered both Chriſt, and Chriſtes word and religion. No man can ſerue two maſters, whye then dooe ye pretend that ye be the ſeruauntes of Chryſt, feynge that ye wyll not forſake the ſeruyce of wycked Mammon? Yf ye be aſhamed to be named, and afrayd to continue the wycked feruauntes of wycked mammon, now ſhew and proue by youre ordinarye callyng, faythfull dealyng, and godly iudgement accordyng to thys example of Paule playnly paynted and ſet[teth] forthe in thys epiſtle vnto the Corinthians, that ye be Chriſtes mynyſters, the ſeruauntes and diſpoſers of gods myſteries and treaſures: for Paule ſhewing hym ſelfe as a good example of Chriſtes feruants, fayth: *Sic nos æſtimet homo, ut miniſtros Chriſti. etc.*[1] So let a man eſteme vs, as the myniſters of Chryſt, and the dyſpoſers of the fecretes of god. No man can come vnto Chriſte Ieſu to be hys myniſter, excepte he be drawen of the father. The father draweth not by force violentlye them that be ſtuborne and frowarde, but by loue them that be gentyll, and come wyllyngly. For when the father ſheweth in Chryſte forgeuenes of ſynnes, grace of amendement, iuſtificacion, and euerlaſtyng lyfe, then thoſe that make theim faſt theim ſelues wyth the bande of loue by defyre of the fame be drawen vnto Chryſt.

As contrary wyſe when the deuyll ſheweth in fleſhlye luſtes and worldly vanytyes, manye voluptuous pleaſures, then they that there wyth be entangled and

[1] 1 Cor. *iv.* 1.

delyted be drawen of the temptour away from Chryſt.
Take hede therfore howe ye haue entred into religion,
profeſſed chryſte, and receyued the goſpell. For if
ye be drawen by loue of mercy, grace and ryghteouſnes,
ye come vnto Chryſt: But by the deſyre of ryches,
welth, and voluptuouſnes, men be drawen and tyſed
away from Chriſte.

He therfore that by the profeſſion of Chriſt, the
zele of hys worde, the fauoure of the goſpell, ſeeketh
couetous gayne, or a carnal liberty, ſurely he is a
ſeruaunt of Mammon, ennemy vnto Chriſte, and a
ſclaunderer of the goſpel. For he that wyll be the
ſeruaunt of Chryſte, muſt folow the example of Chriſt.
He that wyll folowe Chriſt in example of lyuyng, he
muſte forſake hymſelfe, take hys croſſe vpon hys backe
dayly and folow Chriſt. So Chriſtes ſeruaunt ſhalbe
deliuered from the bondage of ſynne, yat he may frely
and wyllyngly contemnyng ye vanities of the world,
and mortifying ye luſts of ye fleſh, ſerue chryſt in
bearyng the croſſe of paynful diligence, to do the duty
of his vocacion.

But all thoſe that delyte in a carnall libertye, or
ſeeke vnlawfull geynes, althoughe they be named
Chryſtians and fauourers of the goſpell, yet be they in
dede not myniſters of Chriſt, but ennemyes vnto
Chriſte: not louers of the Goſpell but ſclaunderers of
the Goſpell, not iuſtyfied by liuelye faythe to be of
that ryghteouſe ſorte for whoſe ſakes G O D ſpareth
and fauoureth a common wealthe, but deceyued with
a dead fayth to be of that vngodlye ſorte, for whoſe
cauſe God plageth and deſtroyeth many a common
welth. And nowe vndoutedly be we in great miſeries
and daunger of deſtruccion, for that we haue many
that be hearers, readers, and talkers of Gods worde,
and fewe or none that do walke and lyue accordyng
to gods worde: we ought truly to eſteme and take
theym onlye to be mynyſters of Chriſte whyche for the
loue of mercy, grace, and ryghtuouſnes ſhewed of the
father vnto theim in Chriſt do kyll the luſtes of theyr

owne fleſhe, dyſpyſe the vanytyes of the whole worlde, and forſakyng theyr own pleaſures and commodities do take the croſſe of paynfull diligence and walke after Chriſt in doynge of theyr dutyes.

All other that haue the name and profeſſion of **Chryſt** without liuyng and conuerſacion accordynge therto, be fayned brethren, in feaſtes wyth Chriſten men to take parte **of** theyr good chere, vnclene ſpots amongeſt honeſt company, feedyng theim ſelues without feare of god, clouds without any moiſture of gods grace, toſſed aboute wyth contrarye wyndes of ſtraunge doctryne, trees paſſyng ſommer tyme without any frutes **of good** workes, twyſe dead without felynge **the** corrupcion of ſynne, or lokynge to be graffed in **the** ſtocke of grace, yea rooted vp from amongeſt ye vynes of the Lord, wilde waues of the ſea frothyng forth vnſhamefaſt brags, and wandryng ſtarres without conſtancie in iudgement and opinion vnto whom the dungeon of darknes is ordeyned for euerlaſtyng dampnacion.

What maruell is it then thoughe the vengeaunce of God be poured forth amongs them of ſuch iniquitie, yea **and** moſt abundantly when as hys word playnely preached, is of theym moſte wickedly abuſed and ſhamefully ſlandered, whych ſay: Lorde, Lorde, and do not **as** they be commaunded of the Lord. Wherfore let vs ſay: *Non nobis domine, non nobis.* Not vnto vs o Lord, not vnto vs, but vnto thy name geue glorye, not for that we by oure dedes haue deſerued, but yat thy name O Chryſte amongeſt vs chriſtians may be honored, pardon our fauts, amende our liues, and indue vs with grace, that the lyghte of oure good workes afore men vpon **the** earthe, may cauſe thee to be gloryſyed O Lorde in heauen. Dearlye beloued in Chriſte for the tender mercyes of god, when as ye ſe carnall goſpellers, couetous ydolaters, greuyng youre conſciences, ſlaunderynge Chriſtes religion, and damnynge theyr owne ſoules, do not of malyce contempne diſdayne and reuyle them, **but** of charitable pitye, lament, ſorow, and pray for

theim, whyche blynded wyth ygnoraunce know not
theim felues, deceyued wyth the deuyll, be drawen from
Chrifte, comforte and faluacion, vnto euerlaftynge deathe
and **damnacion.** Say and **pray for** them: O lorde
fuffer not the enemye thus to lede into captiuitye **owre**
felowes **thy** feruauntes, oure brethren **thy** chyldren, O
Chryft reftore vnto lyberty **them that you haft redeemed**
wythe thy precious blud, **fo** yat we **may** altogether
drawen of ye father, receyued of the **fonne, and** gided
of the holy goft, be minifters of Chryft **in libertye of
the** gofpell, delyuered from fynne frelye to delyte **and**
take pleafure **in a** godly conuerfacion all the dayes of
our lyfe. Nowe let vs after thys takynge of the mynif-
terye of Chryfte, w[h]yich perteineth generally vnto all
chriftians, fpeake of the dyfpofers of Gods myfteryes,
wherein we maye confider feuerally euery mans vocacion.

Paule dyd dyfpofe the fecretes of God by the preach-
ynge of the Gofpell, whych was euer fecretly hydde from
the wyttye, wyfe, and learned in the worlde. Other
men in **other vocacions muft** dyfpofe other treafures of
God by other meanes. As the magiftrate by authorytye
muft dyfpofe the punyfhmente of vyce, and the mayntenaunce of vertue.

The rych man by liberalytye, muft dyfpofe reliefe
and comforte vnto the poore and nedye. The Marchaunt by byinge and fellynge, and the craftes man by
his occupacion, mufte prouyde vnto the common wealthe
of neceffarye wares, fuffyciente plentye. The landelorde
by lettyng of fermes muft dyfpofe vnto the tenants neceffary lands, and houfes of an indifferent rente. The houf-
bandmen by tyllyng of the ground and kepyng of cattel,
muft dyfpofe vnto theyr landlordes, dew rentes, and vnto
them felues and **other,** both córne, **and** other vytals.
So euerye man **by** doynge of hys dutye mufte dyfpofe vnto other that commodytye and benefyte, whiche
is committed of god **vnto theym to** be dyfpofed vnto
other, by the faythful and diligent doyng of theyr dutyes.

The treafures of the Lord be vnmeftrable, his hart
is lyberall, ther can be therefore no lacke amonges hys

people, yf hys ſtewardes vnto whom the dyſpoſing of hys gyftes be committed, be true and faythfull. Thys therfore faythe Paule, is requyred in a ſteward, yat he be faythfull. Who thynke ye, fayth Chriſt, is a faythefull and a wyſe ſtewarde whom the Lorde ſetteth ouer hys houſeholde to geue theim **a due** meaſure of the wheate of neceſſaryes in tyme conuenyente? Bleſſed is that feruaunte **whom the Lorde when** he commeth, ſhall fynde ſo doyng: verelye **I ſaye vnto** you that he wyl make him **lord of all that euer he hath.** Beholde the faythfulnes **of the Lordes ſteward** confyſteth in dylygente prouydynge and myniſtrynge vnto the Lordes famylye **anye** ſuche thynges as bee neceſſary. **The reward of ſuch** faythfulnes is to be put in truſt wyth all **that** his Lord and maſter hath. Then who can defyre a better maſter then the Lorde God or a hygher roume then a ſtewardſhyppe in the houſe of Chriſt, or a greater reward then to haue all the treaſures of God whych be an hundred folde paſſynge any mans deſeruyng here, and furthermore euerlaſtyng lyfe. O that men wold confyder the goodnes of God, the worthines of their offices, the comfortable felowſhyp of the houſhold of Chriſt, and the ioyfull rewarde of the croune of glory, and **ſo be** faythful ſtewardes and dyſpoſers of the manyfold gyftes of God: And not being bleared and blynded **wyth** couetouſneſſe, deſerue to be cut of **from** the company **of** chriſtians, and to haue theyr porcion with hypocrits, wheras ſhalbe waylyng and gnaſhing of teeth. For that ye gredy worme gnawyng the conſcience neuer dyeth, and the flamynge fyre of vntollerable vengeaunce ſhalbe **neuer** quenched.

O brethren, God hath geuen great plentye, and we in Englande fynde greate lacke: therfore the ſtuwards of God be vnfeythfull. Who be gods ſtewardes? They that haue gods gyftes. Suerly **no** man hath all the gyfts of God, and euery man hath fome gyfts of God. Then if all thynges be lackyng, yet can no one man deſerue all the blame, but euery man ſhall be found fauty for that which is amyſſe, for lack of his duty.

Do ye perceyue that the laytie is eyther altogether ygnoraunte and blynd, or els hauyng knowledge to speake fayer, hath no learnynge to do well? Then suerlye the cleargye hath not ben faythfull in preachyng of gods word earnestly, in seson and out of seafon to reproue, besech and blame, in all pacience and token, or dyscyplyne. Do ye see the cleargye hath not wherwithall to mayntayne learnyng, to relieue the pore, to kepe hospytalytye, and too fynde theym selues? Then trewly hath not the layitye sufficientlye prouyded that they whyche preache the Gospell, should lyue on the Gospell, and that they whyche sowe spirituall treasures, myght repe corporall necessaryes.

Do ye see yat they which be in authoritye haue not ben regarded and obedientli serued? Then ye common people haue not done theyr dutyes, dysobeying any man placed in authoryty by gods ordynaunce. Do ye se the people haue hadde iniuries and yet theyr complaintes neglygentlye heard and long delayed? then haue the higher powers omytted ryghteousnes and iudgement, whiche wyl be required at theyr handes of the Lord.

Do ye se that in all maner of thinges ther* is some lack of that whyche is very necessarye? Then be ye sure that all maner of men do leaue or mysufe some parte of theyr dutye. *Quis potest dicere: mundum est cor meum, purus sum a peccato.*[1]

No manne canne say: my hert is cleane, I am pure wythout fautes. Therefore seynge that we be all gyltye, Lette vs not enuye, grudge, or dysdayne one an others faultes, but euery one acknowledge, lament, and mende hys owne fautes.

Do not triumphe and be glad when ye perceyue that other mens fautes be noted or rebuked, but be mooste certayne and suer, that excepte ye spedelye repente and amende, ye shall euerye one be lykewyse serued. If ye haue not those same faultes whyche ye heare by the preacher noted and rebuked, yet yf you take pleasure and be glad to heare other mens euyls, be sure

[1] Prov. xx. 9.

that euen that pleasure takyng is a faute, whyche God hateth and wyll punysh.

Therefore when ye heare anye mannes fautes spoken of, be sorye for theim, and take hede to your selues: so shall you thereby gette good and they haue no harme. If ye so do at thys tyme, I may the more boldely examyne and trye the faythfulnes of some stewardes and disposers of Gods gyftes.

And for the better tryall and assurance[s] of theyr fydelytie I note two thynges to be requyred: fyrste that a stewarde or disposer be, *Quem constituit dominus,* whom the Lord assigneth and maketh: and secondarily, *Vt det cibum in tempore,*[1] that he vse to fede and cheryche, and not to deuoure and hurte theim of the lordes familye. For the fyrste parte, it is to be noted, that euery man in the tyme of hys admyssion, when he shall be put into hys offyce, is set on the hyll of consyderacion and aduysement: where as the Lorde Christ to those whyche he admitteth, sheweth that the haruest is greate, the laborers be fewe, greate paynes muste be taken that muche good may be done: vyle rebukes and greuous afflicions here to be suffered, be the sygnes and tokens of great rewardes in heauen for theym prepared. The ennemy of Christ Satan vnto those whych he would deceyue sheweth all the glory of the worlde, promysyng to geue it a rewarde presently vnto all them that wyl worshyp hym fallyng downe at hys feete, in flattery, crafte, and iniquitye.

Chrifte the Lorde indueth wyth wyll and habilytye to take paynes to do good, those whych he bryngeth in at the dore to be shepherdes of the folde and stewardes of the house: the deuyll the ennemy of Chryst cloketh [clothed] in shepe skynnes of solemne titles to gette gaynes, those whyche he conueyeth not in at the dore, but ouer an other waye to dystroye the flocke, and robbe the house.

Therfore yf thy roume be benefyce, prebende, offyce or authorytie in a christen comminaltye wythin Gods house, and yf thou be brought in at the doore of ordynarye and lawefull callynge, by paynefull dyligence to do good, thou mayest be a faythfull stewarde in that place:

[1] Luke xii. 42.

but yf thou be broughte in ouer and befydes all ordinarye and lawfull callynge, by couetous ambycyon to get gaynes, then muſt thou nedes be a thefe and a robber: for Chryſte whyche fo fayth can be no lyer. I meane yf thou by money or fryndſhyp haue boughte eyther benefyce or offyce, thou canſt not be of Chriſtes inſtitucion, but of the Dyuylles intruſion, not a fayethful dyſpoſer, but a theuyſh extorcioner of Gods gyfts. For Chriſt fayth playnely that he whyche entereth not in at the doore, but clymeth ouer an other way, is a thefe and a robber, and the thefe commeth not but to ſteale, murther, and to deſtroy.

The doore whyche is Chriſte hym felfe, can neuer be entred in at by eyther frendſhyp or money.

Sum perauenture wyl be offended not becauſe I fpeake againſt the biinge of benefices, whyche be fpirituall charges, but for that I alfo include the bying and fellynge of offyces, whych as they faye, be temporall promocions. As for benefyces ye knowe fo well, that I neede not to ſtand about the declaracion or profe in theym.

No, I am fure that ye perceyue howe that through the abufe of one benefyce, the Deuyll ofte tymes is fure to haue many foules.

Fyrſte the patron for hys prefentacion, then the Byſhoppe for admiſſion, the perfon for hys vnworthyneſſe, and a greate manye of the paryſhe that be loſt for lacke of a good Perfons dutye.

But now as concernyng the biynge of offyces, to come thereby vnto the roume of an auditour, Surueiour, Chauncelloure, or anye fuche lyke, furelye no man wyll attempt it, but he whyche is fo couetoufe and ambyciouſſe that he dooeth neyther dread God nor loue man. Whereof commeth the byinge of offyces but of couetoufnes? howe then canne that be a good fruyte whyche fpryngeth oute of the roote of all euyll? Is not euerye Chryſten common wealthe the folde of Chriſtes ſhepe, the houfe of hys famylye? be not then all offycers in a Chryſten common wealthe named by Goddes woorde ſheppeherdes of the fold, and ſtewardes of the famylye of Chryſte? O Lorde what ſhall wee then ſaye to excuſe theim that by and ſel offyces wythyn England? Shall we ſay thoſe offyces be no roumes and places **ordeyned** of god for hys faythefull ſtewardes, therein to **dyſpoſe** hys treaſures and benefytes? or that the vile ſlaues of wycked Mammon for their brybery may law**fully** be promoted **vnto** thoſe **roumes** whyche be ordeyned of God to **hys holy** ſeruauntes for theyr fydelytye? If we ſaye that the offyces be not **meete** for Gods ſeruauntes, then **we confes** that the offycers **whyche** be in theim be gods ennemyes. If we ſaye that they be ordeyned **for** the fayethfull ſeruauntes of god, how can we thynke that they maye **be brought** [bought] **vnto** the brybynge ſeruauntes of wycked mammon? **Lette vs not** ſeeke excuſes to cloke ſynne, no let euerye manne be knowen to be a lyer and ſpecyallye, they that ſay: One manne can ſerue twoo mayſters, Mammon in geuynge or takynge of brybes, and GOD in faythfull dooynge of duty. Let god be iuſtifyed when ye fynde hys worde true, whyche plainly affyrmeth that they whyche clyme into a common offyce of Chryſtes fold **by** the help of Mammon in at the wyndowe **of** bryberye be theues and robbers, commyng to ſteal, murder and deſtroye.

O that no **man** in thys **faute** wer gilty, then myght I be ſure yat no man wold be offended. But and yf any man be greued becauſe hys ſore is touched, let hym remember the ſayinge of the wyſe man: *Meliora ſunt uulnera diligentis,* **quam** *fraudulenta oſcula odientis*:[1] the woundes of the louer be better then the deceyteful kyſſes of the hater. For **the woundes whyche the** frinde openeth, be to hele olde ſores; and the dyſceytfull kyſſes of the ennemyes be to make newe woundes. I ſpeake playnelye to open the wounde, to roote oute **and** heale the dyſeaſe of couetouſnes, whyche wold be to **the** wounded and to euery man, comfort. They that by flattery do couer, kyſſe, and playſter this deepe wounde, **do ſeeke their** owne gayne to the vtter dampnacyon of **the** wounded, and to good mennes greate griefe, yea and to the greate dyſquyetinge of a com-

[1] Prov. *xxvii.* 6.

mune welth: makynge no dyfference betwixt the Lordes feruauntes, and the Lords enemyes. For wythout **dout**, *Non est quem constituit dominus.*

He is none of the **Lordes** appoyntmente or admyffion, whyche entereth **in** to **an offyce** by brybyng, Monye, or flatterynge frendeshyp. **Byinge of an** offyce is an euydente token of vnfayethfulnes. **He that is** once **knowen** by that token **and** marke, shoulde be thrust out of the Lordes foulde, *Ne furetur, mactet, et perdat,*[1] leaste that he robbe, **kyll,** and destroye. But nowe **by the** feconde **note to try** whether that the steward and dyfpoler of goddes treafures be faythfull or not, fe whether that he be **a** feder or deuourer. He that fedeth, **is** fayethfull: **he that deuoureth, is** vnfaythefull. What doeth he **whyche is** vnfaythefull? deuoure goddes shepe, Christen people, the kynges fubiectes; A daungerous **matter,** whiche if it be fpoken of, wyl procure dyfpleafure: **and yf** it be not remedyed, **wyll procure** Goddes vengeaunce. Surelye brethren, I thyncke God would **neuer haue** caufed me to haue **meddeled wyth** thys daungerous matter, **but** that he wyll geue me grace more pacyentlye to **fuffer the loffe** of myne owne lyfe, then the damnacyon **of your foules.**

For yf I lofe my lyfe here, I shall fynde **it in heauen.** But yf you be dampned, and I beynge a watcheman, and feinge your dampnacyon comming, do not geue **warning, you** shal be taken in youre owne fynnes, and your bloude requyred at my hands. If I geue warnyng, **and you take** hede, gods indignacion shalbe appeafed, **and bothe we** faued. Therefore I beynge **a** watcheman and by the lyghte of goddes worde fpying that the abominacion of **ydolatrous couetoufnes** hathe kyndled the indygnacyon **of God to confume** and destroye the people of thys realme, **doo crye out** agaynst Englande by the voyce of the Prophete: *Abiecerunt legem domini,*[2] they haue cast awaye the lawe of the lorde, euery one **framyng** hym **felfe vnto** the fashyon of thys world · *eloquium fancti Ifraell blafphemauerunt.*[2] They haue blafphemed the word of the holy one of Ifraell, by

[1] 1 John x. 10.   [2] Isa. v. 24.

theyr abominable lyuyng. *Ideo incensus est furor domini in populum suum:*[1] therefore is the indignacion of God kindled againſt his people. Therefore doth **all** runne at ſyxe and ſeuen, from euell vnto worſe: therefore doeth goddes worde take no place to do good, but is vnthankefully refuſed, whyche cauſeth more harm. Is gods word receyued in Englande becauſe it is playnlye preache **and taughte, or refuſed and** forſaken becauſe it is not obeyed and folowed? Be we in better caſe then we haue ben afore tyme becauſe papiſtry amongeſt vs is kept vnder, or els worſe then euer we were becauſe couetouſnes raygneth at lybertye? That whych papyſtry abuſed, hath not couetouſnes deſtroy[e]d? is not papiſtry ſuperſticion, and couetouſnes ydolatrye? Then I beſech you be not we well amended yat be come from abuſyng to deſtroying, from ſuperſticion to idolatry? And hath not God geuen vnto vs at the banyſhyng of ſuperſticion, comfortable plenty of his holy worde, and by the ſuppreſſyng of abbeyes excedynge aboundaunce of all maner of landes, ryches, and treaſures? And nowe where is it all become? Surelye it is muche ſpent, waſted and loſt by euyl officers, vnfaithful diſpoſers, whiche be in dede deuourers. Se therefore howe ye haue offended god, begyled the kyng, ſpoyled the realme, and indaungered your ſelues to be accuſed, condemned, and ſuffer as moſt vyle haynous traytours to God, the kyng, and to ye common welth. Wherfore whyles ye haue tyme, before ye be condemned, *Sacrificate ſacrificium iuſtitiæ, et ſperate in domino.*[2] Offer a ſacrifyce of ryghteouſnes, making reſtitucion of yat whych ye haue wrongfullye gotten: then truſte in the Lord, and he wyll ſhew mercy, prouydynge you pardon and ſafegarde, vnto euerye mannes comforte. Here I namynge no man, do meane almoſt euery man: for euery man hath ſome treaſures of the lords to dyſpoſe, and none is ſo faythfull that he maye be able to ſtande vnto the tryall, entryng wyth the Lorde into iudgemente. Therefore I aduertiſe both myniſters of the clergye, offycers in

[1] Isa. v. 25.   [2] Ps. iv. 5.

authoritye, and other people of euerye degre, to acknowledge theyr faultes, and make reſtitucion to ye vttermoſt of theyr power. Firſt vnto the clergy, I ſay: there is none of you al hauing ſo much learninge, wytt, and dylygence, as is poſſyble to be in one man, that can do more then one mans duty: why then do ye take and keepe, ſome foure or fyue mens lyuynges? I do not thyncke that euery man is worthy blame that hath a great lyuynge, nor to be prayſed that hath a litle lyuyng. For as God hath geuen ſome more excellent gyftes of learnynge, wytte and polycy, ſo hathe he prouyded for the ſame better lyuynge with hygher authority: howbeit no man may promote hym ſelfe to procede from a meane lyuyng vnto a better, *quia nemo ſibi ſuimet honorem*, for no man may preſerre hym ſelfe vnto honoure, *niſi qui a deo vocatus eſt*,[1] but he whyche for hys fydelytie in a lytle, is called of God to be truſted wyth more. But it is not a good reſon to ſay that becauſe an honeſt man for hys fydelyty is called of God from the leſſe vnto the more, therefore a couetous manne throughe gredynes, maye kepe leſſe and take more, and ſo ioyne thre or foure of theim together to make dyuers paryſhes in dyuers ſhyres, all one mans lyuynge. The Prophete cryeth: *uæ uobis qui coniungitis domum ad domum, et agrum agro copulatis*.[2] Wo be vnto you that yoine [ioyne] houſe to houſe and knyt fyeld vnto fylde. What reherſeth he no more but houſes and fyeldes? No, for ther was neuer ſuch abominacion in the prophetes times as to ioyne paryſhe to paryſh, prebend to benefyces, and Deanryes vnto knyghtes landes. I pray God that ſome of theim yf they be worthy men in wyſdome, learnynge and iudgemente, may be promoted vnto worthy roumes, and that thoſe meaner lyuynges whiche they haue heaped together to fyll one purſe, beynge ſo far dyſtante in place and condicions that they can neuer bee well ſerued of one mannes dutye, may be deuyded and dyſpoſed vnto meaner men: whych beyng more fitte for theſe lyuynges, maye do more good wyth theym.

[1] Heb. v. 4. [2] Isa. v. 8.

I heare fome complayne and faye that all thynges bee nowe fo chargeable that one benefyce is not able to fynd one [an] honeft man. And yf ye enquyre of the fame man whome they kepe and fynd in theyr **benefyce** they theim felues beyng abfent, they wyll fay a learned curate, and a dyligent farmer both honeft menne. O wycked worldlings condemned by your owne words. The whole benefice yf you fhuld therwyth be content ly[u]ing vpon it, and loke for no more, wolde not fynde **one man**.

But when ye **haue** gotten other promotions befydes that, to lye **in** another place from it, then **a** fmall **porcyon** of it doth ferue two honeft menne whyche ye **leaue in** youre abfence. Herke you that haue **three** or foure benefyces. I wyll fay the beft for you that can be fpoken: Thou lyeft al wayes at one of thy benefyces, thou arte abfente alwayes from three of thy benefyces: thou kepeft a good houfe at one of thy benefyces, thou kepeft no houfe at three of thy benefyces, thou doeft thy deutye at one of thy benefyces, thou doeft no dutye **at** thre of thy benefices. Thou femeft to be a good **manne** in one place, and in dede thou arte founde noughte in thre places. Wo be vntoo you worfe then **Scrybes and Pharifeis** Hypocrytes, whyche fhut vp the kyngedome of heauen afore menne, kepynge the paryfhe fo that neyther you enter in your felfe, neyther fuffer **them** that would enter in and do theyr dewtye, to haue your roumes and commodities. Woo be vnto you **dumme** Dogges, choked **wyth benefyces**, fo that ye be not able to open your mouthes to barcke agaynfte pluralytyes, improperacions, bying of voufons, nor againft anye euyll abufe of the cleargies lyuynges. No, for you* yowre felues myghte go a beggynge **yf** liuynges that be ordeyned for the cleargy wer not abufed, but reftored and beftowed vpon theym onelye that doeth the cleargyes dewtye. Therefore you be the inuenters and procurers of vngodlye ftatutes, and deuelyfhe deuyfes, to gyue Lordes chaplaynes whyche oughte to lyue **vpon** theyr mafters wages, authorytye to lyue vpon the fpoyle of dyuers paryſhes. *Ad erubefcentiam ueſtram dico*,[1] I fpeake to make you aſhamed of youre felues. If gentylmenne that be lordes feruauntes myghte obtayne of the kynge and hys counfel placardes or warrantes to kepe a ſtandyng vpon ſhoters hyll, Salesbury playne, or in any theuyſhe place, to take mens purfes by the way, ſhould not thys be robbery and ſhamfull abhomination to be mayntayned by lawes, ſtatutes and authority? What ſhold a yonge gentleman be aſhamed to robbe one rych mans purfe of forty ſhyllinges once in hys lyfe? and an auncient prelate not once bluſhe whyche robbeth diuers pore paryſhes of forty pounds yerely al the dayes of hys lyfe. You peſtilent prelates whyche by flattery poyfon the hygh powers of authorytye, be ye neyther afrayed nor aſhamed to make the Kynges maieſtye, his lawes and your lordes and maſters whych ſhuld be the miniſters of iuſtice and equitye, to bee the defenders and mayneteyners of your vngodly robbery. Your example and flattery hath caufed the great men and ryche men to take to theim felues the vauntage and profytes, and gèue vnto their chyldren being ignoraunte babes, the names and tytles of Perfonnages, Prebendes, Archedeaconryes, and of all manner of offyces. For euen afwell may the Lorde that cannot, as the Doctoure that wyll not do his dutye, take the profites to hymfelf, and leaue a hyrelyng vnto the paryſh: and yet both be noughte. O that it woulde pleafe God to open the eyes of the hygher powers too perceyue what good doctryne, nay what deuylyſhe dyforder is taught by theim that be double and tryple benefyced. For theyr example teacheth, and theyre preachyng can neuer difwade, to fet and ordeyne ryche robbers and ignoraunt teachers ouer the Chryſten congregacion, goddes people, the kynges fubiectes: yea and as for cyuyll order in all offyces, ambicious couetous men learnyng at theim, take the folempne tytles and good fees vnto them felues, and leaue their dutyes vnto other, fo to be neglected and abufed, as

[1] 1 Cor. *vi.* 5.

causeth al discord and disobedyence. For whoe but offycers shuld set good order, and make quietnes? And how can he set [see] any good order, whyche placeth hym selfe in ten mens roumes? or make other to be quyet wyth nothynge, that wyll neuer quyet hym selfe wyth any one liuynge? Yea how canne he be but a maker of busynes yat thrusteth many menne oute of theyr lyuynges? But for all thys the flatterer wyl say that there is a great number of them that hath many mens lyuynges in theyr handes, whych do much good wyth them, yea and be liberall gentlemen, very good officers and godly preachers. But wotte ye what the scripture sayth: they be *Canes impudentissimi, nescientes saturitatem.*[1] Vnshamefaste dogges, knowynge no measure of gredye gettynge.

Derelinquentes rectam uiam errauerunt secuti uiam Baalam filii Bosor,[2] Leauyng the ryghte way of procedynge vnto greate fees by faythfull diligence in doynge worthye dutyes, do straye in couetousnes, folowyng Balaam the son of Bosor. Leauynge [Louyng] the rewarde of cursed in [and] wycked crafte, O take heede of Baalam you that loue the rewarde of iniquitye, a reward for cursyng the people, whome god would haue blessed. A fee for kepyng those offyces vnto your selues whych god amongst ye people wold haue executed. Can ye say any more for your selues then Balam dyd? *Si dederat mihi Balaac domum suam, plenam argenti et auri.*[3] If Balaac wold geue vnto me hys house full of syluer and gold, I cannot change the word of the lorde my God, to speake more or les. Can ye do any better in the sight of the world then Balaam did vpon the hylles, euen as the lord dyd commaunde hym and none otherwyse? and yet louynge the reward of iniquitye beyng a Prophet, was rebuked of a bruyt beast: as you beyng wyse men ought to learne at a folysh Asse not to ouerburden and lode your selues with far more then ye ar able to beare. Suerlye it is an vngodly and wycked desyre of you, to loke for a rewarde both of god for doyng* of* your* duty and also of Mammon for takynge vpon you farre more

[1] Isa. *lvi.* 11.   [2] 2 Peter *ii.* 15   [3] Num. *xxii.* 18.

then euer ye be able for to dyfcharge. Balaam fought howe too get thanckes of God and a rewarde of Balaac, and in fo doyng he loft the fauoure of God, the rewarde of Balaac, and caufed the people too fynne, fo that the vengeaunce of God dydde fore plague the Ifraelites, and vtterly deftroyed Baalam and Balaac, and al theyr fort. And when as you by heapynge of lyuynges together, do feke to gette the welthe of the world, and alfo the fauour of god by pretendynge to do fo manye dutyes as no man is able to performe, ye lofe the fauor of god, and ye fhal be deceyued of the worlde, and bryng fuch iniquity amongeft ye people as fhall prouoke ye indignacion of god to plage theym, and to diftroy you. O for the tender mercies of god in oure fauioure Iefu Chrifte, although I rufhe and fret your legges vpon the hedge and pales of gods veneyarde, and fpeake playnely beinge but a very affe in comparyfon of your wyfdome, connynge, and experience, yet I befech you dere brethren be affured yat I fpeake not of malyce but of pyty, not of enuy, but of feare: for I fe euydently the aungell of the Lorde with a fworde of vengeaunce redye to deftroye you yf ye doo not ftaye, but procede in thys vngodlye way: Se and behold, *Nifi conuerfi fueritis, gladium fuum acuit, arcum fuum tetendit et parauit illum*,[1] excepte ye turne, he the Lorde hath whet his fword, he hath bente his bowe, and made it readye wyth deadlye dartes. Suerlye brethren this heapynge together of lyuynges maketh you to haue fo many thynges to do, that ye can do nothyng well: it is the readye waye not to edify but to deftroye. Wherefore yf ye cannot efpye your owne fautes in your felues, yet loke one at another: loke you of the layty at them of the cleargye, that feyng the motes in their eyes, ye may learne to pull the beames out of your owne eyes. Do ye not fe how that they of the cleargy by heapyng together manye lyuynges, haue caufed manye poore parifhes to pay their tithes yat lacke their perfons [Parfones]? Do ye not fe how that prebendes whiche were godly founded as mofte conuenient and neceffarye lyuyngs for

[1] Ps. *vii.* 12.

preachers to healp the byſhoppes and the perſons too enſtructe the people, be now vngodly abuſed to corrupte the byſhoppes and the perſonnes that rather ſeke the vauntage of good prebends to enryche them ſelues, then the healp of godly preache[r]s to enſtruct Gods people? Do ye not ſe howe theſe prouiders of pluralities hauynge the cure of Chriſten ſoules in the paryſhe, and ſhepefolde of Chryſt, do leaue the flocke and take the ſpoyle to ſpende in Noble mennes houſes, where as they doo ſe that the keper of horſes in the ſtable, of cattell in the ſyelde, and of dogges in the kenell, doeth lyue on hys maſters wages, and not on the Pyllage of his cure. O ye noble menne do ye geue vnto the kepers of your horſes, cattell, and dogges, wages, leaſte that they ſhoulde ſell youre horſes, kyll youre cattell, or ſleye youre dogges to lyue vpon the ſkynnes: and wyl ye allowe your Chapleynes no wages, but cauſe theym to lyue vpon the murder and ſpoyle of the innocente Lambs of God, redemed and boughte wyth Chriſtes precious blode? Do ye ſe howe by theſe ſeruauntes of Mammon, enemyes of Chryſte, gredy wolues in Lamb ſkynnes, the paryſhes be ſpoyled, the people vntaughte, God vnknowen, hys lyuelye woorde ſette gracyouſlye forthe by the kynges procedynges, is vngracyouſly ſuſpected, hated, and abhorred of the ignorant people?

You of the laytye, when ye ſee theſe ſmall motes in the eyes of the clargye, take heede too the greate beames that be in your owne eyes. But alas I feare leaſt yat ye haue no eyes at all. For as hypocriſy and ſuperſtiticion dooeth bleare the eyes: So couetouſneſſe and ambycyon doeth putte the eyes cleane out. For yf ye were not ſtarke blynd ye would ſe and be aſhamed that where as fyſty tunne belyed Monckes geuen to glotony fylled theyr pawnches, kept vp theyr houſe and relyued the whol country round about them, ther one of your gredye guttes deuowrynge the whole houſe and makyng great pyllage throughoute the countrye, cannot be ſatiſſyed.

If ye had any eies, ye fhould fe and be afhamed to confeffe that yf fome of you fhoulde not haue manye offyces, there woulde not be menne ynoughe founde, to put in. **euerye** offyce one **manne**, mete and able by doynge of theyr dewtyes to ferue **the** kynge, and take good **order** amongeft the people, **where as** there is a greate **number too** manye of your forte **whyche** thyncke your felues mete **and** worthye by takynge **many** Offyces in hande, to burden **the** kynge and the **people** wyth all fees and charges belongyng vnto euery offyce: yea and furdermore **to** requyre perfonages, prebendes, Deanryes and anye manner of lyuynge due vnto the Ecclefiaftycall miniftery, to **be** geuen vnto you **for** feruynge the Kynge in takynge **the** vauntage of many, and doyng the dutyes of **fewe offyces** belongyng vnto ciuyll pollycye.

If ye hadde anye eyes **ye fhoulde fe and** be afhamed that in **the** great **aboundaunce of landes** and goods taken from Abbeis, Colleges and Chauntryes for to ferue the kyng in **all** neceffaryes, and charges, efpecially in prouifion of relyefe **for** the pore, **and** for mayntenaunce of learnynge the kynge is fo dyfapoynted **that bothe** the pore be fpoyled, all mayntenance of learnyng decayed, and you only enryched. But for becaufe ye haue no eyes to fe wyth, I wyll declare that you may **heare** wyth **youre** eares, and **fo** perceyue and **knowe, that were as** God and the kynge hathe bene mofte liberall **to** gyue and beftowe, there you haue bene mofte vnfayethfull **to** dyfpofe and delyuer. For accordyng vnto gods word and the k[y]nges pleafure, the vniuerfities **which be the fcholes** of all godlynes and vertue, fhould haue bene nothyng decayed, **but** much increfed and amended **by thys [the]** reformacion of religion.

As concernynge goddes worde for the vpholdyng **and** increafe of **ye vniuerfities**, I am fure that no man knowyng learnyng and vertue doth doute. And as for the kynges pleafure it dyd well appeare in that he eftablyfhed vnto the vnyuerfityes all Priuileges graunted afore hys tyme, and alfo in all manner of paymentes requyred of the cleargye, as tythes, and fyrſt fruytes, the vnyuerſities be exemted. Yea and the **kynges** mayeſtye that dead is, dyd geue vnto the vniuerſities of Cambryge at **one tyme,** two hundred poundes yerely to the exibition **and** fyndynge of fiue learned menne, to reade and teache dyuynitye, lawe, Phyſycke, Greke and Ebrue.

At an other **tyme. xxx. pounde yerely** *In liberam et puram eliemoſinam.* In fre and pure almes. And fynally for the fuſt dacion [foundation] of a newe Colledge ſo muche as ſhoulde ſerue to buylde it, and replenyſhe it wyth **mo Scholers and better** lyuynges then any other Colledge in the vniuerſitye afore that tyme had.

By the whyche euerye man maye perceyue that **the** kynge geuyng manye thynges and takynge nothinge from the vniuerſityes was very deſirous to haue them increaſed and amended. Howbeit all they that haue knowen the vnyuerſitye of Cambryge ſence that tyme that it dyd fyrſt begynne to receyue theſe greate and manyefolde benefytes from the kynges maieſtye, at youre handes, haue iuſte occaſion to ſuſpecte that you haue deceyued boeth the kynge and vniuerſitie, to enryche youre ſelues. For before that you did beginne to be the diſpoſers of the kinges liberalitye towardes learnyng and pouerty, there was in houſes belongynge vnto the vnyuerſytye of Cambryge, two hundred ſtudentes of dyuynytye, manye verye well learned : whyche bee nowe all clene gone, houſe and manne, young towarde ſcholers, and old fatherlye Doctors, not one of them lefte : one hundred alſo of an other ſorte that hauyng rych frendes or beyng benefyced men dyd lyue of theym ſelues in Oſtles [Oſtries] and Innes be eyther **gon** awaye, or elles ſayne to crepe into Colleges, and put poore men from bare lyuynges. Thoſe bothe be all gone, and a ſmall number of poore godly dylygent ſtudentes nowe remaynynge only in Colleges be not able to tary and contynue theyr ſtudye in ye vniuerſitye for lacke of exibicion and healpe. There be dyuers ther whych ryfe dayly betwixte foure and fyue of the clocke in the mornynge, and from fyue vntyll fyxe of the clocke, vfe common prayer wyth an exhortacion of gods worde in a commune chappell, and from fixe vnto ten of the clocke vfe euer eyther pryuate ftudy or commune lectures. At ten of the clocke they go to dynner, whereas they be contente wyth a penye pyece of byefe amongeft. iiii. hauyng a fewe porage made of the brothe of the fame byefe, wyth falte and otemell, and nothynge els.

After thys flender dinner they be either teachynge or learnynge vntyll v. of the clocke in the euenyng, when as they haue a fupper not much better then theyr dyner. Immedyatelye after the whyche, they go eyther to reafonyng in problemes or vnto fome other ftudye, vntyll it be nyne or tenne of the clocke, and there beyng wythout fyre are fayne to walk or runne vp and downe halfe an houre, to gette a heate on their feete whan they go to bed.

Thefe be menne not werye of theyr paynes, but very forye to leue theyr ftudye : and fure they be not able fome of theym to contynue for lacke of neceffarye exibicion and relefe. Thefe be the lyuyng fayntes whyche ferue god takyng greate paynes in abftinence, ftudye, laboure and dylygence, wyth watching and prayer. Wherfore as Paule, for the Sayntes and brethren at Hierufalem, fo I for your brethren and Saynctes at Cambrydge moofte humblye befeche you make youre colleccions amongeft you rych Marchauntes of this citye, and fend them your oblacions vnto the vnyuerfytye, fo fhall ye be fure to pleafe God, to comfort theim, and prouyde learned men to do muche good throughout all thys realme. Yea and truly ye be detters vnto theim : For they haue fowen amongefte you the fpirituall treafures of goddes worde, for the whyche they oughte to repe of you agayne corporall neceffaries. But to returne vnto them that fhoulde better haue prouyded for learnynge and pouertye in all places, but efpecyally in the vniuerfities.

Loke whether that there was not a greate number of both lerned and pore that myght haue ben kepte, mayntayned, and relyeued in the vniuerfities: whych lackyng **all** healpe or comforte, were compelled to forfake the vniuerfitye, leue their bokes, and feke theyr lyuynge abrode in the country? Yea and in the cuntrey manye Grammer Scholes **founded** of a godly intent to brynge vp poore mennes fonnes in learnynge and vertue, nowe **be** taken aw[a]ye by reafon of the gredye couetoufnes of you that were put in truft by God, and the kynge to erecte and make grammer fcholes in manye places: And had neyther commaundement **nor permiffion to take away** the fcholmafters lyuyng in **anye** place, moreouer muche charitable almes **was there in** manye places yerely to be beftowed in pore townes **and** parifhes vpon goddes people, the kynges fubiectes: whiche almes to ye great dyfpleafure of god and dyshonoure of the kynge, yea and contrarye to goddes worde and the kynges lawes, ye haue taken away. I knowe what ye do faye and bragge in fome places: that ye haue doen as ye were commaunded wyth as muche charytye and lyberalitye towardes both pouertye and learnynge, as your commiffion woulde beare and fuffer.

Take heede whome ye flaunder, for Goddes worde, **and** the kynges lawes and ftatutes be open vnto euery mannes eyes, and be [by?] euery commiffion directed accordynge vnto them, ye both myght and fhould haue geuen much wher as ye **haue** taken much away.

Take hede vnto **the kynges** ftatutes, the actes **of** parliament, there **ye** fhall **fynde that the** Nobles and commons do geue, and the Kynge doth take into hys handes Abbeyes, Colleges and Chauntryes for erectynge of Gramer fcholes, the godly brynging vp of youthe, the farther augmentynge of the vnyuerfytyes, and better prouifyon for the poore. Thys fhall ye fynd in the Actes of parliament, in the Kynges ftatutes: but what fhalbe found in **your** practyfe and in your dedes? Surely the pullyng downe of gramer fcholes, the deuylifhe drownynge of youthe in ignoraunce, the vtter decaye of the vniuerſities, and mooſte vncharitable ſpoyle of prouyſion, that was made for the pore.

Was it not a godly and charitable prouyſion of the Kynge to geue vnto the vniuerſity two hundred poundes yerelye for excellente Readers? three hundred [Thirtie] poundes yerelye in pure almes, **and manye** hundred pounds alſo to the foundacyon and ereccion of a newe Colledge? And was it not a deuiliſhe **deuyſe of** you to **tourne** all thys the kinges bountuouſe liberalitye into improperacions of benefices, whyche be papyſticall and vncharytable ſpoyles of moſt neceſſarye prouyſion for pore paryſhes? *Intelligite inſipientes in populo, et ſtulti aliquando ſapite.*[1]

Learne vnderſtandyng you that playe vnwyſe partes amongeſte the people, and you fooles once waxe wyſe. *Qui plantauit aurem not audiet?*[1]

He that ſette the eares, ſhall he not **heare** the ſorowfull complaynte of pore paryſhes, agaynſte you that **haue by** improperacions clene taken awaye hoſpitalitye, **and** muche impared the due liuynges of gods mynyſters, the peoples inſtructoures and teachers. *Qui figurat oculum non conſiderat?*[1] he that faſhioned the eie, **doth** he not beholde howe that the beſte landes of abbeyes, colleges and chaunteries be in youre handes, **and** euyll improperacions conueyd to the kyng and **to the** vniuerſities and Byſhopes landes? *Qui corripit gentes non arguet?*[1]

He that corrected and punyſheth the heathen lackyng the lyght of gods word for the only **abuſe** of naturall reaſon, wyll he not reproue and condemne you whyche haue **good** reaſonable wyts, gods onely word, the kynges laws, and ſtatut[e]s: and much power and authority geuen **vnto** you to edifye and do good, ſeinge it is abuſed of you to deſtroy and **do** hurt? Shulde not **you** haue amended **the** prouiſion for the pore, the educacyon of youthe, and the condicion of the vniuerſities? **And** be **they** not by you ſore hurte and dekayed? The kynge ſhold and wold haue reformed religion. The fyrſt parte of reformacion is to reſtore

[1] Ps. xciv. 9, 10.

and geue agayne all fuche thynges as haue bene wrongfullye taken and abufed. Surelye the Abbeyes dyd
wrongfullye take and abufe nothynge fo much as the
improperacions of benefices. Nothynge is fo papyftycall as improperacions of benefices **be**: they be the
Popes darlynges and paramors, whiche by the dyuel-
yfhe deuyce of wicked Balaamytes, be fet a brode in this
realme to caufe the lerned men of the vnyuerfities and
all bifhoppes that be godly menne, the Popes enemyes,
to commyt fpirituall fornicacion wyth them. Whye dyd
God deftroye the Madianytes but for their fynne? Why
dyd he plage the Ifraelytes but for ye fame fynne?
Why dyd God caufe the Abeyes to be deftroyed, but
for papyftycall abufes? And why fhoulde not **god**
plage the vnyuerfityes and Byfhops kepynge and med-
delynge wyth improperacions, that bee the fame papyfti-
call and deuelyfh abufes?

O what a bloudye daye fhall it be: when as for thys
abhomynacion, thys fpirituall fornicacion, God fhall
commaunde hys faythfull feruaunte Moyfes the kynges
mayefty to take and hange all the rulers of the people
that haue wittynglye fuffred thefe whoryfhe Madyanytes,
thefe Popyfh abufes? And caufe a zelous Phinees to
fhedde the harte bloude of hym that before Moyfes
and many Ifraelites, before a hygh iuftice and manye
people, taketh a Madianite into hys tent, an improper-
acion into his enheritance. But nowe brethren as
Peter preached vnto the Iewes: *Nunc fratres fcio quod
per ignorantiam feciftis.*[1] Now brethren I knowe that
you haue done thys through ignoraunce: for the Lorde
whych forfeeth all thynges, knoweth that yf you hadde
not bene blynded wyth ignoraunce, ye coulde neuer
for pitye haue executed hys indignacyon and wrathe
in makynge fuche deftruccyon. Seynge therefore that
it was Goddes pleafure thus by one euyll to punyfhe an
other, nowe repent, and amende, that youre fautes maye
be pardoned. It pleafed God by the blynde malyce of
the Iewes, to nayle Chryfte Iefu vpon the croffe: and
yet as many of theim as hearyng that matter opened

[1] Acts *iii*. 17.

by Peter, were greued and pricted in confcience, fo many fayde vnto Peter, and to the other Apoftles what fhall we do? The Apoftolical counfel was: *Agite penitenciam, recipifcite.*¹ Repent and amend. So dere brethren hearynge and knowyng that God hath vfed your gredy couetoufnes to deftr[o]ye Abbeyes, Colleges, and chauntryes, and to plage all thys realme, be greued and fory in your hertes, feynge that ye haue bene *Vafa iræ*,² inftrumentes of wrath to execute vengeance: and purge your felues of thys vyle couetoufneffe, then fhall ye from henceforth be *Vafa honoris*,³ veffels of honoure, to ferue God, *in fanctitate et iufticia*⁴ in holynes and ryghteoufnes all the dayes of your lyfe.

And nowe on the other parte, you that be of the comynaltye, when ye feele that anye plague or punyfhement commeth by thiem that be fette ouer you in offyce, and aucthorytye, knowe that they do it not of theym felues, but be moued and ftyred of God, to worke hys wrath vpon you. For when as God was dyfpleafed wyth the Ifraelytes, then hys dyfplefure caufed Dauyd theyr kynge to take that way that brought a peftilence amongeft the people, whereon dyed. lxx. thoufande: *Addidit furor domini irafci contra Ifrael, commouitque dauid.*⁵ The indignacion of the Lorde waxed whot agaynft Ifrael, and he ftired vp Dauyd. What kyndled the indignacion of God, but the fynnes of the people? The fynnes of the people dyd kyndle the indignacyon of the Lorde: the Lordes indignacyon ftired vp Dauyd in prefumpcyon. Dauids prefumptuoufnes caufed the people to dye on the peftylence. And euen as then God ordeyned yat chrift fhuld be crucifyed be ye malicious blyndnes of the Iewes, the Ifraelites plaged by the prefumption of Dauyd:

So hath he ordeyned that Englande fhoulde be fpoyled wyth gredy couetoufe officers, Looke then, what hath made thys greate fpoyle in England? gredye couetoufnes of officers. What dyd make in theym fuche gredy couetoufnes? the indignacion of God. What kyndled goddes indignacion? the fynnes of the

¹ **Acts** *ii.* 38; Mark *i.* 15. ² Rom. *ix.* 22. ³ 2 Tim. *ii.* 21.
⁴ Luke *i.* 75. ⁵ 2 Sam. *xxiv.* 1.

people. What was the fynne of the people? *Eloquium fancti Ifraell, blafphemauerunt*.[1] They haue blafphemed the holye woorde of GOD, callynge it newe learnynge and heretycall doctryne: *Ideo iratus eft furor domini.*[1] And therefore is the wrath of the Lorde kyndled. Now you people which cry and fay that you are robbed and fpoyled of all that ye haue: Woulde ye haue thys whyche ye call robbyng and fpoyling to be ceaffed? Then quench the indignacion of god whych doth caufe and make it. If ye wyl quench the indignacion of God, *Hodie fi uocem eius audieritis.*[2] To daye, euen nowe yf ye fhal heare hys voyce, harden not your hartes, as in the prouocacion in the daye of temptacyon. Harde heartes, ftyffe neckes, dyfobediente myndes, prouoke, tempte, and ftyre vp the indignacion of God.

Truelye the indignacion of God fhal neuer be quenched, vntyll that you wyth tender hartes, humble, obedyente, and thankefull myndes, receyue, embrace, and conforme your felues vnto the holy worde of God fet forth by the Kynges Mageftye his gracious procedynges.

There is as yet more ftyffe necked ftubburnes, dieuellyfh difobedience, and gredye couetoufnes in one of you of the commune forte that kepeth thys greate fwellynge in the hearte, hauyng no occafion to fette it furth in exercife, then is in ten of the worft of theim that beynge in office and aucthoritye, haue manye occafions to open and fhewe them felues what they be.

When dyd euer anye offycers in authorytye fhewe fuche rebellyous proud myndes, as was of late playnlye perceyued in very manye of the communaltye? I put the cafe that they be fo couetoufe, that one of their gredi guts had fwalowed vp a whole Abbey, houfe, landes and goodes, And yf you had had powers vnto your wylles, ye had deuoured whole countryes, houfes and goodes, men and beaftes, corne and cattell, as ye dyd begynne.

Some of theim kepeth their fermes in theyr owne

[1] Isa. v. 24, 25.   [2] Ps. xcv. 7.

handes, and manye of you kepe youre owne Corne in youre owne barnes. Yea marrye, why fhould we not kepe oure **corne in** oure **owne** barnes? Forfooth ye nowe maye not keepe it for dreade of God, obedience to the Kynges maieſtie, **and pitie of** your poore neighbours: For God fayeth: *Qui abſcondit frumenta, maledicetur in populis: benediƈtio autem ſuper caput uendencium:*[1] He that hydeth vp corne, fhall be accurſed amongeſt [amonges] the people: but bleffynge fhal be vpon theyr heades that bryngeth it furth to the Markettes to fell. Here ye heare the bleffynge and curfe of God.

Ye knowe the kynges gracious Proclamacyon, **ye** maye perceyue youre neyghbours neede, by theyr myferable complaynt. And yet neyther God by blef- **fyng and** curfynge, neither the kyng by proclamacion **and commiffion,** nether **the** pore by praiyng and paying **can caufe you to ferue** ye Markets wyth corne. But let goddes woorde, the Kynges lawes, honeſt order, and charytable prouyfyon be put foorth **of all** markette townes by wycked Mammon, and **let hym** onely kepe the Markets and fet **pryfes for youre purpofes, and** wythoute doubte euerye market **fhalbe ful** of all manner of Corne and vytayles commyng **in** on al **fydes.**

O wycked feruauntes of Mammon, alwayes bothe **ennemyes** and traytoures to G O D and the kyng and the common wealthe. Is it God or Mammon that hath made the Corne to fprynge, and geuen you plentye? **Yf** ye fay Mammon, then ye confeffe playnely whofe feruauntes ye be, what Idolatrye **ye vfe.** If ye fay God, How dare ye confeffe him in **youre** woordes and denye hym in youre deedes? Whye do ye not brynge foorth goddes **corne vnto** goddes people, at goddes **commaundement? Why be ye not** faythfull difpofers **of** Goddes **treafures?** Well, he yat hath no corn thinketh he hath **no** parte, nor **is** not gyltye **in** this matter: **but I can tel** that ther is many of theim, that neither **hath** nor wyll haue corne, whyche make corne moſt **dere.** I haue heard howe that euen this laſt yere, ther was certayn Acres of corne growyng on the ground

[1] Prov. *xi.* 26.

bought for. viii. poundes: he that bought it for. viii. fold it for. x. He that gaue. x. pounds, fold it to an other aboue. xii. poundes: and at laſt, he that caryed it of the ground, payde. xiiii. poundes. Lykewyſe I hearde, that certayne quarters of malte were boughte after the pryce of. iii. ſhyllynges. iiii. pence a quarter to be delyuered in a certayn markette towne vpon a certayne daye. Thys bargayne was ſo oft bought and folde before the daye of deiyueraunce came, that the fame Malte was folde to hym that ſhoulde receyue it there and carrye it awaye, after. vi. s. a quarter. Looke and ſe howe muche a craftes man or anye other honeſte man that muſte ſpend corne in his houſe, by this maner of bargaynynge, payeth, and howe littel the houſbande manne that tylleth the ground, and paieth the rent, receyueth: Then ye may ſe and perceyue it muſt needes be harde for eyther of theim to kepe a houſe, the cra[f]tes man payinge ſo muche, and the huſbandman takynge ſo lytle.

There is a lyke maner of barganyng of them that be leaſemongers, for leaſemongers make the tenaunts to pay ſo muche, and the landlord to take ſo little, that neither of them is wel able to kepe houſe. I heare ſay that within a few miles of London an honeſt gentleman did let his ground by leaſe vnto pore honeſt men after. ii. s. iiii. d. an acar: then commeth a leſemounger, a thefe, an extorcioner, deceiuyng ye tenaunts, bieth theyr leaſes, put theim from the groundes, and cauſeth them yat haue it at hym nowe, to paye after. ix. s. or as I harde ſaye. xix. s. but I am aſhamed to name ſo muche. How be it, couetous extorcioners be aſhamed of no dede be it neuer ſo euyll. **And** as I hear ſay, ther be many leſemongers in London, that heyghthen the rent of bare houſes: and as corne, landes, tenementes and houſes, ſo in al maner of wares, ther be ſuch biers and fellers as cauſe ye prouyders and makers of ye wares to take ſo litle, and the occupiers of the wares too paye ſo muche, that neyther of theim both is able too lyue. All the Marchauntes of myſchyeſe that go betwixt the barke and the tree. Betwixte the houſband man that getteth the corne, and houſholder that occupyeth Corne, betwix the Landlorde, that letteth fermes, **and the** tennauntes that dwell in the fermes. And betwixt the craftes man that maketh, or the marchaunte that **prouydeth wares, and other** men **that** occupieth wares. I ſaye theſe **marchauntes of** miſchiefe commynge betwixte the barke **and** the tree, do make all thinges dere to the byers: **and** yet wonderfull vyle and of ſmall pryce to many, that muſt nedes ſett or ſell that whyche is their owne honeſtlye come bye. Theſe be far worſe than anye other that hath bene mencyoned heretofore: for although benefyced men and offycers haue manye mennes liuynges, yet they do ſome mennes dutyes. But theſe haue euerye mannes lyuyng, and doo no mans duytye. For they haue that whyche is in dede the lyuynge of craftes men, Marchauntmenne, huſbandmen, landelordes and tennauntes, **and do neuer** a one of theſe mens dutyes. Theſe be ydle vacaboundes, lyuyng vpon other mens labours: theſe be named honeſt barginers, and be in dede craftye couetouſe extorcioners. For they that be true marchauntemen **to** by and ſell in dede, ſhoulde **and** doo prouyde great plentye and good chepe by honeſt byenge and ſellynge of theyr wares. But theſe hauynge **the** names of true marchauntes, and beyng in dede crafty theues, do make a ſcarſitye and dearth of all thynges that commeth through theyr handes.

Take awaye all marchauntmen from anye towne or cytye, and ye ſhall leaue almoſt no prouyſyon of thinges that be neceſſarye. Take awaye leaſmongers, regrators and **all** ſuche as by byinge and ſellynge make thyngs more dere, and when they be gone, all thyngs wylbe **more** plentye and better chepe. Now maye ye ſe **who** they be that make a greate dearth in a great plentye. **For who is** it, that heygtheneth the pryce of Corne, the houſbandman that getteth plentye of corne by tyllynge of the grounde? No: the regrator that byeth corne to **make** it dere, growynge vpon the grownde. Who

reyfeth the rentes, ioyneth houfe to houfe, and heapeth
fermes together? The Gentyll manne, that by geuynge
of leafes, letteth forth hys own landes into other mennes
handes? No, the leafemongers, that by felling leafes,
byeth and bryngeth other mennes Landes into their
own hands. Who maketh all manner of wares and
marchandyfes to be very dere? the marchaunt ven-
terer, which with fayethfull dylygence to prouyde for
the commune **weal**th, caryeth furth fuche thynges as
maye well be fpared, and bryngeth home fuche wares
as mufte needes be occupyed in thys **realme?** No,
the **Marchant** of myfchyefe that by craftye conuey-
aunce for his owne gayne, caryeth awaye fuch thinges
as maye not be fpared, and bryngeth agayne fuche
wares as are not nedefull. Take hede you Marchauntes of London that ye be not Marchauntes of
myfchyefe, conueying away to much old lead, wol,
lether and fuch fubftanciall wares as wold fet many
Englyfhmen to work, and do euery manne good
feruyce, and bryngynge home fylkes and fables, cat-
tayls, and folyfhe fethers to fil the realm full of **fuch**
baggage as wyll neuer do ryche or poore good,
and neceffary feruyce. Be ye fure, if thys realme
be rych, ye fhall not nede to be poore, yf thys realme
be poore, you fhall not be able to kepe and enioy
your ryches. Take hede than that your marchaundife
be not a feruynge of folyfh mens fanfies, whyche wyll
deftroye the realme: but lette it be a prouydyng for
honeft difcrete mens commodities, whych wyll be the
vpholdyng and enrychyng of you and the whole realme.
Take hede vnto your vocacions prelates and preachers
Magyftrats and offycers, landlordes and tenaunts,
craftes men and marchauntes, all maner of men take
hede vnto youre felues and to your conuerfacion and
lyuyng: yea dere brethren at the reuerence of god, for a
generall comfort to al partes with out gredye couetoufneffe towards oure felues, or malicious enuye towardes
other, wyth a fyngle eye, of a pure herte, let vs confyder
and acknowledge how that the bountifull liberalitye of

almyghtye God hath geuen vnto thys realme wonderfull plenty of perſonnages, prebends, benefyces, offyces, and all maner of lyuynges: wyth great aboundance of corne, cattell, landes, goodes, and all wares that be good **and** profitable: and howe that it is certeynly the vnfaithfull diſpoſers whyche cauſe a great ſcarſyty, dearth and lacke of all theſe giftes **and treaſures of** God, therfore *dominus de cælo proſpexit, ut uideat ſi eſt intelligens aut requirens deum.*[1]

The Lord loked doun from heauen to ſe yf there **were** any that had vnderſtandyng and ſought to pleaſe God in faythfull dyſpoſynge of Goddes treaſures: but ſeinge that *Omnes ſtudent auaritiæ, a maiore vſque ad minorem.*[2] All be geuen vnto coueteouſnes from the hyeſte vnto the loweſte, ſo that pore people can haue **no** houſes to dwell in, ground to occupye, no nor corne for their moneye. The Lorde hym ſelfe ſpeakyng vnto the earthe, ſheweth wher is the faute: *principes tui infideles.*[3] Thy head rulers and offycers be vnfaythfull diſpoſers. *Socii furum,*[3] theuiſhe fellowes.

Omnes diligunt munera,[3] they all loue brybes, *et ſequuntur retributiones,*[3] and hunte for promocyons. What then O Lorde ſhall be the ende of all thys? *Viuo ego dicit dominus.*[4] As trulye as I lyue ſayeth the Lord *propterea quod facti ſunt greges mei in rapinam,*[4] Becauſe that my flock haue ben ſpoyled, *et oues meæ in deuorationem omnium beſtiarum agri,*[4] and my ſhepe deuoured of all wyld beaſtes of the fyelde, *quia non eſſet paſtor,* Becauſe there was no keper, *Neque enim quæſiuerunt paſtores mei gregem meum,* For thoſe [theſe] which were named my paſtours, dyd take no heede vnto my flocke, *Sed paſtores paſcebant ſemetipſos,* But thoſe paſtours dyd feede theym **ſelu**es prowlyng for profyte, *et greges meos non paſcebant,* and my flocke th[e]y dyd not feede by dooyng of their dutyes. *Propterea paſtores audite uerbum domini.*

Therfore ye keepers heare the word of the Lorde. What worde? that the flocke ſhalbe delyuered, and you ſhalbe deſtroyed: That is a true word: for *qua menſura*

---

[1] Ps. *liii.* 2. [2] Jer. *vi.* 13. [3] Isa. *i.* 23. [4] Ezek. *xxxiv.* 8, 9.

menfi fueritis, remecietur uobis:[1] By [bicaufe] the fame meafure that you haue ferued other, ye youre felues fhall alfo **be** ferued: for as ye haue ferued fuperftycious papiftes, fo fhall you your felues be ferued, beynge couetous Idolaters: yea and haue as muche vauntage **at the** metynge, as is betwixte fuperfticion and Idolatrye. Howe be it, God geuynge you refpite to loke for amendmente: offers more gentelnes, yf ye wyl take it. For in the. xx. of Ieremy he fayth: *Ecce ego do coram uobis uiam uitæ et uiam mortis:*[2] Behold I fet before you the way of lyfe and the way of death: yf ye repent and amend, lyfe: **If ye be** ftyll ftifnecked, death: for the Lorde by Efaye. i. fayeth: *Si uolueritis et audieritis:*[3] Yf ye wyll heare to repent and amend, *Bona terræ comedetis,*[3] ye **fhall eat** the good fruits yat the earth fhall brynge forth, to your comfort. *Si nolueritis, et me ad iracundiam prouocaueritis,*[3] yf ye wyl not, but prouoke me to anger, *gladius deuorabit uos.*[3] The fworde fhall eate you vp. *Quia os domini locutum eft.*[3] For it is Gods owne mouthe that hathe fpoken it. **For Gods** fake beleue it: And do not by an harde hearte voyde of repentance heape vnto your felues the wrathe of god agaynft ye day of vengeance.

But thankfullye enbrafynge the ryches of goddes goodnes, pacience and long fufferyng, acknowlegyng that goddes kyndnes draweth you vnto repentance, yf ye haue fo lytle fpyrituall felyng and ghoftlye vnderftandynge that ye can nothyng be perfwaded or moued by the comfortable promyfes, and terrible thretenynges of the inuifible God: yet hauynge corporall eyes and naturall reafon, confyder the decaye of thys Realme, and the towardnes of the kynges mageftye. Note the decaye of thys realme, and thereby ye fhall learne to knowe that nothynge can make a realme wealthye, **yf** the inhabitauntes therof be couetoufe: for yf [all] landes and goodes coulde haue made a realme happy notwythftandynge mennes couetoufnes, then fhoulde not thys realme foo vnhappylye haue decayed, whenas by the fuppreffion of Abbeis, Colleges and Chaun**teries,** innumerable lands and goodes were gotten.

If goddes worde were ordeyned by anye other meane then by the conuertynge of couetous men, to make that realme happy where couetous men be, then fuerlye fhoulde England now be moft happy, wher gods word is frely fet forth in the **mother toung,** playnly preached in folempne congregacions, **and** commonly vfed in daily communicacion. But vndoubtedlye whereas couetoufe men be, there neyther landes or goodes, no not goddes holye Gofpell canne **doo fo muche** good as couetoufnes doeth harme. Wherefore feyng thys realm by couetoufneffe is foore decayed, leaft it fhoulde alfo by the fame be deftroyed, awaye wyth youre couetoufnes, all you yat loue thys realme. Or yf ye wyll not do it for loue of the realme, yet for the reuerente obedience whyche ye **owe** vnto God and **the** kynges maieftie, away wyth couetoufnes whyche maketh men feruauntes of Mammon, and enemyes vnto **god** and the kynge. Be ye well affured that the kynges Maieftye whyche nowe is, God faue his noble grace, dreadeth god, loueth his people, and abhorreth couetoufnes, whiche in this realme offendeth God, difhonoureth ye kyng, anoyeth the people.

Therefore he doeth partly nowe perceyue and confider, and wyll do better hereafter, that prelates wyth pluralities, and magyftrates wyth manie offices, do burden him and his people wyth paying tithes, fees, and **manye** greate charges, and yet kepe fo many roumes vacant of prechers and officers, that his magefty cannot **be** duly ferued, nor his people well inftructed by the preachyng of gods word, **nor** yet well **ordred** by the myniftracion of iuftice and equitye.

He knoweth that regratours of corne vyttals and of **all** maner of wares, make fuche **dearthe** and fcarcitie, **that no** diligence of good marchauntes by honeft byinge and fellynge canne prouyde anye thynges to be **eyther** good cheap or plentiful. It is well knowen **to** his gracious maiefty, or at the leaft vnto hys honourable councell that leafemungers takynge muche of tenauntes and paying lyttell vnto the landlordes, haue both theyr

lyuynges, and doth the dutyes of neyther. For to
theyr owne pryuate luker they take rentes of tenauntes,
and fermes of landlordes: but when by occafyon they
fhall be requyred to ferue the Kynge for a common
wealth, then they wyll haue neyther landes nor ferme
to do the kyng feruyce. Do not therfore imagyn you
that be eyther of the clergye or of the laytye in hyghe
or lowe degree, that the Kynges Gracious Mageftie
and his honourable councell be fo negligent that they
do not efpye, or fo parcyall that they wyll not punyfhe
thofe whyche in thys realme hynder the prechyng
of gods word, ftoppe the adminyftracion of iuftice
and equitye, caufe of all thynges a dearthe and fcarfytye, and brynge Gentlemenne to poouertye, and hufbandmen vnto beggerye. It is fpyed and mufte be
punyfhed, although it be delayed for a tyme, to fe yf
you of your felues wyllynglye wyll amende it.

Beware therefore that ye ftaye not your felfe vnto a
bryttell ftaffe, for it wyll braft in fpylles and perce
thorowe your handes. Do not ftay your felfe vpon
thys ymaginacion to thynke that althoughe craftelye
contrary to lawe and confcience ye do inuade other
mennes roumes, liuynges and goodes, yet for becaufe
ye be fo many in number that do it, therefore the
kynge and hys councell eyther cannot or wyll not bee
agaynfte you in it: For trulye euen therefore mufte
they nowe neades wythout delaye reforme and amend
it. For as fedicious rebellion, fo couetoufe treafon
beynge in a fewe may be fuffered at the fyrfte in hope
of amendment, fo long as they few by clokynge it
fecretelye, feme to be afhamed of their owne euyll
doynges, or afrayed of the rulers power and authorytye:
but beynge fo many that they all together wythoute
fhame and feare, falle to open fpoylynge of the realme,
then wythoute delaye mufte they needes be repreffed,
althoughe they both fay and fweare, that they be the
kyngs fubiects, and breake no laws. If ye fpoyle be
found in theyr hands, it is neyther fayinge nor fwear-
ynge that can excufe them. Open fpoile hath bene

made of perfonages, prebendes, offices, fermes, wares,
vyctuals, and of all manner of mens liuinges. Therefore there is no long delay to be taken in hope of
amendemente, but fpedye prouifion for redres muft be
made for feare of a generall deftruccion. You then
that for waftynge and abufynge of the Lordes goodes
be worthye and lykely fone to be difplaced, yet in ye
mean tyme whyles ye haue refpyte, playe the parte of
a wyfe fteward. Reftore vnto preachers and **offycers**,
benefyces and offyces: lette landelordes haue their
rentes, and fermoures theyr leafes: caufe byinge and
fellyng to be a prouyfyon of good chepe and plentye,
and not an occafyon of dearthe and fcarfytye. Soo
fhall both God and the kyng perceyuyng your wyfe
prouyfion, allow your wel doyng, pardon your fautes,
and confirme you in your offyces.

O refufe the feruyce, reftore the iniuryes of wycked
Mammon, that ye maye from hencefoorthe ferue God
and the kynge, prouydyng for the people in holynes
and ryghtoufnes all the dayes of youre lyfe: take hede
when ye go from a meaner lyuynge vnto a better, frome
a lower offyce vnto a hygher, that ye goo as menne
called of Chrifte, not as bewitched and allured by
Mammon, fe that God by hygher authoritye perceyu-
ynge your faythfulnes in a lyttell, doo in at the doore
of worthynes and honeftye, admytte and receyue you
to be trufted wyth more: beware leafte that the deuyll
by flatteryng frendfhyppe and couetous ambycion, per-
ceyuynge your worldlynes in a lytle, do in at the wyn-
dow of wycked bryberye conuey and receyue you, to
abufe and be abufed wyth more. Se that ye obey the
commaundement of God, takynge paynes in youre
dutye to feede and doo good. Do not confent vnto
the temptacion of the Deuell, worfhyppynge hym in
worldlynes, for to gette gaynes. Thefe thynges obferued, ye fhal be eftemed and taken as worthye miny-
fters of Chryft, and feruaunts of God, for fo much as
appertayneth vnto the lawfull callyng and admiffion of
you into youre rowmes, and alfo the fayethfull dyly-

gence in vfyng of your felues in your roumes. Furthermore Paule geueth example of a lowly mynde whyche doeth not iuftifye a mans felfe, and iudge euyll of other. For fo it becommeth the feruauntes of God, and the mynyfters of Chryfte, euen when they haue done as they be commaunded, to acknowledge them felues vnprofytable feruaunts. And not as proud Pharifeis, prayinge in the prefence of the Lorde, to make boaft of theim felues, and fynde fautes wyth other men. No, for yf other menne prayfe them, they muft not regarde it, no nor yf theyr owne confcience commende them, excepte **God** alfo allow it. Therfore Paule fayeth. *Mihi pro minimo eft ut a nobis iudicer.* It is one of the leaft thinges wyth me too be iudged of you that be wyth me, eyther in tyme or place. *Vel ab humano die,* eyther of mannes daye, by the experience of theim that fhall haue further tryall in contynuance of tyme. *Sed neque me ipfum iudico.* No nor I doo not iudge my felfe. *Mihi enim nihil confcius fum, fed non ideo iuftificatus fum.* For there is nothyng that I knowe my felfe gylty of, yet through that am **I not** iuftifyed, no not thorow the iudgement of you or of other, or of myne owne confcience. *Qui uero iudicat me dominus eft.*[1] He truly yat iudgeth me, is ye lord iudge **of** all men. *Quare, nihil ante tempus iudicate,*[1] wherefore iudge ye nothyng afore the tyme of iudgemente. *Quando dominus uenerit,*[1] when the Lorde fhall come to iudge. *Qui et illuftrabit occulta tenebrarum,*[1] whyche alfo fhall make bryghte the couertes of darkeneffe and craftye clokynge of fautes. *Et manifeftabit concilia cordis,*[1] and fhall open the thoughtes of the heartes, whiche he only fearcheth. *Et tunc laus erit unicuique **a** deo.*[1] And then prayfe fhall be vnto euery one of God, that geueth prayfe to the prayfe worthy. If Paule, beynge a mynyfter of Chryfte, and a difpofer of Goddes myfteryes, was fo faythefull in hys doynge that neyther all the worlde nor hys owne confcience coulde in any thyng reproue hym, and yet to contynue hys carefull dylygence had euermore a greate refpecte vnto the commyng and

---

[1] 1 Cor. iv. 3, 4, 5.

iudgement of the Lorde: Howe fhall we thynke that
they rede and take thys place, whiche beyng knowen
both to theym felues and vnto the whole worlde to do
very euyl in many thyngs, yet wythout care of amendement, do forget theym felues, the Lord, and his iudgemente? Surely they vnderftand it as Peter fayth: that
many places of Paul be vnderftand of them whych
beyng *indocti καὶ ἄσησιχτοί* vnlearned and vnfetled in
iudgement, ασριβλονσει wraft or wryng vntyll a wrong
pin *in fuam ipforium perniciem*,[1] vnto theyr owne deftruccyon, manye places of Paule, *et reliquas fcripturas*,[1]
and the other fcriptures. For whereas thys place of
Paul fhould be applyed to make men carefull and
diligent, they wraft and wryng it to make for them that
be careles and negligent. For Paul fayth that he doth
very lytle regarde what any man doth iudge of hym,
menyng therby that though all the world wolde commende hym, yet wold he not be vayne glorious, of hys
well doynge. They faye, they paffe lytle what any
man faythe by them, meanyng therby that though all
men fynde fautes wyth theim, yet wyll they neuer be
afhamed of theyr euyll doynge. Paule fayeth that no
man fhoulde iudge, meanynge that no man as concernynge fecretes of the mynde, fhould iudge other to be
yuell, and theim felfes to be iuft: and fo take occafion
to fpeake fhamefully of other, and to glory in theim
felues: they faye that no man fhoulde iudge, meanynge
that neyther preacher nor friende fhoulde fo rebuke
theyr manifeft euyll dedes, as myght geue theym occafion to be afhamed of theym felues, and leue iudgynge
of other. Lette vs not wreft the places of Paule and
of other fcripturs vnto a wrong purpofe. They wreft
the faying of Paule vnto a wrong meanynge, when as
the mercye of God, whyche paffeth all hys works is
denyed of theym vnto anye penytente fynner, by theyr
allegynge of the tenth of Paul vnto the Ebrues. Then
is that place not well applied but wrong wrefted. For
when it is fayde that yf we fynne wylfullye after that
we haue receiued the knoweledge of the trueth, there

[1] II. Peter *iii*. 16.

remayneth no more facrifice for fynne, but a fearefull lookynge for iudgemente and violente fyer, it is a meante that there is remaynynge and leafte in the fcriptures no mencyon of facrifyce for the forgeueneffe of fynnes, but terrible threatnynges of vengeaunce to punyfhe fynners, too bee preached vnto wylfull fynners.

Howbeit there is no condemnacion but alwayes mercye to be preached vnto **theym that** grafted **in** Chrift Iefu, be penitent fynners, how fore and ofte foeuer they fall. For his mercy is aboue all hys workes. Therefore whenfoeuer he fuffereth **the** Deuyll to tempte menne to do fynne, or too plage them for fynne, or whenfoeuer by his worde **wrytten** or preached he doth aggrauate fynne, **all is** done **to** dryue menne vnto mercye. The **deuyll** hathe caufed here in Englande muche fynne and abhominacion, greuous plages, and fore miferies, God hath fent wonderous plenty of hys confortable word. And nowe brethren all this is euen the worke of god: for it is God that worketh al thynges in all men. *Deus eft qui operatur omnia in omnibus.*[1] And yet take good hede to the true interpretacion of thys place leaft that ye make God to be the author of fyn, *Qui non nouit peccatum, nec eft inuentus dolus in ore eius,*[2] whyche knoweth no fynne by experience of doyng it, nor hathe no gyle founde in hys mouthe. But euen as it was God that dyd both geue and take awaye Iobs goodes: So is it God that doth al thyngs, both good and euyll. And as he dyd make Iob ryche, by geuinge him goodes, and poore bi fuffering [and vfyng] the deuill to deftroy thofe goodes: fo doethe he good deedes of hys owne goodnes, and euyll dedes in fufferynge the deuyll to do theym. **Yea** it is euen God that hathe concluded al men under fynne, that hath fuffered the deuyl to tempt al men* to do fynne, yea and *fcriptura conciufit omnia fub peccato,*[3] ye fcriptur of God hath concluded al men vnder fyn, or as Paule fpeaketh in an other place more pla[i]nli αιτοάμεθα. We haue concluded or proued, allegynge good reafon, that both the grekes and the Iewes be vnder fynne. So nowe

[1] 1 Cor. xii. 6   [2] 1 Peter ii. 22.   [3] Gal. iii. 22.

all ye by G O D be concluded vnderneth finne, that is by goddes fuffraunce the deuil hath caufed you to commit finne. By Gods ordinaunce the fcriptures and the preachers of God, do open and declare that ye be all fynners. And this is all done, *ut omnium miferearetur*,[1] that he myght haue mercye vpon **all,** that all mighte receyue the pardon of his mercye without ye which none can be faued, none can **efcape** vengeaunce. For *non eft in aliquo alio falus,* there **is** no health in anye other, *nec aliud nomen datum fub Cælo, in quo oporteat nos faluos fieri,*[2] nor none other name geuen vnder heauen, in the which we fhuld be faued. So yat he whyche wyl haue anye healthe mufte come vnto Chrift, fhewyng him felfe wounded with fin, to ftand in nede of Phificion. He yat wil be faued muft fhew him felfe **a** penytente fynner vnto Chrifte which came not to cal the righteous but fynners to amendmente. But he yat regardeth the flattery of the worlde or the parcialitie of his owne confcience, and therby taketh occafion to glory in his own doynges, he fhal finde no mercy, he can receiue no pardon or forgeuenes fent from god to be deliuered only vnto thofe yat fele and acknowlege them felues to be fickely and vnrighteous finners. Thei therfore that fele and acknowledge ye greateft fins wickednes* and abhominacions in theim felues being **fory** therfore, and entend amendment, be moft worthi **and** fure to receiue ye great pardon of gods mercy, whyche certenly wil deliuer them out of all daunger, kepe them in fafti and bryng them to profperity. Heare therfore and I wil now read my commiffion by ye whiche ye fhall wel perceyue **yat I** fpeake nothyng vpon my own **head,** but euery **thyng** according to the commaundem**ent of** the Lorde your god, whyche hath fent me vnto you hys people. The example of this proclamacion. Ef. lviii. *Clama.*[3] Make proclamation openly, yat al men maye heare: *ne ceffes.*[3] Ceas not for feare of them that may kyll the body, and can not **hurt** the foule, *quafi tuba exalta uocem tuam,*[3] Lifte vp thy voyce as a trumpet, geuinge men knowledge of the

[1] Rom. *xi.* 32.   [2] Act. *iv*   [3] Isa. *lviii.* 1.

commyng of the ennemyes in the tyme of war. So geue them knowlege of the fwerd of vengeance, which fhal folow immediatli after this warning *Et annuncia populo meo fcelera eorum.*[1] And fhew them their fau[l]tes yat in bering of my name, and profeffinge my religion wil be my people. *Et domui Iacob peccata fua,*[1] and vnto the houfe of Iacob their **own** fins: vnto all fortes of men euen thofe fyns which they them felues do vfe. Vnto the clergy, the finnes of ye clergy, vnto the laitye, the fynnes of the layte: and vnto euery degre, ye finnes yat be of that degre vfed. **Shew** ye clergi that thei fede them felues fat with many liuings, and let my flocke be fcatered and vnfed, becaufe ther is few preching paftors yat can and wil fede them.

Shew the clergy that they can neyther teach, nor requyre the king and laitye to prouide new liuings for prechers, vntill they do reftore forth of their own hands thofe which be prouided alredy: fhew fuch of the cleargy as be fatlings puft vp with pluralities, that they neyther haue fed, do fede, or can fede my flocke, yet haue fpoyled, do fpoyle and wyl fpoyle my lambes, ye kynges fubiectes, and theyr own brethren, fo long as thei vfe their pluralities. Shew the laity yat thei haue robbed me theyr lord and god of double honour due vnto my mynifters: for they haue taken awaye the fodder that was prepared for the laborynge oxe, and bene difobedyent vnto my law, pronounced by theim that fate in Moyfes cheire.

Shewe the nobilitie that they haue oppreffed the comminaltye, Kepyng theim vnder in feare and ignorance, by power and aucthoritye, which myght and fhould haue bene louyngly learned their obedience and duty to both God and the kyng by preachyng of the gofpel. Shew the nobility yat they haue extorted and famifhed the commynalty by the heigthening of fynes and rentes of fermes, and decaying of hofpitality and good houfe kepyng. Shew the comminaltye yat they be both traytoures and rebelles, murmuryng and

[1] Isa. *lviii.* 1.

grudgyng agaynſt myne ordinaunces: tel the **comminalty** yat the oxe draweth, the horſe beareth, ye tre bryngeth forth frutes and the earthe corne and **graſſe** to the profyte and comforte of man, as I haue ordained them: but they of the comminaltye in England bye and ſel, make bargaynes, and **do al** thynges to the grefe and hynderaunce of manne, contrary to my commaundemente. Tell the commynaltye that they take **one** anothers ferme ouer their heades, **they** thruſte one an other oute of their houſes, they take **leaſes vnto** theim ſelues, and lette theym dearer vnto other: **they** bye cornes and wares to make other paye more dere for it: they hurte and trouble, eate vp and deuoure one another. Tell all Englande hye and low, riche and poore that **they** euerye one prowlynge for them ſelues, be ſeruaunts vnto Mammon, ennemies vnto god, **diſturbers** of common wealth, and deſtroyers of them **ſelues**. And for all this lette theim knowe that **I haue** no pleaſure in ye death of a ſinner. *Sed magis vt conuertatur et uiuat*,[1] but rather I geue him reſpit and ſend him warning yat he may turne **and** liue, comfortably here vpon earth, and ioifully **in heauen for** euer. Therefore **if** any in Englande do tourne and amende, he ſhall ſaue hym ſelfe. But they which wyll **not** repent and amend ſhal not be ſaued by theyr fathers or frendes, which by repentaunce be as ſure them **ſelues to** be accepted vnto me as was **Noe** Danyel and Iob: but and if all or the mooſt parte of them **in** England, turne and amend them, ſay vnto England: *delectaberis ſuper domino.*[2] From henceforth you ſhalt haue delite and pleſure in ye lord, *et fuſtollam te ſuper aititudines* **terræ,**[2] and I wil lift the higher in honour welth and **power, then any** other realme in or vpon the earth, *et cibabo te hereditate Iacobi patris tui,*[2] **and** ſo wyll I ſede the with **the** inheritaunce of Iacob thy father. I will reſtore vnto ye **whatſoeuer** land or holds in Scotland or in Fraunce dyd at any tyme belonge **vnto** Iacob thy father, vnto the kings of this realme, *os enim domini locutum eſt*,[2] for the Lordes owne mouth

[1] Ezek. xxxiii. 11.   [2] Isa. lviii. 14.

hath fpoken it, which is a better affurance vnto this
commiffion, then though it were figned and feled wyth
ten thoufande mens handes.

Now al you yat entend to be faued by the mercies
of god in our fauioure Iefu Chrift, come when ye be
called from gredy couetoufnes wherwyth ye haue bene
blinded to wreake Gods wrath: receyue mercy and
grace which be now frely offred to make you from
henceforth holy minifters of Chrift, and faithfull difpofers of ye manifolde gyftes of Gods grace and goodnes: and now for fere of forgetfull negligence, when ye
depart hence, replenifh your minds with ye comfortable remembrance of your own greuous myferies, and
of gods great mercies, in fecrete meditation of the
lords praier, here tarying together in quyetnes a littell
for to receyue the Lordes bleffyng.

The god of peace that brought againe from death
our Lord Iefus the greate fhepeheard of the fhepe,
thorow the bloud of the euerlaftyng teftament, make
you perfit in all good workes, to do hys wyll, workyng
in you that which is plefant in his
fyght, through Iefus Chrift.
Amen.

God faue the Kynge.[1]

---

[1] In second edition, 1572.   **God saue the Queene.**

Imprynted at London by Ihon Day dwellyng ouer Alderſgate.

Cum priuilegio ad imprimendum folum Per *ſeptennium.*

In the reprint of 1572, the colophon is—

These bookes are to be solde at the litle North doore ot Paules, at the signe of the blacke Boye.

Muir & Paterson, Printers, Edinburgh.

English Reprints.

WILLIAM WEBBE, Graduate.

A Discourse

of

English Poetrie.

1586.

CAREFULLY EDITED BY

EDWARD ARBER

Associate, King's College, London, F.R.G.S., &c.

LONDON:
QUEEN SQUARE, BLOOMSBURY, W.C.

Ent. Stat. Hall.] 1 December, 1870. [*All Rights reserved.*

CONTENTS.

NOTES of William Webbe,	3
CONTEMPORARY ENGLISH AUTHORS referred to,	5
INTRODUCTION,	7
BIBLIOGRAPHY,	10

A DISCOURSE OF ENGLISH POETRIE, — 11

1. The Epistle to Edward Sulyard, Esquire, — 13
2. A Preface to the noble Poets of England, — 17
3.   A DISCOURSE OF ENGLISH POETRIE, — 21
   - (a) What Poetry is? — 21
   - (b) The beginning of Poetry, and of what estimation it hath always been, — 21
   - (c) The use of Poetry, and wherein it rightly consisted, — 25
   - (d) The Author's judgment of English Poets, — 30
   - (e) 𝕿𝖍𝖊 𝕸𝖆𝖙𝖙𝖊𝖗 𝖔𝖋 𝕰𝖓𝖌𝖑𝖎𝖘𝖍 𝕻𝖔𝖊𝖙𝖗𝖎𝖊, — 38-56
     Ex. Comparison of Thomas Phaer's translation of the *Æneid* with the original text of Virgil.
   - (f) 𝕿𝖍𝖊 𝕸𝖆𝖓𝖓𝖊𝖗 𝖔𝖗 𝕱𝖔𝖗𝖒 𝖔𝖋 𝕰𝖓𝖌𝖑𝖎𝖘𝖍 𝕻𝖔𝖊𝖙𝖗𝖎𝖊, — 56-84
     - A. RHYMED VERSE.
       There be three special notes necessary to be observed in the framing of our accustomed English Rhyme:—
       - (1) *The metre or verse must be proportionate* — 57
         Ex. Criticism of the different sorts of Verse in Spencer's *Shepherds Calender.*
       - (2) *The natural Accent of the words must not be wrested* — 62
       - (3) *The Rhyme or like ending of verses* — 63
     - B. The Reformed kind of ENGLISH VERSE [*i.e.*, in CLASSICAL FEET], — 67-84
       Ex. The Author's translation of the first two *Eglogues* of Virgil into English Hexameters, — 73-79
       Ex. His translation of Hobbinoll's Song in the *Shepherds Calender* into English Sapphics, — 81-84
   - (g) The Canons or general Cautions of Poetry, prescribed by Horace: collected by George Fabricius [*b.* 23 April 1516 at Chemnitz,—*d.* 13 July 1571] — 85-95
4. EPILOGUE, — 96

NOTES
of
WILLIAM WEBBE.

* *Probable or approximate dates.*

Very little is known of the Author of this work. The suggestion that he was the William Webbe, M.A., one of the joint Authors of a topographical book *The Vale Royal*, 1648, fol., is quite anachronistic.

Messrs. Cooper, in *Athenæ Cantabrigiensis, ii.* **12.** *Ed.* 1861, state that our Author "was a graduate of this University, but we have no means of determining his college. One of this name, who was of St. John's College, was B.A. 1572-3 [the same year as Spenser], as was another who was of Catharine Hall in 1581-2. His place of residence is unknown, although it may perhaps be inferred that it was in or near the county of Suffolk. We have no information as to his position in life, or the time or place of his death. He was evidently a man of superior intellect and no mean attainments." [Our Author apparently witnessed *Tancred and Gismund* in 1568, and being evidently acquainted with Gabriel Harvey and Spenser (who left Cambridge in 1578), must be the earlier graduate of the above two Webbes.]

1568. *Tancred and Gismund*, written by five members of the Inner Temple, the first letters of whose names are attached to the several acts, viz., Rod. Staff; Hen. No[well?]; G. All; Ch. Hat[ton?]; and R. W[ilmot]: is 'curiously acted in view of her Maiesty, by whom it was then princely accepted.'

Webbe appears to have been present at the representation: see **1591.** Mr. J. P. Collier in his edition of 'Dodsley's *Old Plays,*' i. 153, prints from a MS. what is apparently a portion of this Tragedy as it was then acted, written in alternate rhymes. He also states in his *Hist. of Dram. Poet.* that it 'is the earliest English play extant, the plot of which is known to be derived from an Italian novel." *iii.* **13.** *Ed.* **1831.**

***1572-3.** Our Author takes his B.A. at Cambridge.

1582. Nov. 28. Gabriel Poyntz presented Robert Wilmott, clerk to the Rectory of North Okendon, Essex: 18 miles from London. *Newcourt Repertorium, ii.* 447. *Ed.* 1710.

Flemyngs is a large manor house in Essex in the parish of Runwell, in the hundred of Chelmsford; from which town it is ten miles distant, and about twenty-nine miles from London. 'This house commands extensive views of some parts of the county and of Kent, including more than thirty parish churches.'

Edward Sulyard succeeded, on the death of his father Eustace in 1546, to Flemyngs and other possessions. He had two sons, Edward and Thomas, and a daughter named Elizabeth. He was knighted on 23 July 1603 at Whitehall by James I, before his coronation: and died in June 1610. Of his two sons, Edward died without issue; Thomas, b. 1573, was knighted, and d. March 1634: leaving a son Edward, who d. 7 Nov. 1692 without issue, 'the last of the house and family.' See *W. Berry, County Gen. Essex*, 64. T. Wright, *Hist. of Essex, i.* 142, 143. *Ed.* 1831. J. P[hilipot] *K'nts. Batch.* made by *James I.* 1660.

***1583 or 4.** Webbe appears to have been at this time private tutor to Mr. Sulyard's two sons, for he presented his MS. translation (now lost) of the *Georgics* to Mr. Sulyard: see *pp.* 55 and 16.

1585. Dec. 2. The Dean and Chapter of St. Paul's appoint Robert Wilmott, M.A., to the Vicarage of Horndon on the Hill, twenty-four miles from London, and a few miles from Flemyngs, where his friend Webbe was a private tutor. *Newcourt, idem. ii.* **343.**

1586. Of 'the pregnant ympes of right excellent hope,' Thomas Sulyard was about thirteen years old, and his brother Edward was older than him.

W. Webbe **writes** the present **work** in the summer evenings.

SEPT. 4. It is thus registered for publication.
"Robt. Walley
John Charlewood, **Rd. of them, for printinge A** Discourse of englishe poetrye . . . . vj^d."
J. P Collier, Extr. of Stat. Co.'s Regrs. ii., 215. *Ed* 1849.

1587. FEB. 5. Margaret, the mother of Mr. Sulyard died. She is buried at Runwell.

1588. Warton quotes "a small black-lettered **tract** entitled *The Touch-stone of Wittes*, chiefly compiled, **with** some slender additions, from William Webbe's *Discourse of English Poetrie*, written by Edward Hake, and **printed at** London by Edmund Bollifant." *p.* 804. *Ed.* 1870.

Our Author—his pupils growing to manhood—then appears to have **gone**, possibly also in the same capacity of private tutor into the family of **Henry** Grey, Esquire [created Baron Grey of Groby, 21 July 1603: *d.* **1614**] at Pirgo, in the parish **of** Havering atte Bower, Essex; fifteen miles from London. Dugdale states that the first husband of one of the daughters **of** this Henry Grey, Esquire, was a *William Sulyard*, Esquire. *Baron. i.* 722. *Ed.* 1675. From this old Palace of the Queenes of England Webbe wrote the following letter to Wilmott, which is reprinted in the revised edition of *Tancred and Gismund* published **in 1592: of** which there **are** copies in the Bodleian, and **at** Bridgewater **House, and an** imperfect **one in** the British Museum (C. 34, e. 44).

1591. AUG. 8. *To his frend R. W.* Master *R. VV.* looke not now for the tearmes of **an intreator, I wil** beg no longer, and for **your** promises, I wil refuse **them as bad** paiment: neither **can I be** satisfied with any thing, **but** a peremptorie performance **of an** old intention of yours, the publishing I meane of **those wast papers (as it** pleaseth you to cal them, but as **I** esteem **them, a most** exquisite inuention) of *Gismunds* Tragedie. Thinke **not to** shift **me** off with longer delayes, nor alledge **more excuses** to get further respite, least I arrest you with my *Actum est,* and commence such a Sute of vnkindenesse against you, **as** when the case **shall** be scand before the Iudges of courtesie, **the** court will crie out of your immoderat modestie. And thus much I tel you before, you shal not be able to wage against me in **the** charges growing vpon this action, especially, if the **worshipful** company of the Inner temple gentlemen patronize **my** cause, **as** vndoubtedly they wil, yea, and rather plead partially for me then let my cause miscary, because themselues are parties. The tragedie was **by** them most pithely framed, and no lesse curiously acted in **view** of her Maiesty, by whom it was then as princely accepted, as of the whole honorable audience notably applauded: **yea,** and of al men generally desired, as a work, either **in** statelines of shew, depth of conceit, or true ornaments **of** poeticall arte, inferior **to** none **of the** best in that kinde: **no,** were the Roman *Seneca* **the** censurer. The braue youths that then (to their high praises) **so** feelingly performed the **same in** action, did shortly after lay vp **the** booke vnregarded, or perhaps let **it** run abroade **(as** many parentes **doe** their children once past dandling) not respecting so **much** what hard fortune might befall it being out of their fingers, as how their heroical wits might againe be quickly conceiued with new inuentions of like worthines, wherof they haue been euer since wonderfull fertill. But this orphan of theirs (for he wandreth as it were fatherlesse,) hath notwithstanding, by the rare and bewtiful perfections appearing in him, hetherto neuer wanted great fauourers, and louing preseruers. Among whom I cannot sufficiently commend your more then charitable zeale, and scholerly compassion towards him, that haue not only rescued and defended him from the deuouring iawes of obliuion, but vouchsafed also to apparrel him in a new sute at your **own** charges, **wherein** he may again more boldly come **abroad**, and by your permission returne **to** his olde parents, **clothed** perhaps not in richer or more costly furniture than **it** went from them, but **in** handsomnes **and** fashion more answer**able** to these times, **wherein fashions are so often altered. Let one** word suffice for **your** encouragement **herein :** namely, your commendable **pains in** disrobing him **of** his antike curiositie, and adorning **him with** the approoued **guise of** our stateliest Englishe **termes** (not diminishing, but augmenting his artificiall colours **of** absolute poesie, deriued from his first parents) cannot but **bee** grateful to most mens appetites, who vpon **our** experience we know highly to esteem such lofty measures of sententiously composed Tragedies.

How much you shal make me, and the rest of your priuate frends beholding **vnto** you, I list not to discourse: and therefore grounding vpon these alledged reasons, that the suppressing of this Tragedie, so worthy for ye presse, were no other thing then wilfully to defraud your selfe of an vniuersall thank, your frends of their expectations, and sweete G. of a famous eternitie. I will cease to doubt of any other pretence to cloake your bashfulnesse, hoping to read it in print (which lately lay neglected amongst your **papers) at our** next appointed meeting.

I bid you heartely farewell. From Pyrgo in Essex, August the eight, 1591. *Tuus fide et facultate.* GUIL. WEBBE.

It may also be noted that Wilmott dedicated this revised tragedy to two Essex ladies: one of whom was Lady Anne Grey, **the** daughter of Lord Windsor, and the wife of the above-mentioned Henry Grey, Esquire of Pirgo.

That the above R. Wilmott, Clergyman, is the same **as** the Reviser of the play appears from the following passage in his Preface.

"Hereupon I have indured some conflicts between **reason and** judgement, whether it were convenient for the commonwealth, and **the** *indecorum* of my calling (as some think it) that the memory of *Tancred's* Tragedy should be again by my means revised, which the oftner I read over, and the more I considered thereon, the sooner I **was** won to consent thereunto; calling to mind that neither the thrice reverend and learned father, M. Beza, was ashamed in his younger **years** to send abroad, in his own name, his Tragedy of *Abraham*, nor that **rare Scot** (the scholar of our age) *Buchanan*, his most patheticall *Ieptha*." '**Dodsley's** *Old Plays*,' ii. 165. Ed. by J. P. Collier, 1825.

If the identity may be **considered as established,** Wilmott the Poet lived on till **1619**: when he was **succeeded on his death** by W Jackson, in the Rectory **of** North Okendon. *Newcourt, idem. ii.* 447.

No later information concerning **W. Webbe than** the above **letter, has yet** been recovered.

CONTEMPORARY ENGLISH AUTHORS
REFERRED TO IN THE FOLLOWING *Difcourfe.*

G. B.	? *The Shippe of Safeguarde*, 1569	35
F. C.	?	35
T. CHURCHYARD.	*Churchyard's 'Chippes*,' 1575; *Churchyard's ' Chance,'* 1580 ; *Churchyard's ' Charge,'* 1580	33
M. D.	[? Mafter Dyer, *i.e.*, Sir Edward Dyer]	33
? DARRELL	?	35

CONTEMPORARY ENGLISH AUTHORS.

R. EDWARDES. *Par. of Dainty Devises*, 1576; *Comedies* . 33
Sir T. ELYOT. *The Governor*, 1538 . . . 42, 43
G. GASCOIGNE. *Posies*, 1572; *The Steele Glas*, &c., 1576 . 33
B. GOOGE. *Eglogs, Epytaphes, and Sonettes*, 1563; translation of *Palingenius* 34
Sir J. GRANGE. *The Golden Aphroditis*, 1577 . . 35
G. HARVEY. 35
HEIWOOD [either JOHN HEYWOOD or JASPER HEYWOOD] 33
W. HUNNIS. *Paradise of Dainty Devises*, 1576, 1578 . 33
? HYLL ? 33
E. K. [*i.e.* EDWARD KIRKE] . . . 33, 53
F. K. [? Fr. Kindlemarsh] *Par. of Dainty Devises*, 1576, 1578 35
J. LYLY. *Euphues*, 1579-80; *Plays* . . . 46
A. MUNDAY. *The Mirrour of Mutabilitie*, 1579; *The Paine of Pleasure*, 1580 35
T. NORTON. Joint Author of *Ferrex and Porrex*, 1561 . 33
C. OCKLANDE. *Anglorum Prælia*, 1580, 1582 . 30
[? DR. E.] SAND[YS]. *Par. of Dainty Devises*, 1576, &c. . 33
E. SPENSER. *Shepheards Calender*, 1579, 1581, 1586 35, 52, 81
HENRY, Earl of SURREY. *Sonnets, &c.*, in *Tottel's Misc.* 1557 33
T. TUSSER. *Five hundred points of Good Husbandrie*, 1557-80 33
THOMAS, Lord VAUX. *Sonnetes, &c.*, *in Tottel's Misc.* 1557; and *Par. of Dainty Devises*, 1576 . . 33
E. VERE, Earl of OXFORD. Unpublished *Sonnets* . 33
G. WHETSTONE. *The Rocke of Regard*, 1576 . . 35
R. WILMOTT. *Tancred and Gismund*, 1568 . . 35
S. Y. [? M. YLOOP, *i.e.* M. POOLY in *Par. of Dainty Devises*] 33

THE TRANSLATORS.

SENECA.

J. HEYWOOD. *Troas*, 1559; *Thyestes*, 1560; *Hercules Furens*, 1561 34
A. NEVILL. *Œdipus*, 1563 34
J. STUDLEY. *Medea*, 1566; *Agamemnon*, 1566 . . 34

OVID.

G. TURBERVILLE. *Heroical Epistles*, 1567 . . 34
A. GOLDING. *Metamorphoses*, 1565 . . 34, 51
T. CHURCHYARD. *Tristia*, 1578 . . . 34
T. DRANT. *Satires*, 1566; *Art of Poetrie*, 1567 . . 34

VIRGIL.

HENRY, Earl of SURREY. *Two Books of the 'Æneid,'* 1557 33
T. PHAER, M.D. 9⅔rd Books of the 'Æneid,' 1558-1562 33, 46-51
T. TWYNE. *The remaining 2⅔rd Books*, 1573 . 34
A. FLEMING. *Bucolicks*, 1575, in rhyme. His *Georgics* referred to at *p.* 55 appeared in 1589 . . 34, 55

A Discourse of English Poetrie

INTRODUCTION.

Apart from the excessive rarity of this work, two copies of it only being known; it deserves permanent republication as a good example of the best form of Essay Writing of its time; and as one of the series of Poetical Criticisms before the advent of Shakespeare as a writer, the study of which is so essential to a right understanding of our best Verse.

Although Poetry is the most ethereal part of Thought and Expression; though Poets must be born and cannot be made: yet is there an art of Poesy; set forth long ago by Horace but varying with differing languages and countries, and even with different ages in the life of the same country. In our tongue—Milton only excepted—there is nothing approaching, either in the average merit of the Journeymen or the superlative excellence of the few Master-Craftsmen, the Poesy of the Elizabethan age. Hence the value of these early Poetical Criticisms. Their discussion of principles is most helpful to all readers in the discernment of the subtle beauties of the numberless poems of that era: while for those who can, and who will; they will be found singularly suggestive in the training of their own Power of Song, for the instruction and delight of this and future generations.

A Cambridge graduate; the private tutor, for some two or three years past, to Edward and Thomas Sulyard, the sons of Edward Sulyard Esquire, of Flemyngs, situated in Essex, some thirty miles distant from London: our Author gave his leisure hours to the study of Latin and English poetry.

He had acquainted himself with our older Poets, and with the contemporary verse: and, thinking for himself, he endeavoured to see exactly what English poetry actually was, and what it might and should become. Doubtless in his walks in the large park surrounding the Old Manor House this subject often occupied his thoughts, and he sat down to commit his opinions to the press, in the presence and quietude of a large and fair landscape stretching far away southward beyond the Thames into Kent, diversified with the spires of many churches and the masts of many passing ships: and all illuminated with the glow and glory of the summer evenings of 1586.

Webbe was as much affected with the 'immoderate modesty' with which, five years later, he charged Wilmot, as any of the writers of that age. He dreads, at *p.* 55, the unauthorized publication of his version of the *Georgics*, and he must have been moved deeply by 'the rude multitude of rusticall Rymers, who will be called Poets' before he ventured to advocate in print 'the reformation of our English Verse,' *i.e.*, the abandonment of Rhyme for Metre.

He calls his work 'a sleight somewhat compiled for recreation in the intermyssions of my daylie businesse,' yet it is the most extensive piece of Poetical Criticism that had hitherto appeared. He had read, for he quotes at *p.* 64, G. Gascoigne's *Certayne Notes, &c.,* 1575: also *Three proper and wittie, familiar Letters,* by Immerito [Edmund Spenser] and G[abriel] H[arvey] 1580, to which he alludes at *p.* 36. He may have heard of Sir P. Sidney's *Apologie for Poetrie* [1582], then circulating in manuscript, or of the young Scotch King's *Reulis and Cautelis of Scottish Poesie*, then being publiſhed at Edinburgh. Yet none of theſe is ſo lengthy, nor deals with the ſame extent of ſubject, nor is illuſtrated by original examples, as is this *Diſcourſe*.

Though the book is an honeſt one, faithfully repreſenting the author's robuſt mind ; it was written under the ſtrong influence of three works ; Aſcham's *Scholemaſter*, 1570 ; Edwardes' *Paradiſe of Dainty Devices*, 1576; and Spenſer's *Shepherdes Calender*, anonymouſly publiſhed, without the author's conſent, by E. K. [*i.e.*, Edward Kirke, as is generally believed] in 1579. He follows Aſcham as to the origin of Rhyme; and alſo in his error as to Simmias Rhodias at *p.* 57, &c. He quotes W. Hunnis' poem at *p.* 66, from the collection of Edwardes. It is alſo Webbe's great merit as a lover and judge of poetry, that he inſtinctively fixes upon the *Shepherdes Calender* (never openly acknowledged by Spenſer in his lifetime) as the revelation of a great poet, as great an Engliſh Poet indeed, as had yet appeared. That Paſtoral Poem gave Webbe a higher reverence for Spenſer than his great Allegory breeds reſpect for him in many, now-a-days.

The facility of Rhyme, at a time when there were many wonderfully facile Rhymers, induced Aſcham, Webbe, and many others to ſeek after a more difficult form of Engliſh verſe. Claſſical feet Webbe himſelf experienced to be a 'troubleſome and unpleaſant peece of labour,' ſo he ſought after ſomething more adapted to the nature of the language, 'ſome perfect platforme or *Proſodia* of verſifying.' Blank verſe would have ſatiſfied him, but he did not recogniſe its merits in Surrey's tranſlation of the *Æneid*. He is, however, warm in his praiſe of Phaer's verſion of that work in hexameters : and gives us three pieces of reformed verſe of his own coinage ; two in hexameters, and one in ſapphics.

Finally, Webbe wrote 'theſe fewe leaues' 'to ſtirre

vppe fome **other** of meete abilitie, to beftowe **trauell in this matter.'** His wifh had been anticipated. Already a Mafter **Critic** was at work—we know **not for certainty** whether it was George Puttenham, or who elfe—who, beginning to write in 1585, publifhed in 1589 *The Arte of Englifh Poefie* : which is the largeft and ableft criticifm of Englifh Poefy that appeared in print, during the reign of Elizabeth.

BIBLIOGRAPHY.

Issues in the Author's lifetime.

I.—*As a separate publication.*

1. 1586. London.   1 vol. 4to.   See title on oppofite page.

Of the two copies known, the one here reprinted is among the Malone books in the Bodleian. The other paffed from hand to hand at the following fales : always increafing in price.

1773. APR. 8. Mr. West's sale, No. 1856, 10s. 6d., to Mr. Pearson.
1778. APR. 22. Mr. Pearson's sale, No. 1888, £3, 5s., to Mr. Stevens.
1800. MAY 19. Mr Stevens' sale, No. 1128, £8, 8s., to the Duke of Roxburghe.
1812. JUNE 2. The Roxburghe sale, No. 3168, £64, to the Marquis of Blandford.

Issues since the Author's death.

I.—*As a separate publication.*

3. 1870. DEC. 1. London. *Englifh Reprints* : fee title at 1 vol. 8vo.   *p.* 1.

II.—*With other works.*

2. 1815. London.   *Ancient Critical Effays.* Ed. by J. Haflewood.   *A Difcourfe of Englifh Poetrie* occupies Vol. ii., *pp.* 13-95.
2 vols. 4to.

A Discourse of English Poetrie.

Together, with the Authors iudgment, touching the reformation of our English Verse.

By VVilliam VVebbe Graduate.

Imprinted at London, by Iohn Charlewood for Robert VValley
1 5 8 6.

To the right vvorſhip=
full, learned, and moſt gentle Gentle-
man, *my verie good Master, Ma.*
Edward Suliard, Eſquire. VV. VV.
wyſheth his harts deſire.
(∴)

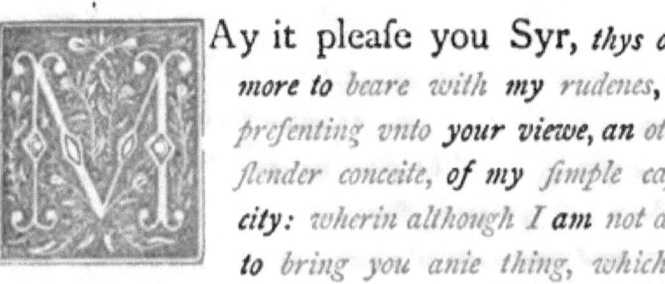Ay it pleaſe you Syr, *thys once more to beare with* my *rudenes*, in *preſenting vnto* your viewe, an *other ſlender conceite,* of my *ſimple capa-* city: *wherin although I* am *not able to bring you anie thing, which is* meete to detaine you from *your more ſerious matters:* yet vppon my *knowledge of your former* courteſy *and your fauourable countenaunce towardes all enterpriſes of Learning, I dare make bold to* craue *your accuſtomed patience, in turning ouer ſome of theſe fewe leaues, which I ſhall* account a greater recompence, then *the wryting thereof may deſerue.*

The firme hope of your wonted gentlenes, not any good lyking of myne owne labour, made me thus presumptuously to craue your worships patronage for my poore booke. A pretty aunswere is reported by some to be made by Appelles *to* King Alexander, *who (in disport) taking vp one of his pensilles to drawe a line, and asking the Paynters iudgment of his draught,* It is doone *(quoth Apelles)* like a King: *meaning indeede it was drawen as he pleased, but was nothing lesse then good workmanshippe. My selfe in like sort, taking vppon me, to make a draught of* English Poetry, *and requesting your worshyps censure of the same, you wyll perhaps gyue* me *thys verdict,* It was doone like a Scholler, *meaning,* as I could, *but indeede more like* to a learner, then one through grounded in Poeticall workmanship.

Alexander *in drawing his lyne, leaned sometime too hard, otherwhyle too soft, as neuer hauing beene apprentice to the Arte: I in drawing this Poeticall discourse, make it some where to straight (leauing out the cheefe colloures and ornaments of Poetry) in an other place to wyde (stuffing in peeces little pertinent to true Poetry) as one neuer acquainted wyth the learned Muses.* What then? *as he being a king, myght meddle in* what Scyence him *listed, though therein* hee had no skyll: *so I beeing a learner, wyll trye my cunning in some parts of Learning, though neuer so simple.*

Nowe, as for my saucie pressing vppon your expected *fauor* in crauing your iudgment, I beseech you let me make thys excuse: that whereas true Gentilitie did neuer withdrawe her louing affection from Lady Learning, so *I* am perswaded, that your worshyppe cannot chuse, but continue your wonted fauourable benignitie towardes all the indeuourers to learning, of which corporation *I* doo indeede professe my selfe one sillie member.

For sith the wryters *of* all ages, haue sought as an vndoubted Bulwarke and stedfast sauegarde the patronage of Nobilitye, (a shielde as sure as can be to learning) **wherin** to shrowde and safelye place their seuerall inuentions: why should not *I* seeke some harbour for my poore trauell to reste and staye vppon, beeing of it selfe vnable to shyft the carping cauilles and byting scornes of lewde controllers?

And in trueth, where myght *I* rather choose a **sure** defence and readye refuge for the same, then where *I* see perfecte Gentilitye, and noblenesse of minde, to be faste lyncked with excellencie of learning and affable courtesye? Moreouer, adde thys **to** the ende of myne excuse: that *I* sende **it** into your sight, not **as** anie wyttie peece of worke that may delight you: but being a sleight somewhat compyled for recreation, in the intermyssions of my daylie businesse, (euen thys Summer Eueninges) as a token of that earnest and vnquenchable desyre *I* haue to shewe my selfe duetifull **and** welwylling towardes you. VVhereunto *I* am continually enflamed more **and** more, when *I* con**sider** eyther your fauourable freendshyppe vsed towardes my ſelfe, or your gentle countenaunce ſhewed to my ſimple trauelles. The one I haue tryed in that homely tranſlation I preſented vnto you: the other I finde true in your curteous putting to my truſt, **and** dooing me ſo great honeſty and credite, with the charge **of** theſe toward young Gentlemen your ſonnes.

To which pregnant **ympes** of right excellent hope, I would I were able, or you myght haue occaſion to **make** triall of my louing minde: who ſhoulde well perceyue my ſelfe to remayne vnto them a faythfull and truſty Achates, euen ſo farre as my wealth my woe, my power or perrill, my penne or witte, my health or lyfe may ſerue to **ferche** myne ability.

Huge heapes of wordes I myght pyle together to trouble **you** withall: eyther of **my ſelfe or of my** dooinges, (as ſome doo) or of your worſhyppes commendable vertues (as the moſte doo) But I purpoſely chuſe rather to let paſſe the ſpreading of that worthy fame which you haue euer deſerued, then to runne in ſuſpicion of fawning flattery which I euer abhorred.

Therefore once againe crauing your gentle **pardon,** and patience in your ouerlooking thys rude Epiſtle: and wyſhing more happineſſe then my penne can expreſſe to you and your whole retinewe, **I rest.**

(∴)

Your worſhippes faithfull
                    Seruant. VV. VV.

A Preface to the noble *Poets of Englande.*

Mong the innumerable fortes of Englyſhe Bookes, and infinite fardles of printed pamphlets, wherewith thys Countrey is peſtered, all ſhoppes ſtuffed, and euery ſtudy furniſhed: the greateſt part I thinke in any one kinde, are ſuch as are either meere Poeticall, or which tende in ſome reſpecte (as either in matter or forme) to Poetry. Of ſuch Bookes therfore, ſith I haue beene one, that haue had a deſire to reade not the feweſt, and becauſe it is an argument, which men of great learning haue no leyſure to handle, or at leaſt hauing to doo with more ſerious matters doo leaſt regarde: If I write ſomething, concerning what I thinke of our Engliſh Poets, or aduenture to ſette downe my ſimple iudgement of Engliſh Poetrie, I truſt the learned Poets will giue me leaue, and vouchſafe my Booke paſſage, as beeing for the rudeneſſe thereof no preiudice to their noble ſtudies, but euen (as my intent is) an *inſtar cotis* to ſtirre vppe ſome other of meete abilitie, to beſtowe trauell in this matter: whereby I thinke wee may not onelie get the meanes which wee yet want, to diſcerne betweene good writers and badde, but perhappes alſo challenge from the rude multitude of ruſticall Rymers, who will be called Poets, the right practiſe and orderly courſe of true Poetry.

It is to be wondred at of all, and is lamented of

manie, that where as all kinde of good learning, haue afpyred to royall dignitie and ſtatelie grace in our Engliſh tongue, being not onelie founded, defended, maintained, and enlarged, but alſo purged from faultes, weeded of errours, and polliſhed from barbarouſnes, by men of great authoritie and iudgement: onelie Poetrie hath founde feweſt frends to amende it, thoſe that can, reſeruing theyr ſkyll to themſelues, thoſe that cannot, running headlong vppon it, thinking to garniſh it with their deuiſes, but more corrupting it with fantaſticall errours. VVhat ſhoulde be the cauſe, that our Engliſh ſpeeche in ſome of the wyſeſt mens iudgements, hath neuer attained to anie ſufficient ripenes, nay not ſul auoided the reproch of barbarouſnes in Poetry? the rudenes of the Countrey, or baſeneſſe of wytts: or the courſe *Dialect* of the ſpeeche? experience vtterlie diſ-proueth it to be anie of theſe: what then? ſurelie the canckred enmitie of curious cuſtome: which as it neuer was great freend to any good learning, ſo in this hath it grounded in the moſt, ſuch a negligent perſwaſion of an impoſſibilitie in matching the beſt, that the fineſt witts and moſt diuine heades, haue contented them-ſelues with a baſe kinde of fingering: rather debaſing theyr faculties, in ſetting forth theyr ſkyll in the cour-ſeſt manner, then for breaking cuſtome, they would labour to adorne their Countrey and aduaunce their ſtyle with the higheſt and moſt learnedſt toppe of true Poetry. The rudenes or vnaptneſſe of our Countrey to be either none or no hinderaunce, if reformation were made accordinglie, the exquiſite ex-cellency in all kindes of good learning nowe flouriſh-ing among vs, inferiour to none other nation, may ſufficiently declare.

The Preface.

That there be as sharpe and quicke wittes in England as euer were among the peerelesse Grecians, or renowmed Romaines, it were a note of no witte at all in me to deny. And is our speeche so courfe, or our phrase so harshe, that Poetry cannot therein finde a vayne whereby it may appeare like it selfe? why should we think so basely of this? rather then of her sister, I meane Rhetoricall *Eloquution*, which as they were by byrth Twyns, by kinde the same, by originall of one descent: so no doubt, as Eloquence hath sounde such fauoures, in the English tongue, as she frequenteth not any more gladly: so would Poetrye if there were the like welcome and entertainment gyuen her by our English Poets, without question aspyre to wonderfull perfection, and appeare farre more gorgeous and delectable among vs. Thus much I am bolde to say in behalfe of Poetrie, not that I meane to call in question the reuerend and learned workes of Poetrie, written in our tongue by men of rare iudgement, and most excellent Poets: but euen as it were by way of supplication to the famous and learned Lawreat Masters of Englande, that they would but consult one halfe howre with their heauenly Muse, what credite they might winne to theyr natiue speeche, what enormities they might wipe out of English Poetry, what a fitte vaine they might frequent, wherein to shewe forth their worthie faculties: if English Poetrie were truely reformed, and some perfect platforme or *Prosodia* of versifying were by them ratifyed and sette downe: eyther in immitation of Greekes and Latines, or where it would skant abyde the touch of theyr Rules, the like obseruations selected and established by the naturall affectation of the speeche. Thus much I say, not to perswade you that are the fauourers of Englishe Poetry but to mooue it to you: beeing not the firste that haue thought vpon this matter, but one that by confent of others, haue taken vppon me to lay it once again in your wayes, if perhaps you may stumble vppon it, and chance to looke fo lowe from your diuine cogitations, when your Mufe mounteth to the starres, and ranfacketh the Spheres of heauen: whereby perhaps you may take compaffion of noble Poetry, pittifullie mangled and defaced, by rude fmatterers and barbarous immitatours of your worthy studies. If the motion bee worthy your regard it is enough to mooue it, if not, my wordes woulde fimply preuaile in perfwading you, and therefore I reft vppon thys onely requeft, that of your courtefies, you wyll graunt paffage, vnder your fauourable corrections, for this my fimple cenfure of Englifh Poetry, wherein if you pleafe to runne it ouer, you shall knowe breefely myne opinion of the moft part of your accuftomed Poets and particularly, in his place, the lyttle fomewhat which I haue fifted out of my weake brayne concerning thys reformed verfifying.

VV: VV:

A Discourse of Eng=
lishe Poetrie.

Ntending to write some discourse of Englissh Poetrie, I thinke it not amysse if I speake something generally of Poetrie, as, what it is, whence it had the beginning, and of what estimation it hath alwayes beene and ought to be among al sorts of people. Poetrie called in Greeke ποετρια, beeing deriued from the Verbe ποίεω, which signifieth in Latine *facere*, in Englissh, to make, may properly be defined, the arte of making: which word as it hath alwaies beene especially vsed of the best of our Englissh Poets, to expresse ye very faculty of speaking or wryting Poetically, so doth it in deede containe most fitly the whole grace and property of the same, ye more fullye and effectually then any other Englissh Verbe. That Poetry is an Arte, (or rather a more excellent thing then can be contayned wythin the compasse of Arte) though I neede not stande long to prooue, both the witnes of *Horace*, who wrote *de arte Poetica*, and of *Terence*, who calleth it *Artem Musicam*, and the very naturall property thereof may sufficiently declare: The beginning of it as appeareth by *Plato*, was of a vertuous and most deuout purpose,

who witnesseth, that by occasion of meeting of a great
company of young men, to solemnize ye feasts which
were called *Panegeryca*, and were wont to be celebrated euery fift yeere, there, they that were most pregnant in wytt, and indued with great gyfts of wysedome
and knowledge in Musicke aboue the rest did vse
commonly to make goodly verses, measured according
to the sweetest notes of Musicke, containing the prayse
of some noble vertue, or of immortalitie, or of some
such thing of greatest estimation: which vnto them
seemed, so heauenly and ioyous a thing, that, thinking such men to be infpyrde with some diuine instinct
from heauen, they called them *Vates*. So when other
among them of the finest wits and aptest capacities
beganne in imitation of these to frame ditties of lighter
matters, and tuning them to the stroake of some of the
pleasantest kind of Musicke, then began there to grow
a distinction and great diuersity betweene makers and
makers. Whereby (I take it) beganne thys difference:
that they which handled in the audience of the people,
graue and necessary matters, were called wise men or
eloquent men, which they meant by *Vates*: and the
rest which sange of loue matters, or other lighter
deuises alluring vnto pleasure and delight, were called
Poetæ or makers. Thus it appeareth, both Eloquence
and Poetrie to haue had their beginning and originall
from these exercises, beeing framed in such sweete
measure of sentences and pleasant harmonie called
Ῥιθμος, which is an apt composition of wordes or
clauses, drawing as it were by force ye hearers eares
euen whether soeuer it lysteth: that *Plato* affirmeth
therein to be contained λοητεία an inchauntment, as
it were to perswade them anie thing whether they would
or no. And heerehence is sayde, that men were first
withdrawne from a wylde and sauadge kinde of life, to
ciuillity and gentlenes, and ye right knowledge of
humanity by the force of this measurable or tunable
speaking.

This opinion shall you finde confirmed throughout

the whole **workes of** *Plato* **and** *Ariſtotle*. And that ſuch was the **eſtimation** of this Poetry at thoſe times, that they ſuppoſed **all** wiſedome and knowledge to be included myſti**cally in that** diuine inſtinction, **wherewith they thought their** *Vates* **to bee** inſpyred. **Wherevpon,** throughout the **noble workes of thoſe moſt excellent** Philoſophers before **named, are the** authorities of Poets very often alledged. **And** *Cicero* **in his** *Tuſculane* queſtions is of that **minde, that a Poet cannot** expreſſe verſes **aboundantly, ſufficiently, and fully,** neither his eloquence **can flowe** pleaſauntly, **or his wordes founde** well and **plenteouſly,** without celeſtiall inſtinction: which **Poets** themſelues **doo** very often **and** gladlie **witnes** of themſelues, as namely *Ouid* **in. 6.** *Faſto:* *Est deus in nobis Agitante calleſcimus illo. etc.* Where**vnto I doubt** not equally to adioyne the authoritye of **our** late famous Engliſh Poet, who wrote the *Sheepheards Calender*, where lamenting the decay of Poetry, at theſe dayes, ſaith **moſt** ſweetely to the ſame.

Then make thee winges of **thine aſpyring wytt,**

And whence thou cameſt flye **back** to heauen apace. etc.

Whoſe fine poeticall witt, and moſt exquiſite learning, as he ſhewed aboundantly in that peece of worke, in my iudgment inferiour to the workes neither **of** *Theocritus* in Greeke, nor *Virgill* **in** Latine, whom **hee** narrowly immitateth: ſo **I** nothing doubt, but if his other workes **were** common **abroade,** which **are as I** thinke in ye cloſe cuſtodie of certaine his freends, we ſhould haue of our **owne** Poets, whom wee might matche in all reſpects with **the** beſt. And among all other his **workes** whatſoeuer, **I** would wyſh to haue the ſight **of hys** *Engliſh Poet*, **which** his freend *E. K.* did **once** promiſe to publiſhe, **which** whether he performed or not, I knowe not, if he **did, my happe** hath not beene **ſo** good as yet to ſee it.

But to returne **to** the eſtimation **of** Poetry. Beſides **ye** great and profitable fruites contained in Poetry, for the inſtruction of manners and precepts of good life (for that was cheefly reſpected in the firſt age of Poetry) this is alſo added to the eternall commendations of that noble faculty: that Kinges and Princes, great and famous men, did euer encourage, mayntaine, and reward Poets in al ages: becauſe they were thought onely to haue the whole power in their handes, of making men either immortally famous for their valiaunt exploytes and vertuous exerciſes, or perpetually infamous for their vicious liues. Wherevppon it is ſaid of *Achilles*, that this onely vantage he had of *Hector*, that it was his fortune to be extolled and renowned by the heauenly verſe of *Homer*. And as *Tully* recordeth to be written of *Alexander*, that with natural teares he wept ouer *Achilles* Tombe, in ioy that he conceiued at the conſideration, howe it was his happe to be honoured wyth ſo diuine a worke, as *Homers* was. *Ariſtotle*, a moſt prudent and learned Philoſopher, beeing appointed Schoolemaſter to the young Prince *Alexander*, thought no worke ſo meete to be reade vnto a King, as the worke of *Homer*: wherein the young Prince being by him inſtructed throughly, found ſuch wonderfull delight in the ſame when hee came to maturity, that hee would not onely haue it with him in all his iourneyes, but in his bedde alſo vnder his pyllowe, to delight him and teache him both nights and dayes. The ſame is reported of noble *Scipio*, who finding the two Bookes of *Homer* in the ſpoyle of Kyng *Darius*, eſteemed them as wonderfull precious Iewelles, making one of them his companion for the night, the other for the day. And not onely was he thus affected to yat one peece or parte of Poetry, but ſo generally he loued the profeſſors thereof, that in his moſt ſerious affayres, and hotteſt warres againſt *Numantia* and *Carthage* he could no whitte be without that olde Poet *Ennius* in his company. But to ſpeake of all thoſe noble and wyſe Princes, who bare ſpeciall fauour and countenaunce to Poets, were tedious, and would require a rehearſall of all ſuch, in whoſe time there grewe any to credite and eſtimation in that faculty. Thus farre therefore may ſuffice for the eſtimation of Poets. Nowe I thinke moſt meete, to ſpeake ſomewhat, concerning what hath beene the vſe of Poetry, and wherin it rightly conſiſted, and whereof conſequently it obteyned ſuch eſtimation.

To begin therefore with the firſt that was firſt worthelye memorable in the excellent gyft of Poetrye, the beſt wryters agree that it was *Orpheus*, who by the ſweete gyft of his heauenly Poetry, withdrew men from raungyng vncertainly, and wandring brutiſhly about, and made them gather together, and keepe company, made houſes, and kept fellowſhippe together, who therefore is reported (as *Horace* ſayth) to aſſwage the fierceneſſe of Tygers, and mooue the harde Flynts. After him was *Amphion*, who was the firſt that cauſed Citties to bee builded, and men therein to liue decently and orderly according to lawe and right. Next, was *Tyrtæus*, who began to practiſe warlike defences, to keepe back enemies, and ſaue themſelues from inuaſion of foes. In thys place I thinke were moſt conuenient to rehearſe that auncient Poet *Pyndarus*: but of the certaine time wherein he flouriſhed, I am not very certaine: but of the place where he continued moſte, it ſhoulde ſeeme to be the Citty of *Thebes*, by *Plinie* who reporteth, that *Alexander* in ſacking the ſame Cittie, woulde not ſuffer the houſe wherein he dwelt to be ſpoyled as all the reſt were. After theſe was *Homer*, who as it were in one ſumme comprehended all knowledge, wiſedome, learning, and pollicie, that was incident to the capacity of man. And who ſo liſte to take viewe of hys two Bookes, one of his *Iliades*, the other his *Odiſſea*, ſhall throughly perceiue what the right vſe of Poetry is: which indeede is to mingle profite with pleaſure, and ſo to delight the Reader with pleaſantnes of hys Arte, as in ye meane time, his mind may be well inſtructed with knowledge and wiſedome. For ſo did that worthy Poet frame thoſe his two workes, that in reading the firſt, that is his *Iliads*, by declaring and ſetting forth ſo liuely the Grecians aſſembly againſt

Troy, together with their proweffe and fortitude againſt their foes, a Prince ſhall learne not onely courage, and valiantneſſe, but difcretion alfo and pollicie to encounter with his enemies, yea a perfect forme of wyfe confultations, with his Captaines, and exhortations to the people, with other infinite commodities.

Agayne, in the other part, wherein are defcribed the manifold and daungerous aduentures of *Vliſſes*, may a man learne many noble vertues: and alfo learne to efcape and auoyde the fubtyll practifes, and perrilous entrappinges of naughty perfons: and not onely this, but in what fort alfo he may deale to knowe and perceiue the affections of thofe which be neere vnto him, and moſt familiar with him, the better to put them in truſt with his matters of waight and importaunce. Therefore I may boldly fette downe thys to be the trueſt, auncienteſt and beſt kinde of Poetry, to direct ones endeuour alwayes to that marke, that with delight they may euermore adioyne commoditie to theyr Readers: which becaufe I grounde vpon *Homer* the Prince of all Poets, therefore haue I alledged the order of his worke, as an authority fufficiently proouing this aſſertion.

Nowe what other Poets which followed him, and beene of greateſt fame, haue doone for the moſte parte in their feuerall workes I wyll briefely, and as my ſlender ability wyll ferue me declare. But by my leaue, I muſt content my felfe to fpeake not of all, but of fuch as my felfe haue feene, and beene beſt acquainted withall, and thofe not all nor the moſte part of the auncient Grecians, of whom I know not how many there were, but thefe of the Latiniſts, which are of greateſt fame and moſt obuious among vs.

Thus much I can fay, that *Ariſtotle* reporteth none to haue greatly flouriſhed in Greece, at leaſt wyfe not left behynd them any notable memoriall, before the time of *Homer*. And *Tully* fayth as much, that there were none wrytt woorth the reading twyce in the Romaine tongue, before ye Poet *Ennius*. And furely

English Poetrie.

as the very fumme or cheefeſt eſſence of Poetry, dyd alwayes for the moſt part confiſt in delighting the readers or hearers wyth pleaſure, ſo as the number of Poets increaſed, they ſtyll inclyned thys way rather then the other, ſo that moſt of them had ſpeciall regarde, to the pleaſantneſſe of theyr fine conceytes, whereby they might drawe mens mindes into admiration of theyr inuentions, more then they had to the profitte or commoditye that the Readers ſhoulde reape by their works. And thus as I ſuppoſe came it to paſſe among them, that for the moſt part of them, they would not write one worke contayning ſome ſerious matter: but for the ſame they wold likewiſe powre foorth as much of ſome wanton or laciuious inuention. Yet ſome of the auncienteſt ſort of Grecians, as it ſeemeth were not ſo much diſpoſed to vayne delectation: as *Ariſtotle* ſayth of *Empedocles*, that in hys iudgment he was onely a naturall Philoſopher, no Poet at all, nor that he was like vnto *Homer* in any thing but hys meeter, or number of feete, that is, that hee wrote in verſe. After the time of *Homer*, there began the firſte Comedy wryters, who compyled theyr workes in a better ſtile which continued not long, before it was expelled by penalty, for ſcoffing too broade at mens manners, and the priuie reuengements which the Poets vſed againſt their ill wyllers. Among theſe was *Eupolis*, *Cratinus*, and *Ariſtophenes*, but afterward the order of thys wryting Comedies was reformed and made more plauſible: then wrytte *Plato, Comicus, Menander*, and I knowe not who more.

There be many moſt profitable workes, of like antiquity, or rather before them, of the Tragedy writers: as of *Euripides*, and *Sophocles*, then was there *Phocitides* and *Theagines*, with many other: which Tragedies had their inuention by one *Theſpis*, and were polliſhed and amended by *Æſchilus*. The profitte or diſcommoditie which aryſeth by the vſe of theſe Comedies and Tragedies, which is moſt, hath beene long in controuerſie, and is ſore vrged among vs at theſe dayes: what

I thinke of the same, perhaps I shall breefely declare anon.

Nowe concerning the Poets which wrote in homely manner, as they pretended, but indeede, with great pythe and learned iudgment, such as were the wryters of Sheepeheards talke and of husbandly precepts, who were among the Grecians that excelled, besides *Theocritus* and *Hesiodus* I know not, of whom the first, what profitable workes he left to posterity, besides hys *Idillia* or contentions of Goteheards, tending most to delight, and pretty inuentions, I can not tell. The other, no doubt for his Argument he tooke in hande, dealt very learnedly and profitably, that is, in precepts of Husbandry, but yet so as he myxed much wanton stuffe among the rest.

The first wryters of Poetry among the Latines, shoulde seeme to be those, which excelled in the framing of Commedies, and that they continued a long time without any notable memory of other Poets. Among whom, the cheefest that we may see or heare tell of, were these. *Ennius, Cæcilius, Næuius, Licinius, Attilius, Turpitius, Trabea, Luscius, Plautus,* and *Terens.* Of whom these two last named, haue beene euer since theyr time most famous, and to these dayes are esteemed, as greate helpes and furtheraunces to the obtayning of good Letters. But heere cannot I staye to speake of the most famous, renowned and excellent, that euer writte among the Latine Poets, *P. Virgill,* who performed the very same in that tongue, which *Homer* had doone in Grecke: or rather better if better might as *Sex. Propert.* in his *Elegies* gallantly recordeth in his praise, *Nescio quid magis nascitur Iliade.* Vnder the person of *Æneas* he expresseth the valoure of a worthy Captaine and valiaunt Gouernour, together with the perilous aduentures of warre, and polliticke deuises at all assayes. And as he immitateth *Homer* in that worke, so dooth he likewyse followe the very steps of *Theocritus,* in his most pythy inuentions of his *Æglogues*: and likewyse *Hesiodus* in his *Georgicks* or bookes of

Hufbandry, but yet more grauely, and in a more decent
ftyle. But notwithftanding hys fage grauity and wonderfull wifedome, dyd he not altogether reftrayne his
vayne, but that he would haue a caft at fome wanton
and fkant comely an Argument, if indeede fuch trifles
as be fathered vppon him were his owne. There followed after him, very many rare and excellent Poets,
whereof the moft part writt light matters, as *Epigrammes* and *Elegies*, with much pleafant dalliance, among
whom may be accounted *Propertius*, *Tibullus*, *Catullus*,
with diuers whom *Ouid* fpeaketh of in diuers places of
his workes. Then are there two Hyftoricall Poets, no
leffe profitable then delightfome to bee read: *Silius* and
Lucanus: the one declaring the valiant proweffe of two
noble Captaines, one enemie to the other, that is, *Scipio*
and *Haniball*: the other likewife, the fortitude of two
expert warriours (yet more lamentably then the other
becaufe thefe warres were ciuill) *Pompey* and *Cæsar*.
The next in tyme (but as moft men doo account, and
fo did he himfelfe) the fecond in dignity, we will ad
ioyne *Ouid*, a moft learned, and exquifite Poet. The
worke of greateft profitte which he wrote, was his
Booke of *Metamorphofis*, which though it confifted of
fayned Fables for the moft part, and poeticall inuentions,
yet beeing moralized according to his meaning, and the
trueth of euery tale beeing difcouered, it is a worke of
exceeding wyfedome and founde iudgment. If one
lyft in like manner, to haue knowledge and perfect
intelligence of thofe rytes and ceremonies which were
obferued after the Religion of the Heathen, no more
profitable worke for that purpofe, then his bookes
De fastis. The reft of his dooinges, though they tende
to the vayne delights of loue and dalliaunce (except
his *Tristibus* wherein he bewayleth hys exile) yet furely
are mixed with much good counfayle and profitable
leffons if they be wifely and narrowly read. After his
time I know no worke of any great fame, till the time
of *Horace*, a Poet not of the fmootheft ftyle, but in
fharpneffe of wytt inferiour to none, and one to whom

all the rest both **before** his time and since, are very much beholding. **About the** same time *Iuuenall* and *Persius,* then *Martial, Seneca* a most excellent wryter of Tragedies, *Boetius,* **Lucretius,** *Statius, Val: Flaccus, Manilius, Ausonius, Claudian,* **and many other,** whose iust times **and feuerall woorkes to speake of in this place, were neither** much **needefull, nor altogeather tollerable,** because I purposed an other argument. **Onely I will adde two** of later **times,** yet not farre **inferiour to the most of** them aforesayde, *Pallengenius,* **and** *Bap. Mantuanus,* **and for a singuler gyft** in a sweete **Heroicall** verse, match **with them** *Chr. Oclan.* the Authour of our *Anglorum* **Prælia.** But nowe least I stray too farre from my purpose, I wyl come to our English Poets, to whom I would I were able to yeelde theyr deserued commendations: and affoorde them **that cenfure, which I know many woulde, which can better, if they were nowe to write in my steede.**

I know **no memorable worke written by any Poet in our English fpeeche,** vntill twenty **yeeres past:** where although Learning was not generally decayde at any time, especially since the **Conquest of** King *William* Duke of *Normandy,* **as it may appeare by many famous works and learned bookes (though not of this kinde) wrytten by** Byshoppes and **others:** yet surelye **that Poetry was in small price** among them, **it is** very **manifest, and no** great **maruayle, for euen that** light of Greeke **and Latine Poets which they had,** they much contemned, **as appeareth** by theyr **rude verfifying,** which **of long** time **was vsed** (a barbarous vse it was) wherin they conuerted the naturall **property of the** sweete Latine verse, to be **a balde kinde of ryming,** thinking nothing **to be learnedly written in verse, which** fell not out in ryme, **that is, in wordes** whereof **the middle worde** of eche verse should sound a **like with the** last, **or of two verses, the ende of both should fall in** the like letters as thus.

O malè viuentes, versus audite sequentes.

English Poetrie.

And thus likewyſe.

Propter hæc et alia dogmata doctorum
Reor eſſe melius et magis decorum:
Quiſque ſuam habeat, et non proximorum.

This brutiſh Poetrie, though it had not the beginning in this Countrey, yet ſo hath it beene affected heere, that the infection thereof would neuer (nor I thinke euer will) be rooted vppe againe: I meane this tynkerly verſe which we call ryme: Maſter *Aſcham* ſayth, that it firſt began to be followed and maintained among the *Hunnes* and *Gothians*, and other barbarous Nations, who with the decay of all good learning, brought it into *Italy*: from thence it came into *Fraunce*, and ſo to *Germany*, at laſt conueyed into *England*, by men indeede of great wiſedome and learning, but not conſiderate nor circumſpect in that behalfe. But of this I muſt intreate more heereafter.

Henry the firſt King of that name in England, is wonderfully extolled, in all aunctient Recordes of memory, for hys ſinguler good learning, in all kinde of noble ſtudies, in ſo much as he was named by his ſurname *Beaucleark*, as much to ſay, as *Fayreclerke* (whereof perhappes came ye name of *Fayreclowe*) what knowledge hee attained in the ſkyll of Poetry, I am not able to ſay, I report his name for proofe, that learning in this Country was not little eſteemed of at that rude time, and that like it is, among other ſtudies, a King would not neglect the faculty of Poetry. The firſt of our Engliſh Poets that I haue heard of, was *Iohn Gower*, about the time of king *Rychard* the ſeconde, as it ſhould ſeeme by certayne coniectures bothe a Knight, and queſtionleſſe a ſinguler well learned man: whoſe workes I could wyſh they were all whole and perfect among vs, for no doubt they contained very much deepe knowledge and delight: which may be gathered by his freend *Chawcer*, who ſpeaketh of him oftentimes, in diuer[s] places of **hys workes.** *Chawcer,* who for that excellent fame which hee obtayned in his Poetry, was alwayes accounted the God of Englifh Poets (fuch a tytle for honours fake hath beene giuen him) was next after, if not equall in time to *Gower,* and hath left many workes, both for delight and profitable knowledge, farre exceeding any other that as yet euer fince hys time directed theyr ftudies that way. Though the manner of hys ftile may feeme blunte and courfe to many fine Englifh eares at thefe dayes, yet in trueth, if it be equally pondered, and with good iudgment aduifed, and confirmed with the time wherein he wrote, a man fhall perceiue thereby euen a true picture or perfect fhape of a right Poet. He by his delightfome vayne, fo gulled the eares of men with his deuifes, that, although corruption bare fuch fway in moft matters, that learning and truth might fkant bee admitted to fhewe it felfe, yet without controllment, myght hee gyrde at the vices and abufes of all ftates, and gawle with very fharpe and eger inuentions, which he did fo learnedly and pleafantly, that none therefore would call him into queftion. For fuch was his bolde fpyrit, that what enormities he faw in any, he would not fpare to pay them home, eyther in playne words, or els in fome prety and pleafant couert, that the fimpleft might efpy him.

Neere in time vnto him was *Lydgate* a Poet, furely for good proportion of his verfe, and meetely currant ftyle, as the time affoorded comparable with *Chawcer,* yet more occupyed in fuperfticious and odde matters, then was requefite in fo good a wytte: which, though he handled them commendably, yet the matters themfelues beeing not fo commendable, hys eftimation hath beene the leffe. The next of our auncient Poets, that I can tell of, I fuppofe to be *Pierce Ploughman,* who in hys dooinges is fomewhat harfhe and obfcure, but indeede a very pithy wryter, and (to hys commendation I fpeake it) was the firft that I haue feene, that obferued ye quantity of our verfe without the curiofity of Ryme.

Since thefe I knowe none other tyll the time of

Skelton, who writ in the time of Kyng *Henry* the eyght, who as indeede he obtayned the Lawrell Garland, so may I wyth good ryght yeelde him the title of a Poet: hee was doubtles a pleasant conceyted fellowe, and of a very sharpe wytte, exceeding bolde, and would nyppe to the very quicke where he once sette holde. Next hym I thynke I may place master *George Gaskoyne*, as painefull a Souldier in the affayres of hys Prince and Country, as he was a wytty Poet in his wryting: whose commendations, becaufe I found in one of better iudgment then my selfe, I wyl sette downe hys wordes, and suppresse myne owne, of hym thus wryteth *E. K.* vppon the ninth *Æglogue* of the new Poet.

Master *George Gaskoyne* a wytty Gentleman and the very cheefe of our late rymers, who and if some partes of learning wanted not (albeit is well knowne he altogether wanted not learning) no doubt would haue attayned to the excellencye of those famous Poets. For gyfts of wytt, and naturall promptnes appeare in him aboundantly. I might next speake of the dyuers workes of the olde Earle of *Surrey*: of the L. *Vaus*, of *Norton*, of *Bristow*, *Edwardes*, *Tusser*, *Churchyard*. VVyl: Hunnis: Haiwood: Sand: Hyll: S. Y. *M. D.* and many others, but to speake of their feuerall gyfts, and aboundant skyll shewed forth by them in many pretty and learned workes, would make my difcourfe much more tedious.

I may not omitte the deserued commendations of many honourable and noble Lordes, and Gentlemen, in her Maiesties Courte, which in the rare deuises of Poetry, haue beene and yet are most excellent skylfull, among whom, the right honourable Earle of *Oxford* may challenge to him selfe the tytle of ye most excellent among the rest. I can no longer forget those learned Gentlemen which tooke such profitable paynes in translating the Latine Poets into our English tongue, whose desertes in that behalfe are more then I can vtter. Among these, I euer esteemed, and while I lyue, in my conceyt I shall account Master *D. Phaer*: without doubt

A Discourse of

the best: who as indeede hee had the best peece of Poetry whereon to sette a most gallant verse, so performed he it accordingly, and in such sort, as in my conscience I thinke would scarcely be doone againe, if it were to doo again. Notwithstanding, I speak it but as myne own fancy, not preiudiciall to those that list to thinke otherwyse. Hys worke whereof I speake, is the englishing of *Æneidos* of *Virgill*, so farre foorth as it pleased God to spare him life, which was to the halfe parte of the tenth Booke, the rest beeing since wyth no lesse commendations finished, by that worthy scholler and famous Phisition Master *Thomas Twyne*.

Equally with him may I well adioyne Master *Arthur Golding*, for hys labour in englishing *Ouids Metamorphosis*, for which Gentleman, surely our Country hath for many respects greatly to gyue God thankes: as for him which hath taken infinite paynes without ceasing, trauelleth as yet indefatigably, and is addicted without society, by his continuall laboure, to profit this nation and speeche in all kind of good learning. The next, very well deserueth Master *Barnabe Googe* to be placed, as a painefull furtherer of learning: hys helpe to Poetry besides hys owne deuises, as the translating of *Pallengenius. Lodiac.* *Abraham Flemming* as in many prety Poesis of hys owne, so in translating hath doone to hys commendations. To whom I would heere adioyne one of hys name, whom I know to haue excelled, as well in all kinde of learning as in Poetry most especially, and would appeare so, if the dainty morselles, and fine poeticall inuentions of hys, were as common abroade as I knowe they be among some of hys freendes. I wyl craue leaue of the laudable Authors of *Seneca* in English, of the other partes of *Ouid*, of *Horace*, of *Mantuan*, and diuers other, becaufe I would haften to ende thys rehearsall, perhappes offensyue to some, whom eyther by forgetfulnes, or want of knowledge, I must needes ouer passe.

And once againe, I am humbly to desire pardon of the learned company of Gentlemen Schollers, and students of the Vniuersities, and Innes of Courte, yf I omitte theyr feuerall commendations in this place, which I knowe a great number of them haue worthely deserued, in many rare deuises, and singuler inuentions of Poetrie: for neither hath it beene my good happe, to haue seene all which I haue hearde of, neyther is my abyding in such place, where I can with facility get knowledge of their workes.

One Gentleman notwithstanding among them may I not ouerslyppe, so farre reacheth his fame, and so worthy is he, if hee haue not already, to weare the Lawrell wreathe, Master *George VVhetstone*, a man singularly well skyld in this faculty of Poetrie: To him I wyl ioyne *Anthony Munday*, an earnest traueller in this arte, and in whose name I haue seene very excellent workes, among which surely, the most exquisite vaine of a witty poeticall heade is shewed in the sweete sobs of Sheepheardes and Nymphes: a worke well worthy to be viewed, and to bee esteemed as very rare Poetrie. With these I may place *Iohn Graunge*, *Knyght*, *VVylmott*, *Darrell*, *F. C. F. K. G. B.* and many other, whose names come not nowe to my remembraunce.

This place haue I purposely reserued for one, who if not only, yet in my iudgement principally deserueth the tytle of the rightest English Poet, that euer I read: that is, the Author of the Sheepeheardes Kalender, intituled to the woorthy Gentleman Master *Phillip Sydney*, whether it was Master *Sp.* or what rare Scholler in Pembrooke Hall soeuer, becaufe himself and his freendes, for what respect I knowe not, would not reueale it, I force not greatly to sette downe: sorry I am that I can not find none other with whom I might couple him in this *Catalogue*, in his rare gyft of Poetry: although one there is, though nowe long since, seriously occupied in grauer studies, (Master *Gabriell Haruey*) yet, as he was once his most special freende and fellow Poet, so becaufe he hath taken such paynes, not onely in his Latin Poetry (for which he enioyed great commendations of the best both in iudgment and dignity in thys Realme) but alſo to reforme our Engliſh verſe, and to beautify the ſame with braue deuiſes, of which I thinke the cheefe lye hidde in hatefull obſcurity: therefore wyll I aduenture to ſette them together, as two of the rareſt witts, and learnedſt maſters of Poetrie in England. Whoſe worthy and notable ſkyl in this faculty, I would wyſh if their high dignities and ſerious buſineſſes would permit, they would ſtyll graunt to bee a furtheraunce to that reformed kinde of Poetry, which Maſter *Haruey* did once beginne to ratify: and ſurely in mine opinion, if hee had choſen ſome grauer matter, and handled but with halfe that ſkyll, which I knowe he could haue doone, and not powred it foorth at a venture, as a thinge betweene ieſt and earneſt, it had taken greater effect then it did.

As for the other Gentleman, if it would pleaſe him or hys freendes to let thoſe excellent *Poemes*, whereof I know he hath plenty, come abroad, as his Dreames, his Legends, his Court of *Cupid*, his Engliſh Poet with other: he ſhoulde not onely ſtay the rude pens of my ſelfe and others, but alſo ſatiſiye the thirſty deſires of many which deſire nothing more, then to ſee more of hys rare inuentions. If I ioyne to Maſter *Haruey* hys two Brethren, I am aſſured, though they be both buſied with great and waighty callinges (the one a godly and learned Diuine, the other a famous and ſkylfull Phiſition) yet if they lyſted to ſette to their helping handes to Poetry, they would as much beautify and adorne it as any others.

If I let paſſe the vncountable rabble of ryming Ballet makers and compylers of ſenceleſſe ſonets, who be moſt buſy, to ſtuffe euery ſtall full of groſſe deuiſes and vnlearned Pamphlets: I truſt I ſhall with the beſt ſort be held excuſed. Nor though many ſuch can frame an Alehouſe ſong of fiue of ſixe ſcore verſes, hobbling vppon ſome tune of a Northen Iygge, or Robyn hoode, or La lubber etc. And perhappes obſerue iuſt number of fillables, eyght in one line, ſixe in an other, and there withall an A to make a iercke in the ende: yet if theſe might be accounted Poets (as it is sayde some of them make meanes to be promoted to ye Lawrell) surely we shall shortly haue whole swarmes of Poets: and euery one that can frame a Booke in Ryme, though for want of matter, it be but in commendations of Copper noses or Bottle Ale, wyll catch at the Garlande due to Poets: whose potticall poeticall (I should say) heades, I would wyshe, at their worshipfull comencements might in steede of Lawrell, be gorgiously garnished with fayre greene Barley, in token of their good affection to our Englishe Malt. One speaketh thus homely of them, with whose words I wyll content my selfe for thys time, becaufe I woulde not bee too broade wyth them in myne owne speeche.

In regarde (he meaneth of the learned framing the newe Poets workes which writt the Sheepheardes Calender.) I scorne and spue out the rakehelly rout of our ragged Rymers, (for so themselues vse to hunt the Letter) which without learning boaste, without iudgment iangle, without reafon rage and fume, as if some inflinct of poeticall fpyrite had newlie rauished them, aboue the meaneffe of common capacity. And beeing in the midft of all their brauery, fuddainly for want of matter or of Ryme, or hauing forgotten their former conceyt, they feeme to be fo payned and trauelled in theyr remembraunce, as it were a woman in Chyldbyrth, or as that fame *Pythia* when the traunce came vpon her. *Os rabidum fera corda domans* etc.

Hus farre foorth haue I aduentured to fette downe parte of my simple iudgement concerning thofe Poets, with whom for the moft part I haue beene acquainted through myne owne reading: which though it may

feeme fomething impertinent to the tytle of my **Booke**, yet I truft the courteous Readers wyll pardon me, confidering that poetry is not of that grounde and antiquity in our Englifh tongue, but that fpeaking thereof only as it is Englifh, would feeme like vnto the drawing of ones pycture without a heade.

Nowe therefore by your gentle patience, wyll I wyth like breuity make tryall, what I can fay concerning our Englifhe Poetry, firft in the matter thereof, then in the forme, that is, the manner of our verfe: yet fo as I muft euermore haue recourfe to thofe times and wryters, whereon the Englifh poetry taketh as it were the difcent and proprietye.

Englifh Poetry therefore beeing confidered according to common cuftome and auncient vfe, is, where any worke is learnedly compiled in meafurable fpeeche, and framed in wordes contayning number or proportion of iuft fyllables, delighting the readers or hearers as well by the apt and decent framing of wordes in equall refemblance of quantity, commonly called verfe, as by the fkyllfull handling of the matter whereof it is intreated. I fpake fomewhat of the beginning of thys meafuring of wordes in iuft number, taken out of *Plato*: and indeede the regarde of true quantity in Letters and fyllables, feemeth not to haue been much vrged before the time of *Homer* in Greece, as *Ariftotle* witneffeth.

The matters whereof verfes were firft made, were eyther exhortations to vertue, dehortations from vice, or the prayfes of fome laudable thing. From thence they beganne to vfe them in exercifes of immitating fome vertuous and wife man at their feaftes: where as fome one fhoulde be appointed to reprefent an other mans perfon of high eftimation, and he fang fine ditties and wittie fentences, tunably to their Mufick notes. Of thys fprang the firft kinde of Comedyes, when they beganne to bring into thefe exercifes, more perfons then one, whofe fpeeches were deuifed Dyalogue wife, in aunfwering one another. And of fuch like exercifes, or as fome wyll needes haue it, long before the other, began the firft Tragedies, and were fo called of τραγος, becaufe the Actor when he began to play his part, flewe and offered a Goate to their Goddeffe: but Commedies tooke their name of κομάζειν και ᾄδειν *comefsatum ire*, to goe a feafting, becaufe they vfed to goe in proceffion with their fport about the Citties and Villages, mingling much pleafaunt myrth wyth theyr graue Religion, and feafting cheerefully together wyth as great ioy as might be deuifed. But not long after (as one delight draweth another) they began to inuent new perfons and newe matters for their Comedies, fuch as the deuifers thought meeteft to pleafe the peoples vaine: And from thefe, they beganne to prefent in fhapes of men, the natures of vertues and vices, and affections and quallities incident to men, as Iuftice, Temperance, Pouerty, Wrathe, Vengeaunce, Sloth, Valiantnes, and fuch like, as may appeare by the auncient workes of *Ariftophanes*. There grewe at laft to be a greater diuerfitye betweene Tragedy wryters and Comedy wryters, the one expreffing onely forrowfull and lamentable Hyftories, bringing in the perfons of Gods and Goddeffes, Kynges and Queenes, and great ftates, whofe parts were cheefely to expreffe moft miferable calamities and dreadfull chaunces, which increafed worfe and worfe, tyll they came to the moft wofull plight that might be deuifed.

The Comedies on the other fide, were directed to a contrary ende, which beginning doubtfully, drewe to fome trouble or turmoyle, and by fome lucky chaunce alwayes ended to the ioy and appeafement of all parties. Thys diftinction grewe as fome holde opinion, by immitation of the workes of *Homer*: for out of his *Iliads*, the Tragedy wryters founde dreadfull euents, whereon to frame their matters, and the other out of hys *Odyffea* tooke arguments of delight, and pleafant ending after dangerous and troublefome doubtes. So that, though there be many fortes of poeticall wrytings, and Poetry is not debarred from any matter, which may be expreſſed by penne or ſpeeche, yet for the better vnderſtanding, and breefer method of thys diſcourſe, I may comprehende the ſame in three ſortes, which are Comicall, Tragicall, Hiſtori[c]all. Vnder the firſt, may be contained all ſuch *Epigrammes, Elegies* and delectable ditties, which Poets haue deuiſed reſpecting onely the delight thereof: in the ſeconde, all dolefull complaynts, lamentable chaunces, and what ſoeuer is poetically expreſſed in ſorrow and heauines. In the third, we may compriſe, the reſte of all ſuch matters, which is indifferent betweene the other two, doo commonly occupy the pennes of Poets: ſuch, are the poeticall compyling of Chronicles, the freendly greetings betweene freendes, and very many ſortes beſides, which for the better diſtinction may be referred to one of theſe three kindes of Poetry. But once againe, leaſt my diſcourſe runne too farre awry, wyll I buckle my ſelfe more neerer to Engliſh Poetry: the vſe wherof, becauſe it is nothing different from any other, I thinke beſt to confirme by the teſtimony of *Horace*, a man worthy to beare authority in this matter: whoſe very opinion is this, that the perfect perfection of poetrie is this, to mingle delight with profitt in ſuch wyſe, that a Reader might by his reading be pertaker of bothe, which though I touched in the beginning, yet I thought good to alledge in this place for more confirmation thereof ſome of hys owne wordes. In his treatiſe *de arte Poetica*, thus hee ſayth.

Aut prodeſſe volunt aut delectare poetæ,

Aut ſimul et iucunda et idonea dicere vitæ.

As much to ſaie: All Poets deſire either by their works to profitt or delight men, or els to ioyne both profitable and pleaſant leſſons together for the inſtruction of life.

And again

English Poetrie.

Omne tulit punctum **qui** *mifcuit vtile dulci,*
Lectorum delectando pariterque mouendo.

That is, He miffeth nothing of his marke **which** ioyneth profitt with delight, as well delighting **his** Readers, **as** profiting them **with** counfell. And that **whole** Epiftle which hee **wryt of his Arte** of Poetrie, among all the parts **thereof,** runneth cheefelie vppon this, that whether **the** argument **which the Poet handleth,** be of **thinges** doone, or fained **inuentions, yet** that they **fhould beare** fuch an Image of **trueth, that** as they **delight** they may likewife profitt. **For thefe are his wordes.** *Ficta voluptatis caufa fint proxima* ***veris.*** **Let** thinges that are faigned for pleafures **fake, haue a** neere refemblance of ye truth. This **precept may you** perceiue **to** bee moft duelie obferued **of** *Chawcer:* for who could with more delight, **prefcribe** fuch wholfome counfaile and fage aduife, where **he** feemeth onelie to refpect the profitte of his leffons and inftructions? or who coulde with greater wifedome, **or** more pithie fkill, vnfold fuch pleafant and delightfome matters **of** mirth, **as** though they refpected **nothing,** but the telling of **a merry** tale? **fo that this is the** very grounde of right poetrie, to giue profitable **counfaile,** yet fo as it muft be mingled with delight. For among all the auncient works of poetrie, though the moft of them incline much to that part of delighting men with pleafant matters of fmall importaunce, yet euen in the vaineft trifles among them, there **is not** forgotten fome profitable counfaile, which a man may learne, either by flatte precepts which therein **are** prefcribed, or by loathing fuch **vile** vices, the enormities **whereof** they largelie difcouer. For furelie, I am of this op**inion,** that the wantoneft Poets of all, in their moft laciuious workes wherein they bufied themfelues, fought rather by that meanes to withdraw mens mindes (efpeciallie the beft natures) from fuch foule vices, then to allure them to imbrace fuch beaftly follies as they detected.

Horace speaking of the generall dueties of Poets, sayth, *Os tenerum pueri balbumque poeta fugitat*, and manie more wordes concerning the profitte to be hadde out of Poets, which becaufe I haue fome of them comprifed into an Englifh tranflation of that learned and famous knight, Sir *Thomas Elyot*, I wyll fet downe his wordes.

> The Poet fafhioneth by fome pleafant meane,
> The fpeeche of children ftable and vnfure:
> Gulling their eares from wordes and thinges vncleane,
> Giuing to them precepts that are pure:
> Rebuking enuy and wrath if it dure:
> Thinges well donne he can by example commend,
> To needy and ficke he doth alfo his cure
> To recomfort if ought he can amende.

And manie other like wordes are in that place of *Horace* to like effect. Therefore poetrie, as it is of it felfe, without abufe is not onely not vnprofitable to the liues and ftudies of menne, but wonderfull commendable and of great excellencie. For nothing can be more acceptable to men, or rather to be wifhed, then fweete allurements to vertues, and commodious caueates from vices? of which Poetrie is exceeding plentifull, powring into gentle witts, not roughly and tirannicallie, but it is were with a louing authoritie. Nowe if the ill and vndecent prouocations, whereof fome vnbridled witts take occafion by the reading of laciuious Poemes, bee obiected: fuch as are *Ouids* loue Bookes, and *Elegies*, *Tibullus*, *Catullus*, and *Martials* workes, with the Comedies for the moft part of *Plautus* and *Terence*: I thinke it eafily aunfwered. For though it may not iuftlie be denied, that thefe workes are indeede very Poetrie, yet that Poetrie in them is not the effentiall or formall matter or caufe of the hurt therein might be affirmed, and although that reafon fhould come fhort, yet this might be fufficient, that the workes themfelues doo not corrupt, but the abufe of the vfers, who vndamaging their

English Poetrie.

owne difpofitions, by reading the difcoueries of vices, refemble foolifh folke, who comming into a Garden without anie choife or circumfpection tread downe the faireft flowers, and wilfullie thruft their fingers among the nettles.

And furelie to fpeake what I verelie thinke, this is mine opinion: that one hauing fufficient fkyll, to reade and vnderftand thofe workes, and yet no ftaie of him felfe to auoyde inconueniences, which the remembraunce of vnlawfull things may ftirre vppe in his minde, he, in my iudgement, is wholy to bee reputed a laciuious difpofed perfonne, whom the recitall of fins whether it be in a good worke or a badde, or vppon what occafion foeuer, wyll not ftaie him but prouoke him further vnto them. Contrariwife, what good leffons the warie and fkylful Readers fhall picke out of the very worft of them, if they lift to take anie heede, and reade them not of an intent to bee made the worfe by them, you may fee by thefe fewe fentences, which the forefayd Sir *Thomas Elyott* gathered as he fayth at all aduentures, intreating of the like argument. Firft *Plautus* in commendations of vertue, hath fuch like wordes.

> Verely vertue doth all thinges excell,
> For if liberty, health liuing or fubftaunce,
> Our Country our parents, and children doo well,
> It hapneth by vertue: fhe doth all aduaunce,
> Vertue hath all thinges vnder gouernaunce:
> And in whom of vertue is founde great plenty,
> Any thing that is good may neuer be dainty.

Terence, in *Eunucho* hath a profitable fpeeche, in blafing foorth the fafhions of harlots, before the eyes of young men. Thus fayth *Parmeno*.

> In thys thing I tryumphe in myne owne conceite,
> That I haue found for all young men the way,
> Howe they of Harlots fhall know the deceite,
> Their witts and manners: that thereby they may
> Them perpetuallie hate, for fo much as they

Out of their owne houfes be frefh and delicate,
Feeding curioufly: at home all day
Lyuing beggerlie in moft wretched eftate.

And many more wordes of the fame matter, but which may be gathered by thefe fewe.

Ouid, in his moft wanton Bookes of loue, and the remedies thereof, hath very many pithie and wife fentences, which a heedefull Reader may marke, and chofe out from ye other ftuffe. This is one.

Tyme is a medicine of it fhall profitt,
VVine gyuen out of tyme may be annoyaunce.
And man fhall irritat vice if he prohibitt,
VVhen time is not meete vnto his vtteraunce.
Therfore if thou yet by counfayle art recuperable,
Fly thou from idlenes and euer be ftable.

Martiall, a moft diffolute wryter among all other, yet not without many graue and prudent fpeeches, as this is one worthy to be marked of thefe fond youthes which intangle theyr wytts in raging loue, who ftepping once ouer fhoes in theyr fancyes, neuer reft plunging till they be ouer head and eares in their follie.

If thou wylt efchewe bitter aduenture,
And auoyde the annoyance of a penfifull hart,
Set in no one perfon all wholly thy pleafure,
The leffe maift thou ioy, but the leffe fhalt thou fmart.

Thefe are but fewe gathered out by happe, yet fufficient to fhewe that the wife and circumfpect Readers may finde very many profitable leffons, difperfed in thefe workes, neither take any harme by reading fuch Poemes, but good, if they wil themfelues. Neuertheles, I would not be thought to hold opinion, that the reading of them is fo tollerable, as that there neede no refpect to be had in making choyfe of readers or hearers: for if they be prohibited from the tender and vnconftant wits of children and young mindes, I thinke

Englifh Poetrie.

it not without great reafon: neyther am I of that deuiliifh opinion, of which fome there are, and haue beene in England, who hauing charge of youth to inftruct them in learning, haue efpecially made choyfe of fuch vnchildifh ftuffe, to reade vnto young Schollers, as it fhoulde feeme of fome filthy purpofe, wylfully to corrupt theyr tender mindes, and prepare them the more ready for theyr loathfome dyetts.

For as it is fayd of that impudent worke of *Luciane*, a man were better to reade none of it then all of it, fo thinke I that thefe workes are rather to be kept altogether from children, then they fhould haue free liberty to reade them, before they be meete either of their owne difcretion or by heedefull inftruction, to make choyfe of the good from the badde. As for our Englifhe Poetrie, I know no fuch perilous peeces (except a fewe balde ditties made ouer the Beere potts, which are nothing leffe then Poetry) which anie man may vfe and reade without damage or daunger: which indeede is leffe to be meruailed at among vs, then among the olde Latines and Greekes, confidering that Chriftianity may be a ftaie to fuch illecibrous workes and inuentions, as among them (for their Arte fake) myght obtaine paffage.

Nowe will I fpeake fomewhat, of that princelie part of Poetrie, wherein are difplaied the noble actes and valiant exploits of puiffaunt Captaines, expert fouldiers, wife men, with the famous reportes of auncient times, fuch as are the Heroycall workes of *Homer* in Greeke, and the heauenly verfe of *Virgils Æneidos* in Latine: which workes, comprehending as it were the fumme and ground of all Poetrie, are verelie and incomparably the beft of all other. To thefe, though wee haue no Englifh worke aunfwerable, in refpect of the glorious ornaments of gallant handling: yet our auncient Chroniclers and reporters of our Countrey affayres, come moft neere them: and no doubt, if fuch regarde of our Englifh fpeeche, and curious handling of our verfe, had beene long fince thought vppon, and from time to time been pollifhed and bettered by men of learning, iudgement, and authority, it would ere this, haue matched them in all refpects. A manifeft example thereof, may bee the great good grace and fweete vayne, which Eloquence hath attained in our fpeeche, becaufe it hath had the helpe of fuch rare and finguler wits, as from time to time myght ftill adde fome amendment to the fame. Among whom I thinke there is none that will gainfay, but Mafter *Iohn Lilly* hath deferued mofte high commendations, as he which hath ftept one fteppe further therein then any either before or fince he fuft began the wyttie difcourfe of his *Euphues*. Whofe workes, furely in refpecte of his finguler eloquence and braue compofition of apt words and fentences, let the learned examine and make tryall thereof thorough all the partes of Rethoricke, in fitte phrafes, in pithy fentences, in gallant tropes, in flowing fpeeche, in plaine fence, and furely in my iudgment, I thinke he wyll yeelde him that verdict, which *Quintilian* giueth of bothe the beft Orators *Demofthenes* and *Tully*, that from the one, nothing may be taken away, to the other, nothing may be added. But a more neerer example to prooue my former affertion true (I meane ye meetneffe of our fpeeche to receiue the beft forme of Poetry) may bee taken by conference of that famous tranflation of Mafter D. *Phaer* with the coppie it felfe, who foeuer pleafe with courteous iudgement but a little to compare and marke them both together: and weigh with himfelfe, whether the Englifh tongue might by little and little be brought to the verye maiefty of a ryght Heroicall verfe. Firft you may marke, how *Virgill* alwayes fitteth his matter in hande with wordes agreeable vnto the fame affection, which he expreffeth, as in hys Tragicall exclamations, what pathe[ti]call fpeeches he frameth? in his comfortable confolations, howe fmoothely hys verfe runnes? in his dreadfull battayles, and dreery byckerments of warres, howe bygge and boyftrous his wordes found? and the like notes in all partes of his worke may be obferued. Which excellent

English Poetrie. 47

grace and comely kind of choyfe, if the tranflatour hath not hitte very neere in our courfe Englifh phrafe iudge vprightly: wee wyll conferre fome of the places, not picked out for the purpofe, but fuch as I tooke turning ouer the Booke at randon. When the Troyans were fo toft about in tempeftious wether, caufed by *Æolus* at *Iunoes* requeft, and driuen vpon the coafte of *Affrick* with a very neere fcape of their liues: *Æneas* after hee had gone a land and kylled plenty of victuals for his company of Souldiours, hee deuided the fame among them, and thus louinglie and fweetely he comforted them. *Æn. Lib. i.*

> *et dictis mærentia pectora* **mulcet**
> *O focii (neque* **ignari** *fumus ante* **malorum***)*
> *O pafsi grauiora: dabit deus his quoque finem*
> *Vos et fcyllæam rabiem, penitufque fonantes,*
> *Accestis fcopulos: vos et cyclopea faxa*
> *Experti, reuocate animos, mæftumque timorem*
> *Mittite,* **forfan et hæc olim** *meminiffe iuuabit.*
> *Per varios cafus, per* **tot** *difcrimina rerum*
> *Tendimus in Latium:* **fedes vbi fata quietas**
> *Ostendunt, illic fas regna* **refurgere troiæ.**
> *Durate, et vofmet rebus* **feruate fecundis.**
> *Talia voce refert, curifque ingentibus æger*
> **Spem vulta** *fimulat, premit altum corde dolorem.*

Tranflated thus.

And then to cheere their heauy harts with thefe words he him bent.
O Mates (quoth he) that many a woe haue bidden and borne ere thys,
Worfe haue we feene, and this alfo fhall end when Gods wyll is.
Through *Sylla* rage (ye wott) and through the roaring rocks we paft,
Though *Cyclops* fhore was full of feare, yet came we through at laft.

Plucke vppe your **harts, and driue** from thence both
feare and care away.
To thinke on this may pleasure be perhapps another day.
By paynes and many a daunger sore, by sundry chaunce
we wend,
To come to *Italy*, where we trust to find our resting ende:
And where the destnyes haue decreed ***Troyes*** Kingdome
eft to ryse
Be bold and harden now your harts, take ease while ease
applies
Thus spake he tho, but in his hart huge cares had him
oppreft,
Dissembling **hope with outward eyes** full heauy was his
breft.

Againe, marke the wounding **of *Dido* in** loue with
Æneas, with howe choyse wordes it is pithily described,
both by the Poet and the translator in the beginning
of the fourth booke.

*At Regina graui iam dudum **faucia cura***

Volnus alii venis, et cœco carpitur igni, etc.

By this time perced satte the Queene so sore with **loues**
desire,
Her wound in euery vayne she feedes, she **fryes in**
secrete fire.
The manhood of the man full oft, full oft his famous lyne
She doth reuolue, and from her thought his face cannot
vntwyne.
His countnaunce deepe she drawes and fixed fast she
beares in breft,
His words also, nor to her carefull hart can come no rest.

And in many places of the fourth booke is the same matter so gallantly prosecuted in sweete wordes, as in mine
opinion the **coppy it** selfe goeth no whit beyond it.
Compare them likewise in the woefull and lamentable

cryes of the Queene for the departure of *Æneas*, towards the ende of that Booke.

Terque quaterque manu pectus percussa decorum
Flauentisque abscissa **comas, proh** *Iupiter, ibit?*
Hic ait, et nostris inluserit aduena Regnis? *etc.*

Three times **her hands fhe** bet, and three times ftrake her comely **breft,**
Her golden **hayre fhe tare and** frantiklike with moode oppreft,
She **cryde,** O *Iupiter,* **O God,** quoth fhe, and fhall a goe?
Indeede? and fhall a flowte me thus within **my** kingdome fo?
Shall not mine Armies out, and all my people them purfue?
Shall they not fpoyle their fhyps and burne them vp with vengance due?
Out people, out vppon them, follow faft with fires and flames,
Set fayles aloft, make out with oares, in fhips, in boates, in frames.
What fpeake **I**? or where am **I**? what furies me doo thus inchaunt?
O *Dydo,* wofull wretch, now deftnyes fell thy head **dooth** haunt.

And a little after preparing **to** kyll her owne felfe.

But *Dydo* quaking fierce with frantike moode and griefly hewe.
With trembling fpotted cheekes, her huge attempting to perfue.
Befides **her** felfe for rage, and towards death with vifage **wanne,**
Her eyes about fhe rolde, as redde as blood they looked than.

At laſt ready to fall vppon *Æneas* ſworde.

O happy (welaway) and ouer happy had I beene,
If neuer Troian ſhyps (ahlas) my Country ſhore had ſeene.
Thus ſayd ſhe wryde her head, and vnreuenged muſt we die?
But let vs boldly die (quoth ſhee) thus, thus to death I ply.

Nowe likewiſe for the braue warlike phraſe and bygge ſounding kynd of thundring ſpeeche, in the hotte ſkyrmyſhes of battels, you may confer them in any of the laſt fiue Bookes: for examples ſake, thys is one about the ninth Booke.

> *Et clamor totis per propugnacula muris,*
> *Intendunt acries arcus, amentaque torquent.*
> *Sternitur omne ſolum telis, tum ſcutæ cauæque*
> *Dant ſonitum flictu galeæ: pugna asper ſurgit?* etc.

A clamarous noyſe vpmounts on fortreſſe tops and bulwarks towres,
They ſtrike, they bend their bowes, they whirle from ſtrings ſharp ſhoting ſhowres.
All ſtreetes with tooles are ſtrowed, than helmets, ſkulles, with battrings marrd.
And ſhieldes diſhyuering cracke, vpriſeth roughneſſe byckring hard
Looke how the tempeſt ſtorme when wind out wraſtling blowes at ſouth,
Raine ratling beates the grownde, or clowdes of haile from Winters mouth,
Downe daſhyng headlong driues, when God from ſkyes with grieſly ſteuen,
His watry ſhowres outwrings, and whirlwind clowdes downe breakes from heauen.

And ſo foorth much more of the like effect.

English Poetrie.

Onely one comparison more will I desire you to marke at your leysures, which may serue for all the rest, that is, the description of Fame, as it is in the 4. booke, towardes the end, of which it followeth thus.

Monstrum horrendum ingens **cui quot sunt** *corpore plumæ* **Tot** *vigilos oculi* **etc.**

Monster gastly great, for euery plume her carkasse, beares,
Like number learing eyes she hath, like number harkning eares,
Like number tongues, and mouthes she wagges, a wondrous thing to speake,
At midnight foorth shee flyes, and vnder shade her found dooth squeake.
All night she wakes, nor slumber sweete doth take nor neuer sleepes.
By dayes on houses tops shee sits or gates of Townes she keepes.
On watching Towres she clymbes, and Citties great she makes agast,
Both trueth and falshood forth she telles, and lyes abroade doth cast.

But what neede I to repeate any more places? there is not one Booke among the twelue, which wyll not yeelde you most excellent pleasure in conferring the translation with the Coppie, and marking the gallant grace which our Englishe speeche affoordeth. And in trueth the like comparisons, may you choose out through the whole translations of the *Metamorphosis* by Master *Golding* who (considering both their Coppyes) hath equally deserued commendations for the beautifying of the English speeche. It would be tedious to stay to rehearse any places out of him nowe: let the other suffice to prooue, that the English tongue lacketh neyther variety nor currantnesse of phrase for any matter.

Wyll nowe speake a little of an other kinde of poetical writing, which might notwithstanding for the variablenesse of the argument therein vsually handled, bee comprehended in those kindes before declared: that is, the compyling *Eglogues*, as much to say as Goteheardes tales, becauſe they bee commonly Dialogues or speeches framed or ſuppoſed betweene Sheepeheardes, Neteheardes, Goteheardes, or ſuch like ſimple men: in which kind of writing, many haue obtained as immortall prayſe and commendation, as in any other.

The cheefeſt of theſe is *Theocritus* in Greeke, next him, and almoſt the very ſame, is *Virgill* in Latin. After *Virgyl* in like ſort writ *Titus Calphurnius* and *Baptiſta Mantuan*, wyth many other both in Latine and other languages very learnedlye. Although the matter they take in hand ſeemeth commonlie in appearaunce rude and homely, as the vſuall talke of ſimple clownes: yet doo they indeede vtter in the ſame much pleaſaunt and profitable delight. For vnder theſe perſonnes, as it were in a cloake of ſimplicitie, they would eyther ſette foorth the prayſes of theyr freendes, without the note of flattery, or enueigh grieuouſly againſt abuſes, without any token of bytterneſſe.

Somwhat like vnto theſe works, are many peeces of *Chawcer*, but yet not altogether ſo poeticall. But nowe yet at ye laſt hath England hatched vppe one Poet of this ſorte, in my conſcience comparable with the beſt in any reſpect: euen Maſter *Sp*: Author of the *Sheepeheardes Calender*, whoſe trauell in that peece of Engliſh Poetrie, I thinke verely is ſo commendable, as none of equall iudgment can yeelde him leſſe prayſe for hys excellent **fkyll, and** fkylfull excellency fhewed foorth **in** the fame, then they would to eyther *Theocritus* or *Virgill*, whom in mine opinion, if the courfenes **of our** fpeeche (I **meane** the courfe of cuftome **which** he woulde not infringe) had **beene no more let vnto** him, then theyr **pure natiue** tongues were vnto them, he would haue **(if it might be)** furpaffed them. What one thing **is there in them** fo worthy admiration, whereunto we **may not** adioyne fome thing of his, of equall defert? Take *Virgil* and **make** fome little comparifon **betweene** them, and **iudge as ye** fhall fee **caufe.**

Virgill hath a gallant **report of** *Auguftus* couertly compryfed in the firft *Æglogue*: the like is in him, of her Maieftie, vnder the name of *Eliza*. *Virgill* maketh **a braue** coloured complaint of vnftedfaft freendfhyppe **in the** perfon of *Corydon*: the lyke is him in his 5 *Æglogue*. Agayne behold the pretty Paftorall **con**tentions of *Virgill* in the third *Æglogue*: of him in ye eight *Eglogue*. Finally, either **in** comparifon **with** them, **or** refpect of hys owne great learning, he may well **were the** Garlande, **and** fteppe **before ye** beft of **all** Englifh **Poets that I haue** feene **or hearde:** for I thinke no **leffe** deferueth **(thus** fayth *E*, *K* in hys commendations) hys wittineffe **in** deuifing, his pithineffe in vttering, his complaintes of loue fo louely, his difcourfes **of** pleafure **fo** pleafantly, **his** Paftrall rudenes, his Morrall wyfeneffe, his due obferuing of *decorum* euery where, **in** perfonages, **in feafon,** in matter, in fpeeche, and generally in **all feemely** fimplicity, of handling hys matter and framing hys wordes. The **occafion** of his worke is a warning to other young men, who being intangled in loue and youthfull vanities, may **learne** to looke to themfelues in time, and to auoyde inconueniences which may breede if they be not **in time** preuented. Many good Morrall leffons are therein contained, as the reuerence which young men owe **to the** aged in the fecond *Eglogue*: the caueate or warning to beware **a** fubtill profeffor of freendſhippe in the fift *Eglogue*: the commendation of good Paſtors, and ſhame and diſprayſe of idle and ambitious Goteheardes in the ſeauenth, the looſe and retchleſſe lyuing of Popiſh Prelates in the ninth. The learned and ſweete complaynt of the contempt of learning vnder the name of Poetry in the tenth. There is alſo much matter vttered ſomewhat couertly, eſpecially ye abuſes of ſome whom he would not be too playne withall: in which, though it be not apparant to euery one, what hys ſpeciall meaning was, yet ſo ſkilfully is it handled, as any man may take much delight at hys learned conueyance, and picke out much good ſence in the moſt obſcureſt of it. Hys notable prayſe deſerued in euery parcell of that worke, becauſe I cannot expreſſe as I woulde and as it ſhould: I wyll ceaſe to ſpeake any more of, the rather becauſe I neuer hearde as yet any that hath reade it, which hath not with much admiration commended it. One only thing therein haue I hearde ſome curious heades call in queſtion: *viz*: the motion of ſome vnſauery loue, ſuch as in the ſixt *Eglogue* he ſeemeth to deale withall (which ſay they) is ſkant allowable to Engliſh eares, and might well haue beene left for the Italian defenders of loathſome beaſtlines, of whom perhappes he learned it: to thys obiection I haue often aunſwered and (I thinke truely) that theyr nyce opinion ouer ſhooteth the Poets meaning, who though hee in that as in other thinges, immitateth the auncient Poets, yet doth not meane, no more did they before hym, any diſordered loue, or the filthy luſt of the deuilliſh *Pederaſtice* taken in the worſe ſence, but rather to ſhewe howe the diſſolute life of young men intangled in loue of women, doo neglect the freendſhyp and league with their olde freendes and familiers. Why (ſay they) yet he ſhold gyue no occaſion of ſuſpition, nor offer to the viewe of Chriſtians, any token of ſuch filthineſſe, howe good ſoeuer hys meaning were: whereunto I oppoſe the ſimple conceyte they haue of matters which concerne learning or wytt, wylling them to gyue

Poets leaue to vfe theyr vayne as they fee good: it is their foolyfh conftruction, not hys wryting that is blameable. Wee muft prefcrybe to no wryters, (much leffe to Poets) in what forte they fhould vtter theyr **conceyts.** But thys wyll be better difcuffed by **fome I hope of** better abillity.

One other forte of Poeticall wryters remayneth yet to bee remembred, that is, The precepts of Hufbandry, learnedly compiled in Heroycall verfe. Such were the workes of *Hefiodus* in *Greeke*, and *Virgils Georgickes* in Latine. What memorable worke hath beene handled in **immitation** of thefe by any Englifh Poet, I know not, (faue onely one worke **of M.** *Tuffer*, **a** peece **furely of** great wytt and experience, and wythal very **prettilye** handled) And **I** thinke the caufe why our **Poets haue not** trauayled in that behalfe, is efpecially, **for that** there haue beene alwayes plenty of other wryters that haue handled the fame argument very largely. Among whom Mafter *Barnabe Googe*, in tranflating and enlarging the moft **profitable** worke of *Hercsbachius*, hath deferued **much commendation, as** well for hys faythfull compyling and learned increafing the noble worke, as for hys wytty tranflation of a good part **of the** *Georgickes* of *Virgill* **into** Englifh verfe.

Among all the tranflations, which hath beene my fortune to fee, **I could neuer yet finde** that worke of the *Georgicks* **wholly** performed. I remember once Abraham Flemming **in** his conuerfion of the *Eglogues*, promifed to tranflate and publifhe it: whether he dyd **or not** I knowe not, **but as** yet I heard not of it. I my **felfe** wott well I beftowed fome **time** in it two or three yeeres fince, turning **it** to that fame Englifh verfe, which other fuch workes were in, though it were rudely: howe beit, **I** did **it** onely for mine owne vfe, and vppon certayne refpectes towardes a Gentleman mine efpeciall freende, to whom I was defirous **to** fhewe fome token **of** duetifull good wyll, and not minding it fhould goe **farre** abroade, confidering howe flenderly I ranne it ouer, yet fince then, hath one gott it in keeping, who as it is told me, eyther hath or wyll vnaduifedly publifhe it: which iniury though he meanes to doo me in myrth, yet I hope he wyll make me fome fuffycient recompence, or els I fhall goe neere to watch hym the like or a worfe turne.

But concerning the matter of our Englyfh wryters, lett thys fuffice: nowe fhall ye heare my fimple fkyl in what I am able to fay concerning the forme and manner of our Englyfhe verfe.

The moft vfuall and frequented kind of our Englifh Poetry hath alwayes runne vpon, and to this day is obferued in fuch equall number of fyllables, and likenes of wordes, that in all places one verfe either immediatly, or by mutuall interpofition, may be aunfwerable to an other both in proportion of length, and ending of lynes in the fame Letters. Which rude kinde of verfe, though (as I touched before) it rather difcrediteth our fpeeche, as borrowed from the *Barbarians*, then furnifheth the fame with any comely ornament: yet beeing fo ingraffed by cuftome, and frequented by the moft parte, I may not vtterly diffalowe it, leaft I fhould feeme to call in queftion the iudgement of all our famous wryters, which haue wonne eternall prayfe by theyr memorable workes compyled in that verfe.

For my part therefore, I can be content to efteeme it as a thing, the perfection whereof is very commendable, yet fo as wyth others I could wyfh it were by men of learning and ability bettered, and made more artificiall, according to the woorthines of our fpeeche.

The falling out of verfes together in one like founde, is commonly called in Englifh, Ryme, taken from the Greeke worde Ρυθμος, which furely in my iudgment is verye abufiuelye applyed to fuch a fence: and by thys, the vnworthineffe of the thing may well appeare, in that wanting a proper name, wherby to be called, it borroweth a word farre exceeding the dignitye of it,

and not appropriate to fo rude or bafe a thing. For
Ryme is properly, the iuft proportion of a claufe or
fentence, whether it be in profe or meeter, aptly comprifed together : wherof there is both **an naturall and**
an artificiall compofition, in any **manner** or kynde of
fpeeche, eyther French, **Italian,** Spanifh **or** Englifh :
and is propper not onely **to Poets,** but alfo to Readers,
Oratours, Pleaders, or any which are to pronounce or
fpeake any thing **in pu**blike audience.

The firft **begynning** of **Ryme** (as we nowe terme **it**)
though **it be fomewhat** auncient, yet nothing famous.
In Greece **(they** fay) **one** *Symias Rhodias*, becaufe he
would be finguler in fomthing, wryt poetically of the
Fable, contayning howe *Iupiter* beeing in fhape **of a**
Swanne, begatte the Egge **on** Leda, wherof **came**
Caftor, Pollux, and Helena, whereof euery verfe ended
in thys Ryme, and was called therefore ὠον but thys
foolyfhe attempt was fo contemned and difpyfed,
that the people would neither admitte the Author nor
Booke any place in memory of learning. Since that
it was not hearde **of, till** ye time ye *Hunnes* **and**
Gothians **renued** it agayne, and **brought it** into Italie.
But howfoeuer or wherefoeuer it beganne, certayne it
is, that in our Englifh tongue it beareth as good grace,
or rather better, then **in any other :** and is a faculty
whereby many may **and doo** deferue great prayfe and
commendation, though our fpeeche be capable of a
farre more learned manner of verfifying, as I wyl **partly**
declare heereafter.

There be three fpeciall notes neceffary to be **obferued**
in the framing of our accuftomed Englifh Ryme : the
firft **is,** that one meeter **or** verfe be aunfwerable to an
other, **in** equall number of feete or fyllables, or pro-
portiona**ble** to the tune whereby it is to be reade or
meafured. The feconde, to place **the** words in fuch
forte, as **none** of them be wrefted contrary to the
naturall inclination or affectation of the fame, or more
truely ye true quantity thereof. The thyrd, to make
them fall together mutually in Ryme, that is, in wordes

of like founde, but so as the wordes be not disordered for the Rymes sake, nor the sence hindered. These be the most pryncipall obseruations, which I thinke requisite in an English verse: for as for the other ornaments which belong thereto, they be more properly belonging to the seuerall gyfts of skylfull Poets, then common notes to be prescribed by me: but somewhat perhaps I shall haue occasion to speake heereafter.

Of the kyndes of English verses which differ in number of syllables, there are almost infinite: which euery way alter according to hys fancy, or to the measure of that meeter, wherein it pleaseth hym to frame hys ditty. Of the best and most frequented I wyll rehearse some. The longest verse in length, which I haue seene vsed in English consisteth of sixteene syllables, eache two verses ryming together, thus.

Wher vertue wants and vice abounds, there wealth is but a bayted hooke,
To make men swallow down their bane, before on danger deepe they looke.

Thys kynde is not very much vsed at length thus, but is commonly deuided, eche verse into two, whereof eche shal containe eyght syllables, and ryme crosse wyse, the first to the thyrd, and the second to the fourth, in this manner.

> Great wealth is but a bayted hooke.
> VVhere vertue wants, and vice aboundes:
> VVhich men deuoure before they looke,
> So them in daungers deepe it drownes.

An other kynd next in length to thys, is, where eche verse hath fourteene syllables, which is the most accustomed of all other, and especially vsed of all the translatours of the Latine Poets for the most part thus.

My mind with furye fierce inflamde of late I know not howe,
Doth burne Parnassus hyll to see, adornd wyth Lawrell bowe.

Which may likewyse and so it often is deuyded, eche

Englifh Poetrie.

verfe into two, to [the?] firft hauing eyght fillables, the fecond fixe, wherof the two fixes fhall alwayes ryme, and fometimes the eyghtes, fometimes not, according to the wyll of the maker.

> My minde with furye fierce inflamde,
>   Of late I knowe not howe :
> Doth burne *Pernaffus* hyll to fee,
>   Adornd wyth Lawrell bowe.

There are nowe wythin this compaffe, as many fortes of verfes as may be deuifed differences of numbers: wherof fome confift of equall proportions, fome of long and fhort together, fome of many rymes in one ftaffe (as they call it) fome of croffe ryme, fome of counter ryme, fome ryming wyth one worde farre diftant from another, fome ryming euery thyrd or fourth word, and fo likewyfe all manner of dytties applyable to euery tune that may be fung or fay'd, diftinct from profe or continued fpeeche. To auoyde therefore tedioufneffe and confufion, I wyll repeate onely the different fortes of verfes out of the *Sheepeheardes Calender*, which may well ferue to beare authoritie in thys matter.

There are in that worke twelue or thirteene fundry forts of verfes, which differ eyther in length, or ryme, of deftinction of the ftaues: but of them which differ in length or number of fillables not paft fixe or feauen. The firft of them is of tenne fillables, or rather fiue feete in one verfe, thus,

> A Sheepheards boy no better doo him call,
> When Winters waftfull fpight was almoft fpent.

This verfe he vfeth commonly in hys fweete complayntes, and mornefull ditties, as very agreeable to fuch affections.

The fecond fort hath naturally but nyne fyllables, and is a more rough or clownifh manner of verfe, vfed moft commonly of him if you mark him in hys satyricall reprehenfions, and his Sheepeheardes homelyeſt talke, ſuch as the ſecond *Æglogue* is.

> Ah for pitty wyll rancke **Winters** rage,
> Theſe bytter blaſts **neuer gynne to** aſſwage.

The number of nine fillables in **thys verſe is very** often altered, and ſo it may without any **diſgrace to** the fame, eſpecially where the ſpeeche fhould be moſt **clowniſh** and ſimple, which is much obſerued of hym.

The third kynd is a pretty rounde **verſe, running** currantly together, commonly feauen fillables **or ſome**time eyght in one verſe, as many in the next, **both** ryming together: euery two hauing one the like verſe after them, but of rounder wordes, **and** two of them likewyſe ryming mutually. That verſe expreſſeth notably, light and youthfull talke, **fuch** as is the thyrde *Æglogue* betweene two Sheepheardes boys concerning loue.

> *Thomalin* why ſitten we ſo
> As weren ouerwent with woe
> Vpon ſo fayre a morrowe?
> The ioyous time now nigheth faſt
> That wyll allay **this** bitter blaſt
> And flake the Winter ſorrow.

The fourth fort containeth in eche **ſtaffe** manie vnequall verſes, but **moſt** fweetelie falling together: which the Poet calleth the tune of the waters fall. Therein is his ſong In **prayſe** of *Eliza.*

> Ye daintie Nymphes which in this bleſſed brooke
>   doo bathe your breſt,
> Forſake your **watrie** bowres **and hether** looke,
>   at my **requeſt**.
> And eke yee Virgins that on *Parnafs* dwell,
> Whence floweth *Helicon* the learned Well,
>   helpe **me to** blaze
>   her **woorthy praiſe**
> That in her **fex doth all excell**. etc.

English Poetrie.

The fift, is a deuided verfe of twelue fillables into two verfes, whereof I fpake before, and feemeth moft meete for ye handling of a Morrall matter, fuch as is the praife of good Paftors, and the difpraife of ill in the feauenth *Æglogue*.

The fixt kinde, is called a round, beeing mutuallie fung betweene two: one fingeth one verfe, the other the next, eche rymeth with himfelfe.

> **Per.** It fell vppon a holie eue
> **Wyl.** Hey ho holliday
> **Per.** When holie fathers wont to fhrieue,
> **Wyl.** Thus ginneth our Rondelay. etc.

The feauenth forte is a verie tragicall mournefull meafure, wherein he bewayleth the death of fome freend vnder the perfon of *Dydo*.

> Vp then *Melpomene* the mournfulft Mufe of nyne,
>   fuch caufe of mourning neuer hadft afore:
> Vp griefly ghoftes, and vp my mournfull ryme:
>   matter of myrth now fhalt thou haue no more.
>   *Dydo* my deere alas is dead,
>   Dead and lyeth wrapt in leade:
>   O heauie hearfe
> Let ftreaming teares be powred out in ftore
>   O carefull vearfe.

Thefe fortes of verfes for breuities fake haue I chofen foorth of him, whereby I fhall auoide the tedious rehearfall of all the kindes which are vfed: which I thinke would haue beene vnpoffible, feeing they may be altered to as manie formes as the Poets pleafe: neither is there anie tune or ftroke which may be fung or plaide on inftruments, which hath not fome poetical ditties framed according to the numbers thereof: fome to Rogero, fome to Trenchmore, to downe right Squire, to Galliardes, to Pauines, to Iygges, to Brawles, to all manner of tunes which euerie Fidler knowes better then my felfe, and therefore I will let them paffe.

Againe, the diuersities of the staues (which are the number of verses contained with the diuisions or partitions of a ditty) doo often times make great differences in these verses. As when one staffe containeth but two verses, or (if they bee deuided) foure: the first or the first couple hauing twelue sillables, the other fourteene, which versifyers call Powlters measure, because so they tall[i]e their wares by dozens. Also, when one staffe hath manie verses, whereof eche one rimeth to the next, or mutuallie crosse, or distant by three, or by foure, or ended contrarye to the beginning, and a hundred sortes, whereof to shewe seuerall examples, would bee too troublesome: nowe for the second point.

The naturall course of most English verses seemeth to run vppon the olde Iambicke stroake, and I may well thinke by all likelihoode, it had the beginning thereof. For if you marke the right quantitie of our vsuall verses, ye shall perceiue them to containe in sound ye very propertie of Iambick feete, as thus.

∪ — ∪ — ∪ — ∪ — ∪ — ∪ — ∪ —
I that my slender oaten pipe in verse was wont to sounde:

For transpose anie of those feete in pronouncing, and make short either the two, foure, sixe, eight, tenne, twelue sillable, and it will (doo what you can) fall out very absurdly.

Againe, though our wordes can not well bee forced to abyde the touch of *Position* and other rules of *Prosodia*, yet is there such a naturall force or quantity in eche worde, that it will not abide anie place but one, without some foule disgrace: as for example try anie verse, as thys,

∪ — ∪ — ∪ — ∪ — ∪ — ∪ — ∪ —
Of shapes transformde to bodies strange I purpose to intreate.

Make the first sillable long, or the third, or the fift and so foorth: or contrariwise make the other sillables to admitte the shortnesse of one of them places, and see

English Poetrie.

what a wonderfull defacing it wil be to the wordes, as thus.

— ͝ — ͝ — ͝ — ͝ — ͝ — ͝ — ͝
Of ſtrange bodies tranſformd to ſhapes purpoſe I to intreat.

So that this is one eſpeciall thing to be taken heede of in making a good Engliſh verſe, that by diſplacing no worde bee wreſted againſt his naturall propriety, wherevnto you ſhal perceyue eche worde to be affected, and may eaſilie diſcerne it in wordes of two ſillables or aboue, though ſome there be of indifferencie, that wyll ſtand in any place. Againe, in chouching the whole ſentence, the like regarde is to be had, that wee exceede not too boldly in placing the verbe out of his order, and too farre behinde the nowne: which the neceſſitie of Ryme may oftentimes vrge. For though it be tollerable in a verſe to ſette wordes ſo extraordinarily as other ſpeeche will not admit, yet heede is to be taken, leaſt by too much affecting that manner, we make both the verſe vnpleaſant and the ſence obſcure. And ſure it is a wonder to ſee the folly of manie in this reſpect, that vſe not onely too much of thys ouerthwart placing, or rather diſplacing of wordes, in theyr Poemes and verſes, but alſo in theyr proſe or continued writings: where they thinke to rolle moſt ſmoothlie, and flow moſt eloquently, there by this means, come foorth theyr ſentences dragging at one Authors tayle as they were tyde together with poynts, where often you ſhall tarrie (ſcratching your heade) a good ſpace before you ſhall heare hys principall verbe or ſpeciall word, leaſte hys ſinging grace, which in his ſentence is contained ſhould be leſſe, and his ſpeeche ſeeme nothing poeticall.

The thyrd obſeruation is, the Ryme or like ending of verſes: which though it is of leaſt importance, yet hath won ſuch credite among vs, that of all other it is moſt regarded of the greateſt part of Readers. And ſurely as I am perſwaded, the regarde of wryters to this, hath beene the greateſt decay of that good order of verſifying, which might ere this haue beene eſtabliſhed

in our fpeeche. In my iudgment, if there be any **ornament in the fame, it is rather to** be attributed to the
plentifull fulneffe **of** our fpeeche, which **can** affoorde
ryming words fufficient for the handling of any matter,
then **to the thing it** felfe **for any** beautifying it bringeth
to **a worke:** which might bee adorned with farre more
excellent collours then ryming is. Notwithftanding I
cannot but yeelde vnto it (as cuftome **requireth)** the
deferued prayfes, efpecially where it is with **good iudgement** ordered. And I thinke them right **worthy** of
admiration, for their readines and plenty of wytt **and**
capacity, who can with facility intreate at large, **and
as** we call it *extempore*, in good and fencible ryme,
vppon fome vnacquainted matter.

The ready fkyll of framing anie thing in verfe, befides
the naturall promptneffe which many haue therevnto,
is much helped by Arte, and exercife of the memory:
for as I remember, **I** reade once among *Gaskoynes*
workes, a little inftruction to **verfifying,** where is prefcribed as **I** thinke thys **courfe of** learning to verfifye
in Ryme.

When ye haue one verfe well fetled, and decently
ordered which you may difpofe at your pleafure, to
ende it with what word you wyll: then what foeuer **the
word is,** you may fpeedilie runne **ouer the** other wordes
which are aunfwerable therevnto, (for more readines
through all the letters Alphabetically) whereof you may
choofe that which wyll beft fitte the fence of your matter
in that **place:** as for example: if your **laft worde** ende
in Booke, you may ftraightwayes in your minde runne
them ouer thus. Brooke, Cooke, crooke, hooke, looke,
nooke, pooke, rooke, forfooke, **tooke,** awooke etc.
Nowe it is twenty to one, **but alwayes** one of thefe fhall
iumpe with your **former worde and** matter in **good
fence.** If not, then **alter the firft.**

And indeede **I thinke, that** next to the Arte **of**
memory, thys is the readyeft way to attaine **to the**
faculty of ryming well Extempore, efpecially if it be
helped with thus much paynes. Gather together all

manner of wordes especially *Monasillables*, and place them Alphabetically in some note, and either haue them meetely perfectly by hart (which is no verye laboursome matter) or but looke them dilligently ouer at some time, practising to ryme indifferent often, whereby I am perswaded it wil soone be learned, so as the party haue withall any reasonable gyft of knowledge and learning, whereby hee want not bothe matter and wordes altogether.

What the other circumstaunces of Ryming are, as what wordes may tollerably be placed in Ryme, and what not: what words doo best become a Ryme, and what not, how many sortes of Ryme there is: and such like I wyll not stay nowe to intreate. There be many more obseruations and notes to be prescribed, to the exacte knowledge of versifying, which I trust wilbe better and larger laide forth by others, to whom I deferre manie considerations in this treatise: hoping that some of greater skill will shortlie handle this matter in better sorte.

Nowe the sundry kindes of rare deuises, and pretty inuentions which come from ye fine poeticall vaine of manie in strange and vnacustomed manner, if I could report them, it were worthie my trauell: such are the turning of verses: the infolding of wordes: the fine repititions: the clarklie conueying of contraries, and manie such like. Whereof though I coulde sette downe manie: yet becaufe I want bothe manie and the best kindes of them, I will ouerpasse: onelie pointing you to one or two which may suffice for example.

Looke vppon the rufull song of *Colin* sung by *Cuddie* in the *Sheepheardes Calender*, where you shall see a singuler rare deuise of a dittie framed vpon these sixe wordes *VVoe, sounde, cryes, pact, sleep, augment*, which are most prettilie turned and wounde vppe mutually together, expressing wonderfully the dolefulnesse of the song. A deuise not much vnlike vnto the same, is vsed by some, who taking the last wordes of a certaine number of verses, as it were by the rebound

of an *Echo*, ſhall make them fall out in ſome prettie
fence.

Of this ſorte there are ſome deuiſed by *Iohn Graunge*,
which becauſe they be not long I wyll rehearſe one.

If feare oppreſſe howe then may hope me ſhielde?
Denyall ſayes, vayne hope hath pleaſed well,
But as ſuch hope thou wouldeſt not be thine,
So would I not the like to rule my hart.
For if thou loueſt it bidds thee graunt forthwith
Which is the ioy whereof I liue in hope.

Here if you take the laſt worde of euerie verſe, and
place them orderlie together, you ſhall haue this ſentence: *Shielde well thyne hart with hope.* But of
theſe *Echoes* I knowe indeede verie daintie peeces of
worke, among ſome of the fineſt Poets this day in London: who for the rareneſſe of them keepe them priuelie
to themſelues, and wil not let them come abroad.

A like inuention to the laſt rehearſed, or rather a
better, haue I ſeene often practiſed in framing a whole
dittie to the Letters of ones name, or to the wordes of
ſome two or three verſes which is very witty, as for
example this is one of *W. Hunnis*, which for the
ſhortnes I rather chuſde then ſome yat are better.

If thou deſire to liue in quiet reſt,
Gyue eare and ſee, but ſay the beſt.

Theſe two verſes are nowe as it were reſolued into
dyuers other, euery two wordes or ſillables being the
beginning of an other like verſe, in this ſort.

If thou   ⎧ delight in quietnes of life,
Deſire   ⎪ to ſhunne from brawles, debate and ſtrife:
To liue   ⎨ in loue with G O D, with freend and foe,
In rest   ⎩ ſhalt ſleepe when other cannot ſo.

Gyue eare ⎧ to all, yet doo not all beleeue,
And ſee   ⎪ the end and then thy ſentence gyue:
But ſay   ⎨ For trueth of happy liues aſſignde
The best ⎩ hath he that quiet is in minde.

Thus are there infinite fortes of fine conueiances (as they may be termed) to be vfed, and are much frequented by verfifyers, as well in compofition of their verfe, as the wittines of their matter: which all I will referre to the confideration of euerie pleafant headded Poet in their proper gifts: onelie I fett downe thefe fewe fortes of their formes of verfifying, which may ftand in fteede to declare what manie others may be deuifed in like forte.

But nowe to proceede to the reformed kind of Englifh verfe which manie haue before this, attempted to put in practife, and to eftablifh for an accuftomed right among Englifh Poets, you fhall heare in like manner my fimple iudgment concerning the fame.

I am fully and certainlie perfwaded, that if the true kind of verfifying in immitation of Greekes and Latines, had beene practifed in the Englifh tongue, and put in vre from time to tyme by our Poets, who might haue continually beene mending and pollyfhing the fame, euery one according to their feuerall giftes: it would long ere this haue afpyred to as full perfection, as in anie other tongue whatfoeuer. For why may I not thinke fo of our Englifh, feeing that among the Romaines a long time, yea euen till the dayes of *Tully*, they efteemed not the Latine Poetrie almoft worth any thing, in refpecte of the Greeke, as appeareth in the Oration *pro Archia Poeta*: yet afterwardes it increafed in credite more and more, and that in fhort fpace: fo that in *Virgilles* time, wherein were they not comparable with the Greekes? So likewife, now it feemeth not currant for an Englifh verfe to runne vpon true quantity, and thofe feete which the Latines vfe, becaufe it is ftraunge, and the other barbarous cuftome, beeing within compaffe of euery bafe witt, hath worne it out of credite or eftimation. But if our wryters, beeing of learning and iudgment, would rather infringe thys curious cuftome, then omitte the occafion of inlarging the credite of their natiue fpeeche, and theyr owne prayfes, by practifing that commendable kind of wryting in true verfe: then no doubt, as in other partes of learning, fo in Poetry, fhoulde not ftoupe to the beft of them all in all maner of ornament and comlineffe. But fome obiect that our wordes are nothing refemblaunt in nature to theirs, and therefore not poffible to bee framed with any good grace after their vfe: but cannot we then as well as the Latines did, alter the cannon of the rule according to the quality of our worde, and where our wordes and theyrs wyll agree, there to iumpe with them, where they will not agree, there to eftablifh a rule of our owne to be directed by? Likewife, for ye tenor of the verfe might we not (as *Horace* dyd in the Latine) alter their proportions to what fortes we lifted, and to what we fawe wold beft become the nature of the thing handled, or the quallity of the words? Surely it is to be thought that if any one, of found iudgment and learning, fhoulde putt foorth fome famous worke, contayning dyuers formes of true verfes, fitting the meafures, according to the matter: it would of it felfe be a fufficient authority without any prefcription of rules, to the moft part of Poets, for them to follow and by cuftome to ratify. For fure it is, that the rules and principles of Poetry, were not precifely followed and obferued of the firft beginners and wryters of Poetry, but were felected and gathered feuerally out of theyr workes, for the direction and behoofe of their followers. And indeede, he that fhall with heedefull iudgment make tryall of the Englifh wordes, fhall not finde them fo groffe or vnapt, but that they wyll become any one of ye moft accuftomed fortes of Latine or Greeke verfes meetely, and run thereon fomewhat currantly.

    I my felfe, with fimple fkyll I confeffe, and farre vnable iudgment, haue ventured on a fewe, which notwithftanding the rudenes of them may ferue to fhewe what better might bee brought into our fpeeche, if thofe which are of meete abilitye woulde beftowe fome trauell and endeuour thereuppon. But before I fette them downe, I wyll fpeake fomewhat of fuch obferuations as

I could gather neceſſary to the knowledge of theſe kinde of verſes, leaſt I ſhould ſeeme to runne vpon them raſhly, without regarde either of example **or** authority.

The ſpeciall poyntes of a **true** verſe, are the due obſeruations of the feete, and place of the feete.

The foote of a verſe, is a meaſure of two ſillables, or of three, diſtinguiſhed by time which is eyther long or ſhort. A foote **of two** ſillables, is eyther ſimple or mixt, that is, of like time or of diuers. A ſimple foote of two ſillables is likewiſe twofolde, eyther of two long ſillables called *Spondæus*, as – – *goodneſſe*, **or of** two ſhort called *Pyrrichius* as ◡ ◡ *hyther*. A myxt foote of **2.** ſillables, is eyther of one ſhort and one long called *Iambus* as ◡ – *dying*: or of one long and one ſhort, called *Choreus* as – ◡ *gladly*. A foote of 3. ſillables in like ſorte is either ſimple or myxt. The ſimple is eyther *Moloſſus*, that is of three long, as – – – *forgiuenes*: or *Trochæus*, that is of 3. ſhort, as ◡ ◡ ◡ *merylie*. The mixt is of 6. diuers ſortes, **1.** *Dactylus*, of one **long**, and two ſhort, as – ◡ ◡ *happily*. 2. *Anapætus*, **of two** ſhorte, and one long, as ◡ ◡ – *t[r]auelers*. 3. *Bacchius*, **of** one ſhort, and two long, as ◡ – – *remembrers*. 4. *Palimbachius*, of two long and one ſhort, as – – ◡ *accorded*. 5. *Creticus* of a long, a ſhort, and a long, – ◡ – *daungerous*. 6. *Amphibrachus*, of a ſhort, a long, and a ſhort, as ◡ – ◡ *reioyced*.

Many more deuiſions of feete are vſed by ſome, but theſe doo more artificially comprehende all quantities neceſſary to the ſkanning of any verſe, according to *Tallæus* in hys Rethorique. The place of the feete is the diſpoſing of them in theyr propper roomes, whereby may be diſcerned the difference of eche verſe which is the right numbring of the ſame. Now as for the quantity of our wordes, therein lyeth great difficultye, and the cheefeſt matter in this faculty. For in truth there being **ſuch** diuerſity betwixt our words and the Latine, it cannot ſtande indeede with great reaſon that they ſhoulde frame, wee beeing onelie directed by ſuch rules

… as ſerue for onely Latine words, yet notwithſtanding one may well perceiue by theſe fewe, that theſe kinde of verſes would well become the ſpeeche, if ſo bee there were ſuch Rules preſcribed, as woulde admitt the placing of your apteſt and fulleſt wordes together. For indeede excepting a fewe, of our *Monaſyllables*, which naturally ſhoulde moſt of them be long, we haue almoſt none, that wyll ſtande fitlie in a ſhort foote: and therfore if ſome exception were made againſt the preciſe obſeruation of *Poſition*, and certaine other of the rules, then might we haue as great plenty and choyſe of good woordes to furniſh and ſette foorth a verſe, as in any other tongue.

Likewiſe if there were ſome derection in ſuch wordes, as fall not within the compaſſe of Greeke or Latine rules, it were a great helpe, and therefore I had great miſſe in theſe few which I made. Such as is the laſt fillable in theſe wordes, *able*, *noble*, or *poſſible* and ſuch like: againe for the nature and force of our *W.* of our *th*, of our *oo*, and *ee*, of our wordes which admytte an *e* in the ende after one or two Conſonantes, and many other. I for my part, though (I muſt needes confeſſe) many faultes eſcaped me in theſe fewe, yet tooke I as good heede as I coulde, and in trueth did rather alwaies omitt the beſt wordes and ſuch as would naturally become the ſpeech beſt, then I wolde committe any thing, which ſhoulde notoriouſly impugne the Latine rules, which herein I had onely for my direction. Indeede moſt of our *Monaſyllables* I am forced to make ſhort, to ſupply the want of many ſhort wordes requiſite in theſe verſes. The Participle *A*, being but the Engliſh article adioyned to Nownes, I alwayes make ſhort, both alone and in compoſition, and likewiſe the wordes of one fillable ending in *E*, as *the*, when it is an article, *he*, *ſhe*, *ye*, etc. *we* I thinke ſhould needes be alwayes long becauſe we pronounce continually *VVe*. *I*, beeing alone ſtanding for the Pronowne *Ego*, in my iudgment might well be vſed common: but becauſe I neuer ſawe it vſed but ſhort I ſo obſerued it. Words ending in *y*

Englifh Poetrie.

I make fhort without doubt, fauing that I haue marked in others one difference which they vfe in the fame, that is to make it fhort in the ende ◡ of an Aduerb, as *gladly*, and long in the ende – of an Adiectiue as *goodly*: but the reafon is as I take it, becaufe the Adiectiue is or fhould be moft commonly written thus *goodlie*. *O*, beeing an Aduerbe is naturally long: in the ende of wordes both *Monafyllables* and **other** I thinke it may be vfed **common**. The firft of *Pollifyllables* I directed according **to the** nature of the worde, **as** I thought moft auniwerable **to** Latine examples, fauing that **fomewhere** I am conftrayned to ftraine curtefy with the prepofition of a **worde** compounded or fuch like, which breaketh **no** great fquare: as in *defence* or *depart*, etc. The myddle fillables which are not very many, come for the moft part vnder the precinct of *Pofition*, whereof fome of them will not poffibly abide the touch, and therfore muft needes be a little wrefted: fuch are commonly ye Aduerbs of three fillables, as *mournfully, fpyghtfully* and fuch like words, deriued of this Adiectiue, *full*: and therfore if there be great occafion to vfe them, **they** muft be reformed by detracting onely (*l*) and then **they** ftand meetely currant, as *mournfuly*. The laft fillables I wholly directed fo neere as I could to the touch of common rules.

The moft famous verfe of all the reft, is called *Hexametrum Epicum*, which confifteth of fixe feete, wherof the firft foure are indifferently either *Spondæi* or *Dactyli*, the fift is euermore a *dactyl*, aud the fixt a *Spondæ*, as thus.

— ◡ — — ◡ ◡ — — — — — ◡ ◡ — —
Tyterus happily thou liest tumbling vnder **a** *beetchtree.*

Thys kinde of verfe I haue onely feene to be practifed in our Englifh fpeeche: and indeede wyll ftand fomewhat more orderlye therein then any of the other kindes, vntill we haue fome tolleration of wordes made by fpeciall rule. The firft that attempted to practife thys verfe in Englifh, fhould feeme to be the Earle of **Surry**, who tranflated fome part of *Virgill* into verfe indeede, but without regard of true quantity of fillables. There is one famous *Diſtichon*, which is common in the mouthes of all men, that was made by one Maſter VVatſon, fellowe of S. *Iohns* Colledge in Cambrydge about 40. yeeres paſt, which for the ſweetnes and gallantnes therof in all reſpects doth mat[c]h and ſurpaſſe the Latine coppy of *Horace*, which he made out of *Homers* wordes, *qui mores hominum etc.*

— ‿ ‿ — — — ‿ ‿ — — — — ‿ ‿ — —
All trauellers doo gladlie report great praiſe to Vliſſes

— ‿ ‿ — ‿ ‿ — — — — ‿ ‿ — —
For that he knewe manie mens maners, and ſavv many citties.

Which two verſes if they be examined throughout all the rules and obſeruations of the beſt verſifying, ſhall bee founde to attaine the very perfection of them all. There be two other not much inferiour to theſe, which I found in ye Gloſſe of *E. K.* vppon the fift *Æglogue* of the newe Poet: which Tully tranſlated out of Greeke into Latine, *Hæc habui quæ edi etc.*

All that I eate did I ioy and all that I greedilie gorged.

— — — ‿ ‿ — — — — ‿ ‿ — —
As for thoſe manie goodlie matters left J for others.

Which though they wyll not abide the touch of *Synalæpha* in one or two places, yet perhappes ſome Engliſh rule which might wyth good reaſon be eſtabliſhed, would make them currant enough, and auoyde that inconuenience which is very obuious in our **wordes.** The great company **of** famous **verſes** of thys **ſort,** which Maſter *Haruey* made, **is not** vnknowne to any and are to be viewed at all times. **I** for my part, ſo farre as thoſe examples would leade me, and mine owne ſmall ſkyll affoorde me, haue blundered vppon theſe fewe, whereinto I haue tranſlated the two firſt Æglogues of Virgill: becauſe I thought no matter of mine owne inuention, nor any other of antiquitye more fitte for tryal of thys thyng, before there were ſome more ſpeciall direction, which might leade to a leſſe troubleſome manner of wryting.

The Argument of the first
Æglogue.

Vnder the perfonne of *Tityrus Vyrgill* beeing figured himfelfe, declareth to *Melibeus* an nother Neateheard, the great benefittes he receyued at *Auguſtus* hand, who in the ſpoyle of *Mantua* gaue him hys goods and ſubſtaunce againe.

𝕸𝖊𝖑𝖎𝖇𝖆𝖈𝖚𝖘.   𝕿𝖎𝖙𝖞𝖗𝖚𝖘.

*T Ityrus, happilie thou lyste tumbling vnder a **beech tree**,
All in a fine oate pipe thefe fvveete fongs lustilie chaunting:
VVe, poore foules goe to wracke, and from thefe coastes beremooued,
And fro our pastures fvveete:* **thou** *Tityr, at eafe in* **a shade plott**
Makst thicke groues to refound vvith **fonges** *of braue* Amarillis.

𝕿𝖎𝖙𝖞𝖗𝖚𝖘.

O Melibæus, *he vvas no man but a God vvho receeude me:*
Euer he shalbe my God: from this fame Sheepcot his alters
Neuer, a tender Lambe shall vvant, with blood to bedevv them.
This good gift did he giue, to my steeres thus freelie **to** *vvander,*
And to my felfe (thou feest) **on** *pipe to refound vvhat* 𝓕 *lifted.*

Melibaeus.

*Grutch thee sure **I** doo not, but this thing makes me to wonder,*
Whence comes all this adoo: with grieeuous paine not a little
*Can I **remooue** my Goates: here, Tityre skant get I forward*
Poore olde crone, two twyns at a clappe ith boysterous hasilles
*Left she behind, best hope i' my flock laid **hard on a bare** stone.*
*Had not a luckleffe lotte poffest **our** mindes, I remember*
*Warnings oft fro the blast burnt oake we sawv to **be sent vs.***
*Oft did a left hand crow foretell these thinges **in her** hull **tree,***
But this God let vs heare what he was, good Tityre tell me.

Tityrus.

That fame Cittie so braue which Rome was wont to be called,
Foole did I thinke, to be like this of ours, where we to the pastures
Wonted were to remooue from dammes our young prettie Cattell.
Thus did I thinke young whelpes, and Kids to be like to the
    mothers,
*Thus did I wont compare manie great thinges with many **little**.*
*But this aboue all townes **as** loftily mounteth her **high** head,*
*As by the **lowe** base shrubbes tall Cypreffe shooteth aboue **them**.*

Melibaeus.

And what did thee mooue that needes thou must goe to see Rome?

Tityrus.

*Freedome: which **though** late, yet once **lookt** backe to my pore*
    state,
After time when haires from my beard did ginne to be whitish:
Yet lookt back at last and found me out after a long time.
When Amarill was once obtainde, Galatea departed:
*For (for **I will** confeffe) whilst as Galatea did hold mee,*
Hope did I not for freedome, and care had I none to my cattell.
*Though manie faire young beastes **our** folde **for the** aulters aforded*

And manie cheeses good fro my presse **vvere** *sent* **to the** *Cittie:*
Seldome times **did** *I bring anie store of pence fro the markett.*

Melibaeus.

O Amarill, *vvherefore, to thy Gods (very much did I meruaile)*
Heauilie thou didst praie: ripe fruites vngathered all still:
Tityrus is not at home: these Pyne **trees** *Tityre mist thee.*
Fountaines longd **for thee***: these hedgrovves* **vvisht** *thy return home*

Tityrus.

VVhat vvas then to be doone? from bondage could not J vvind out:
Neither *I could haue found such gentle Gods any vvhere els.*
There did **I** *see (Meliboee) that youth vvhose hestes I* **by** *course still.*
Fortnights whole to obserue on the Alters sure will I not faile.
Thus did he gentlie graunt to my sute when first I demaunded.
Keepe your heardes poore slaues as erst, let bulles to the makes still.

Melibaeus.

Happy olde man, then thou shalt haue thy farme to remaine still,
Large and **large** *to thy selfe, others nought but stonie grauell:*
And foule slymie rush wherewith their lees be besprinkled.
Here no *vnwoonted foode shall grieue young theaues who be laded,*
Nor the infections foule of neighbours flocke shall annoie them.
Happie **olde** *man. In shaddowy bankes and coole prettie places,*
Heere by the quainted floodes and springs most holie remaining.
Here, these quicksets fresh which lands seuer out fro thy neighbors
And greene willow rowes which Hibloe bees doo reioice in,
Oft fine whistring noise, shall bring sweete sleepe to thy fences.
Vnder a Rock side here will proyner chaunt merrie ditties.
Neither on highe Elme trees, thy beloude Doues loftilie fitting,
Nor prettie Turtles **trim***, vvill cease to crooke with a good cheere.*

Tityrus.

*First, **therefore** swift **buckes** shall flie for foode **to the** skies ward,
And from **fis**h with drawn broade seas themselues shal auoid
    hence:
First, (both borders broke) Araris shal **run** to the Parthanes,
And likewise Tygris shall againe runne backe to the Germanes:
Ere **his** countnaunce sweete shall slippe once out from my hart roote.*

Melibaeus.

*VVe poore soules, **must** some to the land **cald** Affrica packe hence.
Some to the farre Scythia, and some must **to** the swift flood Oaxis.
Some **to** Britannia coastes quite parted **farre** fro the whole world.
Oh **these pastures** pure shall I nere **more** chance to behold yee?
And **our cottage** poore with warme turues couerd about trim.
Oh these trim tilde landes, shall a rechlesse souldier haue them?
And shall a Barbarian haue this croppe? see what a mischiefe
Discord vile hath araisde? for whom was **our** labour all tooke?
Novv Meliboee ingraft pearie stocks, sette vines **in an** order.
Now goe (my braue flocke **once** that were) O now goe my
    kidlings.
Neuer againe shall **I** now in a greene bowre **sweetelie** reposed
See ye in queachie briers farre a loose clambring on **a** high hill.
Now shall I sing no Iygges, nor whilst I doo fall to my iunkets.
Shall ye my Goates, cropping sweete flowres and leaues sit
    about me.*

Tityrus.

*Yet thou maist tarrie heere, and keepe me companie this night,
All on a leauie couch: good Aples ripe I **doo** not lacke,
Chestnutts sweete good **store**, and plentie **of** curddes will I set thee.
Marke i' the Towne how chimnie tops doo beginne to be smoaking,
And fro the Mountaines high how shaddowes grow **to be** larger.*

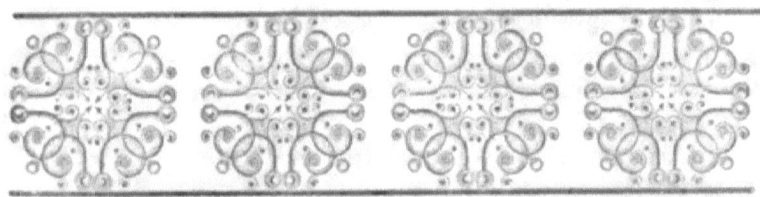

The seconde Æglogue called
Alexis.

The Argument.

Virgill in the personne of *Corydon* as some thinke, complayneth that he is not so gratious with Augustus as he would bee: or els it is to be referred to a youth *Alexander*, which was giuen him of *Asinius Pollio*, whom he blameth for the vnstedfastnes of his witt and wandering appetite, in refusing the freendly counsayle which he vsed to giue him.

THat Sheepheard **Corydon** did burne in loue with Alexis,
All his mastersdeare: and nought had he whereby to hope
Onely in beechen groues, and dolesome shaddowy places. [for.
Dailie resorted he: there these rude disordered outcryes,
Hylles and desert woodes throughout thus mournfully tuned.
O hard harted Alex, hast thou no regard to my sweete song?
Pyttiest me not a whitt: yea makst me now that I shall dye.
Yet doo the beastes find out fine shades and trim pretty
  coole plottes,
And fro the sun beames safe lie lyzardes vnder a bushtufte:
And for workmen toughe with boyling heate so beparched,
Garlick sauery sweete and coole hearbes plenty be dressed.
But, by the scorcht banke sydes i' thy foote steppes stil I goe
  plodding.

Hedgerowes hott doo refound with Grafhops mournfully fqueak-
O had I not ben better abyd Amarillis her anger? [ing,
And her proude difdaine? yea better abyde my Menalcas?
What though brown did he feeme? yea what though thou be
 fo gallant
O thou fine chery cheekt child truft not t' much to thy beauty.
Black violetts are tooke when dayfes white be refufed.
Me thou doft defpife vnknowne to thy felfe yet Alexis:
What be my riches greate in neate, in milke what aboundance.
In Sicill hylles be my Lambes of which there wander a thoufand.
All times, colde and hote yet frefh milke neuer I wanted.
Such be my Muficke notes, as (when his flockes he recalling)
Amphion of Dirce did vfe on fhore Aracynthus.
Much mifhapt I am not, for late in a bancke I behelde me,
VVhen ftill feas were calme, to thy Daphnis neede not I giue
 place
No, though thou be the iudge, if pictures haue any credite.
O were thou content to remaine with me by the downes heere,
In thefe lodgings fmall, and helpe me proppes to put vnder,
And trym kydling flocke with me to driue to the greene fieldes:
Pan in finging fweete with me fhouldft brauely refemble:
Pan, was firft the inuenter, pypes to adioyne in an order:
Pan, poore flockes and Sheephearedes to moft duly regardeth.
Thofe fine lips thou needft not feare to brufe with a fweete pype:
VVhat dyd Amynt forfake i'this excercife to be cunning?
One pype with feauene fundry ftops matcht fweetly together.
Haue I my felfe, Damætas which ats death he bequeathd me,
And fayd, heere, thou art now the fecond which euer hath ought
So fayd Damætas: but Amyntas fpightfully fcornde it. [it.
Alfo, two pretty fmall wyld kyddes, moft goodlie befpotted
Haue I, that heere i' the dales doo runne skant fafe I doo
 feare me.
Twyce in a day two teates they fuck: for thee will I keepe them:
Wondrous faine to haue had them both was Theftylis of late.
And fo fhe fhall: for I fee thou fcornft whatfo-euer I giue thee.
Come hyther O thou fweete face boy: fee fee, to thy felfe heere
How fayre Nymphes in baskets full doo bring manie Lillies:
White violets fweete Nais plucks and bloomes fro the Poppies,
Narcyfs, and dyll flowres moft fweete that fauoureth alfo.

Cafia, broade mary Goldes, with pancyes, and Hyacinthus.
And I my felfe rype peaches foft as filke will I gather.
And fuch Chefnutts as Amarill was wont to reioyce at.
Ploms **wyll** I bring likewife: that fruite fhall be honored alfo.
And **ye O** Lawrell twygges that I croppe, and **myrte thy felfe** next.
For ye be wont, (bound both in a bunch) moft fweetely to fauour.
Thou art but a Clowne Corydon: thefe gifts efteemes not Alexis:
Nor by thy gifts to obtaine art meete to incounter Iolas.
VVretch (ahlas) whats this that I wifh? fouth blafts **to the** yong flowers
Or cleere cryftall ftreames with loathfome fwyne to be troubled.
Ah mad boy from whom dooft runne? why Gods ithe woods **dwelt:**
And Paris erft of Troy: Pallas moft gladly reioyfeth,
In thefe bowres: and in trym groues we all chiefely delight **vs.**
Grym Lyoneffe doth courfe curft woolues, fo wolues doo the kydlinges.
And thefe wanton Kyddes likewife thefe faire Cytifus flowers.
Thee Corydon (O Alex) fome pleafure euery wight pulles.
See thefe yoked fteeres fro the plough nowe feeme to be lett loofe.
And thefe fhadowes large **doo** declare thys fun to depart hence
Styll **I** doo burne in loue. What meane in loue to be lookt for?
Ah Corydon Corydon, what raging fury dooth haunt thee,
Halfe cropt downe be thy vynes and broade brauncht elmes ouerhang them.
Rather about fome needefull worke now bufy thy felfe well,
Either on Ofyers tuffe or bulrufh weaue pretty basketts.
And if Alexis fcorne thee ftill, mayft hope for another.

I durſt not enterpryſe to goe any further with this rude tranſlation: beeing for the reſpects aforeſayd a troubleſome and vnpleaſant peece of labour: And therefore theſe ſhall ſuffice till further occaſion ſhall ſerue to imploy ſome profitable **paynes** in this behalfe.

The next verſe in dignity to the *Hexameters*, is ye *Carmen Elegiacum* which conſiſteth of **foure feete** and **two od** ſillables: viz: the two firſt feete, eyther *Dactyli* or *Spondæi* indifferent, the one long ſillable: **next two** *Dactyli* and an other long ſillable $---\cup\cup--\cup\cup-\cup\cup-$ ſome doo meaſure it in this ſorte (and more truely yet **not** ſo readily to all) accounting firſt two indifferently either *Dactyli* or *Spondæi*, then one *Spondæi*, and two *Anapæſti*. But it commeth all to one reckoning. Thys **verſe** is alwayes vnſeperably adioyned vnto the Hexameter, and ſerueth eſpecially to the handling of loue and dalliances, whereof it taketh the name. It will not frame altogether **ſo currantlye** in our Engliſh as the other, becauſe the **ſhortneſſe** of the ſeconde *Penthimimer* will hardly be framed to fall together in good ſence, after the Latine rules. I **haue** not ſeene very many of them made by any, **and** therefore one or two for example ſake ſhall be ſufficient.

This *Diſtichon* out of *Ouid*.

> *Ingenium quondam fuerat pretioſius auro,*
> *At nunc barbaries grandis habere nihil.*

May thus be tranſlated.

Learning once was thought to be better then any gold was,
Now he that **hath not** wealth **is but a** barbarian.

And thys

> *Omnia ſunt hominum tenui pendentia filo:*
> *Et ſubito caſu quæ valuere ruunt.*

Tis but a ſlender thread, which all mens ſtates do depend on:
And moſt goodly thinges quickly **doo fall to** decay.

As for the verses *Phalocium* and *Iambicum*, I haue not as yet made any tryall in them: but the *Sapphic* I assure you, in my iudgment wyl doo very pretty, if ye wants which I speake were once supplied. For tryall of which I haue turned the new Poets sweete song of *Eliza* into such homely *Sapphick* as I coulde.

Thys verse consisteth of these fiue feete, one *Chore*, one *spondæ*, one *dactyl*, and two *Chorcis*, with this addition, that after euery third verse be sette one *Adonium* verse, which consisteth of a *dactyl* and a *spondæ*. It is more troublesome and tedious to frame in our speeche by reason they runne without difference, euery verse being a like in quantity throughout, yet in my iudgement standeth meetely well in the same. I pray looke the Coppy which I haue translated in the fourth *Æglogue* of the *Sheepheardes Calender*: ye song of *Colins* making which *Hobbinoll* singeth in prayse of the Queenes maiesty, vnder the name of *Eliza*.

YE dainty Nymphes that in this blessed brooke,
    doo bathe your brest:
Forsake your **watry bowres and hether looke,**
    at my request:
And onely you Virgins that on *Parnass* dwell.
Whence floweth *Helicon* the learned well,
    helpe me to blase
    her worthy praise
That in her sex doth all excell.

Of fayre *Eliza* be your siluer song
    that blessed wight:
The flowre of Virgins, may she flourish long,
    in princely plight.
For she is *Syrinx* daughter without spott,
Which *Pan* the Sheepheards God on her begot:
    so sprang her grace,
    of heauenly race,
No mortall blemish may her blott.

See where she sittes, etc.

A Discourse of

The *Saphick* verse.

```
— υ — — — υ υ — υ — —
— υ — — — υ υ — υ — —
— υ — — — υ υ — υ — —
            — υ υ — —
```

O ye Nymphes most fine who resort to this brooke,
For to bathe there your pretty breasts at all times :
Leaue the watrish bowres, hyther and to me come
                        at my request nowe.

And ye Virgins trymme who resort to *Parnafs*,
Whence the learned well *Helicon* beginneth :
Helpe to blase her worthy deserts, that all els
                        mounteth aboue farre.

Nowe the siluer songes of *Eliza* sing yee,
Princely wight whose peere not among the virgins
Can be found : that long she may remaine among vs.
                        now let vs all pray.

For *Syrinx* daughter she is, of her begotten
Of the great God *Pan*, thus of heauen aryseth,
All her exlent race : any mortall harde happe
                        cannot aproche her.

See, she sittes most seemely in a grassy greene plott,
Clothed in weedes meete for a princely mayden,
Boste with Ermines white, in a goodly scarlett
                        brauely beseeming.

Decked is that crowne that vpon her head standes
With the red Rose and many Daffadillies,
Bayes, the Primrose and violetts, be sette by : how
                        ioyfull a sight ist.

Say, behold did ye euer her Angelike face,
Like to *Phœbe* fayre ? or her heauenly hauour
And the princelike grace that in her remaineth ?
                        haue yee the like seene ?

Medled ist red rose with a white together
Which in either cheeke do depeinct a trymme cheere,
Her maiestie and eye to behold so comely, her
                        like who remembreth ?

Phœbus once peept foorth with a goodly guilt hewe,
For to **gaze**: but when he fawe the bright beames
Spread abroade fro' her face **with** a glorious grace,
      it did **amaze** him.

When another funne he behelde belowe heere,
Blufht he red for fhame, nor againe he durft **looke**:
Would he durft bright beames of his owne with hers match,
     for to be vanquifht.

Shew thy felfe **now** *Cynthia* with thy **cleere rayes**,
And behold her: **neuer** abafht be thou fo: [beauty, how
When fhe fpreades thofe beames **of** her heauenly
    thou art **in a dump** dafht?

But I will take heede that I match not her grace,
With the *Laton* feede, *Niobe* that once **did**,
Nowe fhe doth therefore in a ftone **repent: to** all
     other a warning.

Pan he may well boafte that he did begit **her**
Such a noble wight, to *Syrinx* is it ioy,
That fhe found fuch **lott with a** bellibone **trym**
     for to be loaden.

When my younglinges firft to **the dammes doo** bleat out,
Shall a milke white Lambe to my **Lady be offred**: [grome.
For my Goddeffe fhee is **yea I** my felfe her Heard-
    though but a rude Clowne.

Vnto that place *Caliope* **dooth** high her,
Where my Goddeffe fhines: to the fame the Mufer
After her with fweete Violines **about them**
     cheerefully tracing

Is not it Bay braunche that aloft in handes they haue,
Eune to giue them fure to **my** Lady *Eliza*:
O fo **fweete** they play—and **to** the fame doo fing too
     heaunly to heare ift.

See, the Graces trym to the ftroake doo foote it,
Deftly dauncing, and meriment doo make them,
Sing to the inftruments to reioyce the more, but
     wants not a fourth grace?

Then the daunce wyll be eune, to my Lady therefore
Shalbe geune that place, for a grace she shall be
For to fill that place that among them in heaune, she
                                      may be receiued.

Thys beuy of bright Nymphes, whether ist goe they now?
Raunged all thus fine in a rowe together?
They be Ladies all i' the Lake behight foe?
                                    they thether all goe.

One that is there chiefe that among the rest goes,
Called is *Chores* of Olyues she beares a
Goodly Crownett, meete for a Prince that in peace
                                        euer abideth.

All ye Sheepheardes maides that about the greene dwell,
Speede ye there to her grace, but among ye take heede
All be Virgins pure that aproche to deck her,
                                    duetie requireth.

When ye shall present ye before her in place,
See ye not your selues doo demeane too rudely:
Bynd the fillets: and to be fine the waste gyrt
                                    fast with a tawdryne

Bring the Pinckes therewith many Gelliflowres sweete,
And the Cullambynes: let vs haue the Wynesops,
With the Cornation that among the loue laddes
                                    wontes to be worne much.

Daffadowndillies all a long the ground strowe,
And the Cowslyppe with a prety paunce let heere lye.
Kyngcuppe and Lillies so beloude of all men
                                    And the deluce flowre.

   One verse there remaineth vntranslated as yet, with some other of this sorte, which I meant to haue finished, but by reason of some let which I had, I am constrained to defer to some other time, when I hope to gratify the Readers with more and better verses of this sort: for in trueth I am perswaded a little paine taking might furnish our speeche with as much pleasaunt delight in this kinde of verse, as any other whatsoeuer.

Heere followe the Cannons or generall cautions of Poetry, prefcribed by Horace, firft gathered by *Georgius Fabricius Cremnicenfis*: which I thought good to annex to thys Treatife, as very neceffary obferuations to be marked of all Poets.

In his Epiſtle ad Piſones
de arte Poetica.

Irſt let the inuention be meete for the matter, not differing, or ftraunge, or monftrous. For a womans head, a horfe necke, the bodie of a dyuers coloured Byrd, and many members of fundry creatures compact together, whofe legges ending like a Fyfhes tayle: this in a picture is a wonderful deformitie: but if there be fuch diuerfitye in the frame of a fpeeche, what can be more vncomely or ilfauoured?

2. The ornaments or colours muft not bee too many, nor rafhly aduentured on, neither muft they be vfed euery where and thruft into euery place.

3. The proprietie of fpeeche muft bee duely obferued that wayghty and great matters be not fpoken flenderly, or matters of length too briefly: for it belongeth much both to the comlineffe and nature of a matter: that

in big matters there be lykewife vfed boyfterous wordes.

4. In Poeticall defcriptions, the fpeeche muft not exceede all credite, nor any thing fainedlie brought in, againft all courfe of nature.

5. The difpofing of the worke muft be fuch, that there be no offence committed, as it were by too exquifite dilligence: for many thinges may be oft committed, and fome thing by too curious handling be made offenciue. Neyther is it in one part to be well furnifhed, and in another to be neglected. Which is prooued by example of a Caruer, who expreffed very artificially the heade and vpper part of a body, but the reft hee could not make an ende of. Againe, it is prooued thus, that a body fhould not be in other partes beautifull, and yet bee deformed in the crooked nofe: for all the members in a well fhapen bodie muft be aunfwerable, found, and well proportioned.

6. He that taketh in hande to write any thing muft firft take heede that he be fufficient for the fame: for often vnwary fooles through their rafhnes are ouertooke with great want of ability

7. The ornament of a worke confifteth in wordes, and in the manner of the wordes, are either fimple or mixt, newe or olde, propper or tranflated. In them all good iudgment muft be vfed and ready wytt. The chiefeft grace is in the moft frequented wordes, for the fame reafon holdeth in wordes, as doth in coynes, that the moft vfed and tried are beft efteemed.

8. The kinde of verfe is to be confidered and aptly applied to the argument, in what meafure is moft meete for euery fort. The moft vfuall kindes are foure, the *Heroic, Elegiac, Iambick,* and *Lyric.*

9. One muft vfe one kynde of fpeeche alike in all wrytings. Sometime the *Lyric* ryfeth aloft, fometime the comicall. To the Tragicall wryters belong properly the bygge and boyfterous wordes. Examples muft be interplaced according fitly to the time and place.

10. Regarde is to be had of affections: one thing

becommeth pleafant perfons, an other fadde, an other wrathfull, an other gentle, which muft all be heedefully refpected, Three thinges therefore are requifite in verfes, beauty, fweetnes, and the affection. *Theophraftus* fayth that this beauty or delectableneffe is **a** deceyt, and Ariftotle calleth it τυραννία ολιγοκρονίον, a momentany tyrany. Sweetneffe retayneth a Reader, affection moueth him.

11. Euery perfon **muft be** fitted accordingly, and the fpeeche well ordered: wherein are to be confidered the dignity, age, **fex,** fortune, condition, place, Country, etc. of eche perfon.

12. The perfonnes are eyther to be fayned by the **Poets them** felues, or borrowed of others, if he borrow **them,** then muft hee obferue **το ὅμοιον, that is,** that **he folow that** Author **exactly** whom he purpofeth **to** immitate, and whereout he bringeth his examples. But if he fayne newe perfonnes, then muft he keepe his το ὁμαλόν, that is equallie: fo bringing them in eche place, that it be alwayes agreeable, and the laft like vnto the firft, and not make one perfon nowe a **bolde** boafter, and the fame ftraightwaies a wife warie **man,** for that is paffing abfurd. Againe, euery one muft obferue το ἁρμοστον, which is interpreted *conuenientiam*, **fitneffe:** as it is meete and agreeable euery where, a man to be ftoute, **a woman** fearefull, a feruant crafty, a young man gentle.

13. Matters which are common may be handled by a Poet as they may **be** thought propper to himfelfe alone. All matters **of themfelues are open to** be intreated of **by** any man: but if **a** thing be handled of fome one in fuch fort, as he thereby obtaine great prayfe, he maketh it his owne or propper to himfelfe, as many did write of the Troiane war, but yet *Homer* made matter which was common to all, propper to himfelfe.

14. Where many thinges are to be taken out of auncienter tongues, as the Latines tooke much out of the Greekes, the wordes are not fo precifelie to be followed, but that they bee altered according to the iudg-

ment and will of the Immitator, which precept is borrowed of Tully, *Non verbum verbo necesse est reddere.*

15. The beginning must not be foolishly handled, that is, straungly or too long.

16. The proposition or narration let it not be far fetched or vnlikely, and in the same forget not the differences of ages and persons.

17. In a Comedie it is needfull to exhibite all the actions openlie, as such as are cruell, vnhonest, or ougly, but such thinges may better bee declared by some meete and handsome wordes, after what sorte they are supposed to bee doone.

18. If a Commedye haue more Actes then fiue, it is tedious, if fewer, it is not sufficient.

It sytteth not to bring in the persones of Gods, but in verie great matters. *Cicero* sayth, when the Tragedy wryters cannot bring theyr matters to good passe, they runne to God. Let not more persones speake together then foure for auoyding confusion.

The *Chori* must be well garnished and sette foorth: wherein eyther menne are admonished, or reprehended, or counsayled vnto vertue. Such matter must bee chosen for the *Chorus*, as may bee meete and agreeable to that which is in hand. As for instruments and singing, they are Reliques of olde simplicitye. For the Musicke commonlye vsed at Theaters and the licencious nesse of theyr songes, which together wyth theyr wealth increased among the Romaines, is hurtfull to discipline and good manners.

19. In a *Satyr* the clownish company and rurall Gods, are brought in to temperate the Heauinesse of Tragedies, wyth some myrth and pastyme. In iesting it must be obserued that it bee not lacyuious or Rybaldlike, or slaunderous, which precept holdeth generallie in all sortes of wrytynges.

In a *Satyr* greate heede is to be taken, of the place, of the day, and of the persones: as of *Bacchus, Silenus,* or the *Satyres.* Againe of the vnmeetnesse or inconuenience of the matter, and of the wordes that they be fitted according to the persons: of *Decorum*, that he which represented some noble personage in the Tragedie, **bee** not some busy foole in the *Satyr*: finallie of **the** hearers, least they bee offended by myxing filthy matters with iestes, wanton toyes wyth vnhonest, **or** noysome with merry thinges.

20. The feete are **to** be applied propper to euery kinde of verse, **and therin a** Poet must not vse too much licence or boldnes. The auncient writers in *Iambick* **verses vsed** at first pure *Iambicks*: Afterwards *Spondæus* was admitted into *Locos impares*, but at last such **was the** licentious custome, that they woulde both *Spondæus* where they listed, and other **feete** without regarde.

21. In compyling of verses great care and circumspection must be vsed.

Those verses which be made Extempore, are of no great estimation: those which are vnartificiall, are vtterly repelled as too foolish. Though many doo lightlie regard our verses, yet ought the Carelesnesse **of** the hearers to bee no cause in vs **of errour and negligence.** Who desireth to make any thing **worthy to be** heard of learned eares, **let** hym reade Greeke **Authors** heedefullie and continually.

22. Artes **haue their** increasinges euen as other things, beeing naturall, **so** haue Tragedies which were first rudely inuented by *Thespis*, **at** last were much adorned by *Æschylus*: at the first **they** were practised in Villages of the Countrey, afterwardes brought to stages in great Citties.

23. Some **Artes doo** increase, some doo decay by a **certayne naturall course.** The olde manner of Commedies decayde, by reason of slaundering which therein they vsed against many, for which there was a penaltie appointed, least their bitternes should proceede too farre: In place of which among the Latines came the *Satyres*.

The auncient Authors of Comedies, were *Eupolis*, *Cratinus*, and *Aristophanes*, of the middle sorte *Plato*

Comicus, of the laſt kinde *Menander*, which continued and was accounted the moſt famous.

24. A Poet ſhould not content himſelfe onely with others inuentions, but himſelfe alſo by ye example of old wryters ſholde bring ſomething of his owne induſtry, which may bee laudable. So did they which writte among the Latines the Comedies called *Togatæ*, whoſe arguments were taken from ye Greekes, and the other which wrytt the *Pretextatæ*, whereof the arguments were Latine.

25. Heedefulneſſe and good compoſition maketh a perfecte verſe, and that which is not ſo may be reprehended. The faculty of a goode witte exceedeth Arte.

26. A Poet that he may be perfect, hath neede to haue knowledge of that part of Philoſophy which informeth ye life to good manners. The other which pertaineth to naturall thinges, is leſſe plauſible, hath fewer ornaments, and is not ſo profitable.

27. A Poet to the knowledge of Philoſophie ſhoulde alſo adde greater experience, that he may know the faſhions of men and diſpoſitions of people. Thys profit is gott by trauelling, that whatſoeuer he wryteth he may ſo expreſſe and order it, that hys narration may be formable.

28. The ende of Poetry is to wryte pleaſant thinges, and profitable. Pleaſant it is which delighteth by beeing not too long, or vneaſy to be kept in memory, and which is ſomewhat likelie, and not altogether forged. Profitable it is, which ſtyrreth vppe the mindes to learning and wiſedome.

29. Certaine eſcapes are to be pardoned in ſome Poets, ſpecially in great workes. A faulte may bee committed either in reſpect of hys propper Arte, or in ſome other Arte: that a Poet ſhoulde erre in precepts of hys owne arte, is a ſhamefull thing, to committe a faulte in another Arte is to be borne withal: as in *Virgil*, who fayneth that *Æneas* comming into *Affrica* ſlew with hys darte certaine Stagges, whereas

indeede *Affrica* hath in it none of thofe beaftes. Such errours doo happen eyther by vnheedefulnes, when one efcapeth them by negligence: or by the common fragility of man, becaufe none there is which can know all thinges. Therefore this laft kinde of errour is not to be ftucke vppon.

30. A good Poet fhould haue refpect to thys, how to retaine hys Reader or hearer. In a picture fome thing delighteth beeing fette farre of, fomething nearer, but a Poet fhould delight in all places as well in funne as fhaddowe.

31. In a Poet is no meane to be admitted, which if hee bee not he of all is the worft of all.

32. A Poeme if it runne not fweetely and fmoothly is odious: which is proued by a *fimile* of the two fenfes, hearing and tafting, as in fweete and pleafaunt meates. And the Poem muft bee of that forte, that for the fweeteneffe of it may bee acceptable and continue like it felfe vnto the ende, leaft it wearye or driue away a Reader.

33. He that would wryte any thing worthy the pofteritye, let him not enterprife any thing wherevnto his nature is not agreeable. *Mercury* is not made of wood (as they fay) neyther doth *Minerua* fauour all ftudies in euery one. In all Artes nature is the beft helpe, and learned men vfe commonly to fay that *A Poet is as well borne as made a Poet.*

34. Let no man efteeme himfelfe fo learned, but that he may fubmytte hys wrytinges to the iudgments of others, and correct and throughly amend the fame himfelfe.

35. The profitte of Poetry fprang thus, for that the auncient wyfe men fet downe the beft things that pertained to mans life, manners, or felicity, and examining and proouing the fame by long experience of time, when they are aged they publifhed them in wrytinges. The vfe of Poetry what it was at the firft, is manifeft by the examples of the mofte learned men: as of *Orpheus* who firft builded houfes: of *Amphion* who

made Citties, of *Tyrtæus* who firſt made warre: of *Homer*, who wryt moſt wyſely.

36. In an artificiall Poet three thinges are requiſite, nature, Arte, and dilligence.

37. A wryter muſt learne of the learned, and he muſt not ſticke to confeſſe when he erreth: that the worſe he may learne to auoyde, and knowe howe to follow the better.

The confeſſion of an errour betoken a noble and a gentle minde. *Celſus* and *Quintillian* doo report of *Hippocrates*, that leaſt he ſhould deceiue his poſterity, he confeſſed certayne errours, as it well became an excellent minded man, and one of great credite. For (as ſayth *Celſus*) light witts becauſe they haue nothing, wyll haue nothing taken from them.

38. In making choiſe of ſuch freendes as ſhould tell vs the trueth, and correct our wrytinges, heedefull iudgment muſt bee vſed: leaſt eyther we chooſe vnſkylfull folke, or flatterers, or diſſemblers. The vnſkilfull know not how to iudge, flatterers feare to offende, diſſemblers in not prayſing doo ſeeme to commende.

39. Let no man deceiue himſelfe, or ſuffer himſelfe to be deceiued, but take ſome graue learned man to be iudge of his dooing, and let him according to hys counſayle change and put out what hee thinketh good.

40. He which will not flatter and is of ability to iudge, let him endeuour to nothing ſo much, as to the correction of that which is wrytten, and that let be doone with earneſt and exquiſite iudgment. He which dooth not thus, but offendeth wilfully in breaking his credite too raſhly, may be counted for a madde, furious, and franticke foole.

41. The faultes commonly in verſes are ſeauen, as either they be deſtitute of Arte, of facility, or ornament: or els, they be ſuperfluous, obſcure, ambicious, or needeleſſe.

Englifh Poetrie.

Out of the Epiftles ad Mecænatem, Auguftum, et Florum.

42. An immitation fhould not be too feruile or fuperftitious, as though one durft not varry one iotte from the example: neyther fhould it be fo fenceleffe or vnfkilfull, as to immitate thinges which are abfurde, and not to be followed.

43. One fhould not altogether treade in the fteppes of others, but fometime he may enter into fuch wayes as haue not beene haunted or vfed of others. *Horace* borrowed ye *Iambick* verfe of *Archilocus*, expreffing fully his numbers and elegant[l]y, but his vnfeemely wordes and pratling tauntes hee moftewyfhlye fhunned.

44. In our verfes we fhould not gape after the phrafes of the fimpler forte, but ftriue to haue our writings allowable in the iudgments of learned menne.

45. The common peoples iudgments of Poets is feldome true, and therefore not to be fought after. The vulgar fort in *Rome* iudged *Pacuuious* to be very learned, *Accius* to bee a graue wryter, that *Affranius* followed *Menander*, *Plautus*, *Epicharmus*: that *Terence* excelled in Arte *Cæcilius* in grauity: but the learned forte were not of this opinion. There is extant in *Macrobius* (I knowe not whether *Angellius*) the like verdite concerning them which wryt *Epigrammes*. That *Catullus* and *Caluus* wrytt fewe thinges that were good, *Næuius* obfcure, *Hortenfius* vncomely, *Cynna* vnpleafant, and *Memmius* rough.

46. The olde wryters are fo farre to be commended, as nothing be taken from the newe: neyther may we thinke but that the way lyeth open ftyll to others to

attaine to as great matters. Full well fayd *Sidonius* to *Eucherius*, I reuerence the olde wryters, yet not fo as though I leffe efteemed the vertues and defertes of the wryters in this age.

47. Newnes is gratefull if it be learned: for certaine it is, Artes are not bothe begunne and perfected at once, but are increafed by time and ftudie. which notwithftanding when they are at the full perfection, doo debate and decreafe againe.

Cic. de orat. There is nothing in the world which burfteth out all at once, and commeth to light all wholly together.

48. No man fhould dare to practife an Arte that is daungerous, efpecially before he haue learned the fame perfectly: fo doo guyders of Shyppes: fo doo Phifitions: but fo did not manie Romaine Poets (yea fo doo not too many Englifh wryters) who in a certaine corragious heate gaped after glory by wryting verfes, but fewe of them obtayned it.

49. A Poet fhould be no leffe fkylfull in dealing with the affectes of the mynde, then a tumbler or a Iuggler fhoulde bee ready in his Arte. And with fuch pyth fhoulde he fette foorth hys matters, that a Reader fhoulde feeme not onely to heare the thing, but to fee and be prefent at the dooing thereof. Which faculty *Fabius* calleth ὑποτασιν and *Ariftotle* προ ομματον θεσιν ἡ ποίησιμ.

50. Poets are either fuch as defire to be liked of on ftages, as Commedie and Tragedie wryters: or fuch as woulde bee regeftred in Libraries. Thofe on ftages haue fpeciall refpect to the motions of the minde, that they may ftirre bothe the eyes and eares of their beholders. But the other which feeke to pleafe priuately with[in] the walles, take good aduifement in their workes, that they may fatiffy the exact iudgments of learned men in their ftudies.

51. A Poet fhoulde not bee too importunate, as to offende in vnfeafonable fpeeches: or vngentle, as to contemne the admonitions of others: or ambicious, as

to thinke too well of his owne dooinges: or too wayward, as to thinke, reward enough cannot be gyuen him for his deferte, or finally too proude, as to defyre to be honoured aboue meafure.

52. The emendations of Poemes be very neceffary, that in the obfcure poyntes many thinges may be enlightned, in the bafer partes many thinges may be throughly garnifhed. Hee may take away and put out all vnpropper and vnfeemely words, he may with difcretion immitate the auncient wryters, he may abridge thinges that are too lofty, mittigate thynges that are too rough, and may vfe all remedies of fpeeche throughout the whole worke. The thinges which are fcarce feemely, he may amende by Arte and methode.

53. Let a Poet firft take vppon him, as though he were to play but an Actors part, as he may bee efteemed like one which wryteth without regarde, neyther let him fo pollifh his works, but that euery one for the bafeneffe thereof, may think to make as good. Hee may likewyfe exercife the part of gefturer, as though he feemed to meddle in rude and common matters, and yet not fo deale in them, as it were for variety fake, nor as though he had laboured them thoroughly but tryfled with them, nor as though he had fweat for them, but practifed a little. For fo to hyde ones cunning, that nothing fhould feeme to bee laborfome or exquifite, when notwithftanding, euery part is pollifhed with care and ftudie, is a fpeciall gyft which *Ariftotle* calleth κρῆψν.

54. It is onely a poynt of wyfedome, to vfe many and choyfe elegant words, but to vnderftand alfo and to fet foorth thinges which pertaine to the happy ende of mans life. Wherevppon the Poet *Horace*, calleth the Arte poeticall, without the knowledge of learning and philofophy, a *prating vanity*. Therfore a good and allowable Poet, muft be adorned with wordes, plentious in fentences, and if not equall to an Orator, yet very neere him, and a fpecial louer of learned men.

F I N I S.

Epilogus.

His small trauell (courteous Reader) I desire thee take in good worth: which I haue compyled, not as an exquisite censure concerning this matter, but (as thou mayst well perceiue, and) in trueth to that onely ende that it might be an occasion, to haue the same throughly and with greater discretion, taken in hande and laboured by some other of greater abilitie: of whom I knowe there be manie among the famous Poets in London, who bothe for learning and leysure, may handle this Argument far more pythilie then my selfe. Which if any of them wyll vouchsafe to doo, I trust wee shall haue Englishe Poetry at a higher price in short space: and the rabble of balde Rymes shall be turned to famous workes, comparable (I suppose) with the best workes of Poetry in other tongues. In the meane time, if my poore skill, can sette the same any thing forwarde, I wyll not cease to practise the same towardes the framing of some apt English *Prosodia:* styll hoping, and hartelie wishing to enioy first
the benefitte of some others iudgment,
whose authority may beare greater
credite, and whose learn-
ing can better per-
forme it.

(∴)

1 October 1870.

Please oblige, by showing this List to your friends.

Works in English Literature

PUBLISHED OR TO BE PUBLISHED BY

EDWARD ARBER,

Associate, King's College, London, F.R.G.S., &c.

AT

5 QUEEN SQUARE, **BLOOMSBURY**, LONDON, **W.C.**

Sold by all Booksellers in the United Kingdom, and by the following, abroad :—

Berlin : N. Asher.	Montreal : Dawson Brothers.
Bombay : Thacker, Vining & Co.	New York : Scribner, Welford & Co.
Boston : Little, Brown & Co.	Philadelphia : C. J. Price.
Calcutta : Thacker, Spink & Co.	San Francisco : A. L. Bancroft & Co.
Melbourne : George Robertson.	Toronto : Adam, Stevenson & Co.

*** Foreign booksellers selling these publications can have their names added to **the above, in** the next List, upon application.

Chronological List.	2

For Students of English Literature.

To Students.	3
Facsimile Texts.	4
English Reprints, Foolscap size. . . .	5–12
Demy size. . . .	13
Imperial size. . . .	14
Annotated Reprints. (**The** Paston Letters.)	15

For General Readers.

Leisure Readings in English Literature. . .	16
Choice Books.	16

These publications are all edited by Mr. Arber, unless otherwise stated.

Any single work may be obtained separately. In ordering quote the Number, Title, and Price (the author's name is unnecessary).

All orders **must** be accompanied by a remittance; which, if under 10s., can be made in *Postage Stamps*; if above that sum, in P.O.O., made payable at High Holborn Office, **or** Cheques crossed London and County Bank.

These publications are always on sale; and may be obtained through your own Bookseller; or, *in any number,* post-free *by return*, **on** remitting to Mr. Arber, *the prices,* as stated in this List.

The usual allowance to Colleges and Schools.

All inquiries must be accompanied by a Stamp for reply.

Subscriptions, of not less than One Guinea, can **be** paid in advance of the appear**ance of** the Publications ordered.

This List cancels all previous ones, as regards Works not yet published.

CHRONOLOGICAL LIST.

Richard II.
1196. 1486. *The Revelation to the Monk of Evesham.* No. 18

Henry VI.—Henry VII.
1422-1509. *The Paston Letters.*

Henry VIII.
1516. 1566. Sir T. More. *Utopia.* 14
1527. W. Roy. *Rede me and be nott wrothe.*
1530. [Roy?] *A proper dyaloge between a Gentillman, etc.*
1545. R. Ascham. *Toxophilus.* 7

Edward VI.
1549. Bp. H. Latimer. *The Ploughers.* . . . 2
1549. Do. *Seven Sermons before Ed. VI.* . 13
1550. Rev. T. Lever. *Sermon in the Shrouds of St. Pauls.* 25
1550. Do. *Sermon before Ed. VI.* . . 25
1550. Do. *Sermon at Paul's Cross.* . . 25
1553. N. Udall. *Roister Doister.* . . . 17

Philip and Mary.
1553. R. Eden. *Translation from S. Munster (1532).*

1555. R. Eden. *Translations from Peter Martyr (1516).*
Oviedo y Valdes (1521). A. Pigafetta (1532), etc.
1557. Tottel's Miscellany. *Songes and Sonettes, etc.* . 24

Elizabeth.
1562. 1563. B. Googe. *Eglogs, Epytaphes, etc.*
1570. R. Ascham. *The Scholemaster.* . . . 23
1575. G. Gascoigne. *Notes of Instruction in Eng. verse.* 11
1576. G. Gascoigne. *The complaynt of Philomene.* . 11
1576. Do. *The Stele Glasse.* . . . 11
1577. G. Whetstone. *A Remembrance of G. Gascoigne.* 11
1579. J. Lyly. *Euphues. The Anatomy of Wit.* . 9
1579. S. Gosson. *The Schoole of Abuse.* . . 3
1579. Do. *An Apologie for the School of Abuse.* 3
1580. J. Lyly. *Euphues and his England.* . . 9
1557-1580. T. Tusser. *Fine Hundred Points of Good Husbandrie.* 4
1582. 1595. Sir P. Sidney. *An Apologie for Poetrie.* . 21
1582. T. Watson. *The Ἑκατομπαθια.*

1583. Rev. P. Stubbes. *The Anatomie of Abuses.*
1583. Do. *2d Part of the Anatomie of Abuses.*
1585. James VI. *The Essayes of a Prentise in. . . Posie* 19
1586. W. Webbe. *A Discourse of English Poetry.* 26

1589. G. Puttenham. *The Arte of English Poesie,* No. 15
1590. Ubaldini.—Ryther. *Concerynge the Spanishe fleete.* 21
1590. T. Watson. *Meliboeus.* . . . 21
1590. Do. *An Eclogue, &c.* . . . 5
1591. E. Webbe. *His Wonderful Travailes.*
1592. 1593. Sir W. Ralegh. *The Fight in the 'Revenge.'*
1593. T. Watson. *The Teares of Fancy or Love disdained.* 21
1593. *The Phœnix Nest.* Ed. by R. S.
1595. G. Markham. *The Tragedie of Sir R. Grenville.*
1597. F. Bacon. *Essayes.*

James I.
1604. [James I.] *A Counterblaste to Tobacco.* . 19
1607-12. Sir F. Bacon. *The Writings, &c.* Harl. MS. 5106.
1612. *The Essaies of Sir F. Bacon,* Knt.
? Sir R. Naunton. *Fragmenta Regalia.* . 20

Charles I.
1625. Francis Lord Verulam, *Essayes or Counsels.*
1628-33. Bp. J. Earle. *Microcosmographie.* . 12
1625-45. 1689. J. Selden. *Table Talk.* . . . 6
1634-40. W. Habington. *Castara.* . . . 22
1637. F. Quarles. *Enchyridion.*
1640. Star Chamber. *Decree concerning Printing.* 1
1641. J. Milton. *The Reason of Church Government, etc.*
1642. J. Howell. *Instructions for Forreine Travell.* 16
1643. Lords and Commons. *Order regulating of Printing.*
1644. J. Milton. *On Education.*
1644. Do. *Areopagitica.* 1
1645. J. Howell. *Epistolæ Ho-Elianæ.* Book I.
1647. J. Howell. *Epistolæ Ho-Elianæ.* Book II.

Commonwealth.
1650. J. Howell. *Epistolæ Ho-Elianæ.* Book III.
1650. Do. *Instructions for travelling into Turkey.* 16
1655. Do. *Epistolæ Ho-Elianæ.* Book IV.

Charles II.
1671. 1672. G. Villiers, Duke of Buckingham, *The Rehearsal.* 10

William and Mary.
1694. E. Phillips. *Life of John Milton.*

Anne.
1712. J. Addison. *Criticism on Paradise Lost.* . 8

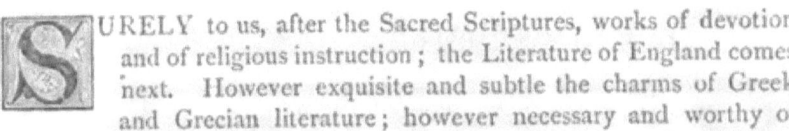URELY to us, after the Sacred Scriptures, works of devotion and of religious instruction; the Literature of England comes next. However exquisite and subtle the charms of Greek and Grecian literature; however necessary and worthy of study the language and literature of Rome; the writings of our Forefathers come home to every Englishman. What a mighty Literature have we inherited! How little is it known, save to a few, who have devoted all their leisure to its exploration! Authors mighty in Prose and Verse! Writers full of aëry fancies and graceful similitudes! **Men whose** Prose marches with the tramp and strength of a Roman legion: men whose Song is sung by a Puck or an Ariel; or who sing in it of Patient Grissell, of Fair Geraldine, or of Una and her Red Cross Knight. Above all the English Bible, so clung unto by our ancestors—with its infinite early editions and their most heroic story.

What present nation has so ancient, so vast, so varied a body of writings as England? In which are contained not only the productions of our Arch-Poets, Chaucer, Spenser, Shakespeare, Milton, Dryden; but those of an almost uncountable number of authors, inferior indeed **to these,** but of high rank among ordinary minds.

Good books, besides affording enjoyment, provoke to like excellence. No man writeth unto himself. Each worthy writer is trained, assimilated, and influenced by those who have gone before: each returning a like benefit to posterity. To trace the continuous chain **of** influence, **of** cause and effect, link by link, forms a part of the History of English Literature. That History that we may soon hope to possess, for the first time adequately in our language, in Professor HENRY MORLEY's work *English Writers*: of which we have already received the earlier instalment, down to Dunbar. What is designed in the *Facsimile Texts*, the *English Reprints*, and the *Annotated Reprints* is to **represent** the later literature by giving, at as cheap a price as can be, Exact Texts sometimes of books already famous, sometimes of those quite forgotten: in some cases, of works that illustrate the Literary History; in other instances, of those that in a sense, constitute it.

The result is already, that these Reproductions are unique in English Bibliography for their accuracy and cheapness, as well as for the unlimited numbers offered constantly for sale: and *so far as they are yet published*, they constitute the best of all introductions to our **old** Authors, from the time of Caxton to that **of** Addison.   E. A.

P.S.—A word in furtherance of the *Early English Text*, the *Chaucer*, and the *Ballad* Societies. No one knows the extent of the unprinted Literature of England. These Societies are recovering for us book **after** book; and **laying us all** under great obligation **to** their able Editors, who labour gratuitously. For further information, apply to **F. J.** Furnivall, M.A., 3 St. George's Square, London, N.W.

Facsimile Texts.

In Varying Sizes, following the Originals.

OF European publications there are not a few which the mere outward appearance, their countenance so to speak, **possess** an extreme **interest**. Either from the excessive rarity of the book itself, or the drollery or quaintness of its illustrations; **either from** the literary importance of the work or its significance in the history of our Country or in the progress of the World: there arises at the sight of it the keenest attention, one might almost say an inexpressible sympathy with the book itself. In all such cases: Sun-Portraits confer exquisite and perpetual enjoyment.

Hitherto Cost has debarred photolithographed books from general use: **but I trust** to offer from time to time, at *ordinary book-prices*, works of this supreme interest, though necessarily of an infinitely diverse character. In which effort, I trust to receive a thorough support from the large number of readers who have sustained the *English Reprints*. Both being like attempts to make forgotten books known; and known books, more perfectly and perpetually obtainable.

Early in November, will be published in Fcp. 4to., Half **Calf**, Illuminated sides, pp. xxxii.-64.

[WILLIAM TYNDALE, assisted by WILLIAM ROY.

The First *printed* English New Testament. Cologne—Worms. 1525. 4to.]

Photo-lithographed, by the permission of the Trustees of the British **Museum, from** the *unique* fragment in the Grenville Collection.

Briefly told, the story of this profoundly interesting work is as follows:—In **1524 Tyndale went from London** to Hamburg; where remaining for about a year, he journeyed on to Cologne; and there assisted by William Roy, subsequently the author of the Satire on Wolsey, *Rede me and be nott wrothe* [see p. 11], he began this first edition in 4to: *with glosses* of the English New Testament. A virulent enemy of the Reformation, Cochlæus, at that time an exile in Cologne, learnt, through giving wine to the printer's men, that P. Quentel the printer had in hand a secret edition of three thousand copies of the English New Testament. In great alarm, he informed Herman Rinck, **Senator** of the city, who moved the Senate to stop the printing; but Cochlæus could **neither** obtain a sight of the Translators, nor a sheet of the impression.

Tyndale and Roy, fled with the printed sheets, up the Rhine to Worms; and there **completing this edition, produced also another in** Octavo, *without glosses*. Both editions were in England in Jan.-March, **1526:** and of the six thousand copies of which they together were composed, there remain but this fragment of the First commenced edition; **and of the** Second edition, one complete copy in the Library of the Baptist College at Bristol, and an imperfect one **in** that of St. Paul's Cathedral, London.

The price of this *Facsimile Text*, will be only Six Shillings.

English Reprints.

THE great importance to the increasing study of English Literature, of constantly adding to, and constantly keeping on sale (a more difficult task than at first would appear) at the lowest practicable prices, these Exact Texts; has led to a full consideration of the past three years' progress, in an experiment which has been successful beyond anticipation. The following alterations have been found advisable, in order to place this designedly very cheap Series upon a permanent basis.

The changes to take effect from 1st October 1870.

Small Paper, in Foolscap Octavo.

1. **The public choice** has passed so generally from *Cut* to *Uncut* edges: that future issues will be in *Uncut* edges only. This will also apply to all reimpressions, as soon as the existing *Cut-edged* copies have been sold.

2. **No** Sixpenny Reprints will be issued in future. The trouble is **out of all proportion to the price.**

3. The *maximum* number of pages for Shilling works will be about One hundred and twenty-eight. Experience has proved that number **to be** the *very utmost* limit practicable for such closely packed works **in the** costly old spelling, &c.

∴ The result of these changes to the public will be simply, that some future Reprints will be increased in price, by an extra Sixpence. A trifling contribution to enable me to go on for years. Yet I **very** reluctantly decide on this augmentation: this series being my personal free offering to a more perfect knowledge of English Literature.

All existing issues will be maintained at the present prices.

Large Paper, in Foolscap Quarto.

Nos. 19 to 24 in Large Paper are now ready. A single Large Paper copy **can be** obtained.

Demy Quarto.

Works in this size **will** be issued bound in Cloth. When published, copies will however be obtainable in Sheets, for binding, by remitting the price *direct* to me.

There is a great cause for thankfulness in the progress already made. Works which some of our most experienced English scholars never hoped **to** see reprinted; have **been put into** *general* circulation. Much more may be accomplished, **by** a personal advocacy of this Series by *each* Purchaser; with a generous permission to print, from possessors of rare or unique English books; and with unwearying effort on my own part. Maintaining herein the ancient and worthy fame of England; may we lead very many to understand how much pure and unadulterated Delight is to be **found in our** Old English Authors.

English Reprints.

ORDINARY ISSUE IN OCTAVO.
Durable Cases, in Roxburghe style, to hold four or five Reprints. **One Shilling each.**

BOUND VOLUMES IN OCTAVO.
Two or three of such works, collected into occasional Volumes.

LARGE PAPER EDITION IN QUARTO.
*The same texts, beautifully printed on thick toned paper, with ample margins suitable for **purposes** of study. Issued in Stiff covers, uncut edges. When bound to the purchaser's **own taste**; these Large Paper Copies form most handsome books.*

ANY SINGLE WORK OR VOLUME MAY BE HAD SEPARATELY.

Quarto.	FOOLSCAP.	Octavo.
Large Paper Edit.		Stiff Covers. Uncut Edges. / Green Cloth, Red Edges.
	1. JOHN MILTON.	
	(1) A decree of the Starre-Chamber, concerning Printing, made the eleuenth day of July last past. London, 1637.	
	(2) An Order of the Lords and Commons assembled in Parliament **for** the regulating of Printing, &c. London, 14 June, 1643.	
1/6	(3) *AREOPAGITICA:* A speech of Mr. **John** Milton for the liberty **of Vnlicenc'd** Printing, to the **Parliament** of England. London. [24 November]. 1644. <u>Sixpence</u>.	**Vol. I.**
	2. HUGH LATIMER, *Ex-Bishop of Worcester.*	Milton,
1/6	*SERMON ON THE PLOUGHERS.* A notable Sermon of ye reuerende father Master Hughe Latimer, whiche he preached in ye Shrouds at paules churche in London, on the xviii daye of Januarye. ☾ The yere of our Loorde MDXLviii. <u>Sixpence</u>.	Latimer, Gosson.
	3. STEPHEN GOSSON, *Stud. Oxon.*	
	(1) *THE SCHOOLE OF ABUSE.* Conteining a pleasaunt invective against Poets, Pipers, Plaiers, Jesters, and such like Caterpillers of a Commonwealth; Setting up the Flagge of Defiance to their mischievous exercise, and ouerthrowing their Bulwarkes, by Prophane Writers, **Naturall** reason, and common experience. A discourse as pleasaunt for gentlemen that fauour learning, as profitable for all that wyll follow vertue. London. [August?] 1579.	**2/**
1/6	(2) *AN APOLOGIE **OF** THE SCHOOLE OF ABUSE*, against Poets, **Pipers**, and their Excusers. London. [December?] **1579**. <u>Sixpence</u>.	
	4. SIR PHILIP SYDNEY.	
1/6	*AN APOLOGIE FOR POETRIE.* Written by the right noble, **vertuous** and learned Sir Philip Sidney, Knight. London. **1595**. <u>Sixpence</u>.	

ENGLISH REPRINTS—FOOLSCAP.

Quarto.
Large Paper Edit. | *TITLES, PRICES, etc., etc.* | *Octavo.*
Stiff Covers, Uncut Edges. | Green Cloth, Red Edges.

5. EDWARD WEBBE, *Chief Master Gunner.*

The rare and most vvonderful thinges which Edward Webbe an Englishman borne, hath seene and passed in his troublesome trauailes, in the Cities of Ierusalem, Damasko, Bethelem, and Galely: and in the Landes of Iewrie, Egipt, Gtecia, Russia, and in the land of Prester Iohn. Wherein is set foorth his extreame slauerie sustained many yeres togither, in the Gallies and wars of the great Turk against the Landes of Persia, Tartaria, Spaine, and Portugall, with the manner of his releasement, and comming into London in May last. London. 1590.
Sixpence.

1/6

Vol. II.

Sidney,

Webbe,

Selden.

2/6

6. JOHN SELDEN.

TABLE TALK: being the Discourses of John Seldon Esq.; or his Sence of various Matters of Weight and High Consequence relating especially to Religion and State. London. 1689.
One Shilling.

2/6

7. ROGER ASCHAM.

TOXOPHILUS. The schole of shooting conteyned in tvvo bookes. To all Gentlemen and yomen of Englande, pleasaunte for theyr pastime to rede, and profitable for theyr use to folow, both in warre and peace. London. 1545.
One Shilling.

2/6

Vol. III.

Ascham,

Addison.

2/6

8. JOSEPH ADDISON.

CRITICISMS OF MILTON'S PARADISE LOST. From *The Spectator*: being its Saturday issues between 31 December, 1711, and 3 May, 1712. One Shilling.

2/6

9. JOHN LYLY, M.A.

(1) ☾ *EUPHUES. THE ANATOMY OF WIT.* Verie pleasaunt for all Gentlemen to read, and most necessarie to remember. Wherein are contained the dedelightes that Wit followeth in his youth by the pleasantnesse of loue, and the happinesse he reapeth in age, by the perfectnesse of Wisedome. London. 1579.

(2) ☾ *EUPHUES AND HIS ENGLAND.* Containing his voyage and aduentures, myxed with sundrie pretie discourses of honest Loue, the Description of the Countrey, the Court, and the manners of that Isle. Delightful to be read, and nothing hurtful to be regarded : wher-in there is small offence by lightnesse giuen to the wise, and lesse occasion of loosenes proferred to the wanton. London, 1580. Collated with early subsequent editions.
Four Shillings.

9/

Vol. IV.

Lyly.

5/

ENGLISH REPRINTS—FOOLSCAP.

Quarto.   Octavo.
Large Paper Uncut Edges Edit.   *TITLES, PRICES, etc., etc.*   *Stiff Covers. Uncut Edges.*   *Green Cloth, Red Edges.*

10. GEORGE VILLIERS, *Duke of Buckingham.*
    THE REHEARSAL. As it was acted at the Theatre Royal London, 1672. With Illustrations from previous plays, &c.   **One Shilling.**

2/6

11. GEORGE GASCOIGNE, *Esquire.*
    (1) A remembravnce of the wel imployed life, and godly end of George Gaskoigne, Esquire, who deceassed at Stalmford in Lincoln shire, the 7 of October 1577. The reporte of GEOR. WHETSTONS, Gent an eye witness of his Godly and Charitable End in this world. Lond. 1577.
    (2) Certayne notes of Instruction concerning the making of verse or rime in English, vvritten at the request of Master *Edouardi Donati.* 1575.
    (3) *THE STEELE GLAS.* A Satyre compiled by George Gasscoigne Esquire [Written between Apr. 1575 & Apr. 1576]. Together with
    (4) *THE COMPLAYNT OF PHYLOMENE.* An Elegie compyled by George Gasscoigne Esquire [between April 1562 and 3rd April 1575.] London. 1576.
                                 One Shilling.

Vol. V.

Villiers,

Gascoigne,

Earle.

3/6

2/6

12. JOHN EARLE, M.A.: *afterwards in succession Bishop of Worcester, and of Salisbury.*
    MICRO-COSMOGRAPHIE, or a Peece of the World discovered, in Essays and Characters. London. 1628. With the additions in subsequent editions during the Author's life time.   **One Shilling.**

2/6

13. HUGH LATIMER, *Ex-Bishop of Worcester.*
    SEVEN SERMONS BEFORE EDWARD VI.
    (1) ❡ The fyrste sermon of Mayster Hugh Latimer, whiche he preached before the Kynges Maiest. wythin his graces palayce at Westmynster. M.D.XLIX. the viii of Marche. (,',)
    (2) The seconde [to seventh] Sermon of Master Hughe Latimer, whych he preached before the Kynges maiestie, withyn hys graces Palayce at Westminster ye. xv. day of March. M.cccc.xlix.   **Eighteen Pence.**

4/

Vol. VI.

Latimer.

More.

14. SIR THOMAS MORE.
    UTOPIA. A frutefull pleasaunt, and wittie worke, of the best state of a publique weale, and of the new yle, called Utopia : written in Latine, by the right worthie and famous Sir Thomas More knyght, and translated into Englishe by RAPHE ROBYNSON, sometime fellowe of Corpus Christi College in Oxford, and nowe by him at this seconde edition newlie perused and corrected, and also with diuers notes in the margent augmented. London. [1556].   **One Shilling.**

2/6

3/

ENGLISH REPRINTS—FOOLSCAP. 9

Quarto. Large Paper Edit.	TITLES, PRICES, etc., etc.	Octavo.
		Stiff Covers. Uncut Edges. / Green Cloth. Red Edges.
	15. GEORGE PUTTENHAM. *THE ARTE OF ENGLISH POESIE.* Contriued into three Bookes: The first of Poets and Poesie, the second of Proportion, the third of Ornament. London. 1589. Two Shillings.	Vol. VII. Puttenham.
5/		2/6
	16. JAMES HOWELL, *Historiographer Royal to Charles II.* *INSTRUCTIONS FOR FORREINE TRAVELL.* Shewing by what *cours,* and in what *compasse of time,* one may take an **exact** Survey of the Kingdomes and States of Christendome, **and arriue** to the practicall knowledge of the Languages, to good purpose. London. 1642. Collated with the edition of 1656; and in its 'new Appendix for Travelling into **Turkey** and the *Levant* parts' added. Sixpence.	Vol. VIII.
1/6		
	17. The earliest known English comedy. NICHOLAS UDALL, *Master of* **Eton.** *ROISTER DOISTER,* [from the unique copy at Eton College]. **1566.** Sixpence.	Howell, Udall,
1/6		
	18. *THE REVELATION TO THE MONK OF EVESHAM.* Here begynnyth a marvelous revelacion that was schewyd of almighty god by sent Nycholas to a monke of Euyshamme yn the days of Kynge Richard the fyrst. And the yere of our lord. M.C.Lxxxxvi. [From the unique copy, printed abont 1482, in the British Museum]. One Shilling.	Monk of Evesham James VI.
2/6		3/6
	19. JAMES VI. *of Scotland,* **I.** *of England.* (1) *THE ESSAYES OF A PRENTISE, IN THE DIVINE ART OF POESIE.* Edinburgh 1585. (2) *A COUNTER BLASTE TO TOBACCO.* London. 1604. One Shilling.	
2/6		
	20. SIR ROBERT NAUNTON, *Master of the Court of Wards.* *FRAGMENTA REGALIA:* or, Observations on the late Queen Elizabeth, her Times, and Favourites. [Third Edition. London] 1653. Sixpence.	Vol. IX.
1/6		
	21. THOMAS WATSON, *Student at law.* (1) *THE* Ἑκατομπαθια or Passionate Centurie of Loue. Divided into two parts: whereof, the first expresseth the Authors sufferance in Loue: the latter, his long farewell to Loue and all his tyrannie. Composed by *Thomas Watson* Gentleman; and published at the request of certaine Gentlemen his very frendes. London [1582.]	Naunton, Watson. 2/6

ENGLISH REPRINTS—FOOLSCAP.

Quarto. Large Paper Edit.	TITLES, PRICES, etc., etc.	Octavo. Stiff Covers. Uncut Edges.	Green Cloth, Red Edges.
4/	(2) *MELIBŒUS* T. Watsoni, Ecloga in obitum F. Walsinghami, &c. Londini, 1590. (3) *AN EGLOGUE*, &c., Written first in latine [the above MELIBŒUS] by *Thomas Watson* Gentleman and now by himselfe translated into English. London 1590. (4) *THE TEARS OF FANCY*, or Loue disdained. [From the unique copy, wanting Sonnets ix.-xvi., in the possession of S. Christie-Miller, Esq.] London, 1593. <u>Eighteen Pence.</u>		
	22. WILLIAM HABINGTON.		
2/6	*CASTARA.* The third Edition. Corrected and augmented. London. 1640. With the variations of the two previous editions. <u>One Shilling.</u>		Vol. XI Habington,
	23. ROGER ASCHAM.		
2/6	*THE SCHOLEMASTER*, Or plaine and perfite way of teachyng children, to vnderstand, write, and speake, the Latin tong, but specially purposed for the priuate bryngyng vp of youth in Ientlemen and **Noble** mens houses, commodious also for all such, as haue forgot the Latin tongue, and **would**, by themselues, without a Scholemaster, in short tyme, and with small paines, recouer a sufficient habilitie, to vnderstand, write, and speake Latin. London. 1570. <u>One Shilling.</u>		Ascham. 2/6
	24. Tottel's Miscellany.		Vol. XI.
6/6	*SONGES AND SONETTES*, written by the ryght honorable Lorde HENRY HAWARD, late Erle of Surrey, and other. [London, 5 June] 1557. <u>Half-a-crown.</u>		Tottel. 3/
	25. REV. THOMAS LEVER, M.A.: *afterwards Master of St John's College, Cambridge.*		
4/	*SERMONS.* (1) A fruitfull Sermon made in Paules churche at London in the Shroudes, the second of Februari. 1550. (2) A Sermon preached the thyrd [or fourth] Sunday in Lent before the Kynges Maiestie, and his honourable counsell. 1550. (3) A Sermon preached at Pauls Crosse, the xiiii. day of December 1550. <u>Eighteen Pence.</u>		Vol. XII. Lever, Webbe.
	26. WILLIAM WEBBE, *Graduate.*		
2/6	*A DISCOURSE OF ENGLISH POETRIE.* Together, with the Authors iudgment, touching the reformation of our English Verse. London. 1586. <u>One Shilling.</u>		3/

∴ *The following works are designed for publication in time to come. Their prices cannot be fixed with precision, but are approximately given.* Ferrex and Porrex *has been postponed; and*

ENGLISH REPRINTS—FOOLSCAP.

Newes from the North by F. T. [FRANCIS THYNNE], with RICHARD BARNFIELD'S Poems *have not been inserted; some of the Texts* **not** *being accessible, at the present time.* J. HOWELL'S Epistolæ Ho-Elianæ *will be put to press as soon as No.* 27 BACON'S Essayes, &c., *is finished.*

Large Paper Edit.			
	27. FRANCIS BACON. *Stiff Covers. Uncut Edges.*		*Green Cloth, Red Edges.*
	A harmony of the *ESSAYES*, &c. The four principle texts appearing in parallel columns. ; (1) Essayes. Religious Meditations. Places of perswasion and disswasion. London 1597. (10 Essays.) Of the Coulers of good and euill a fragment. 1597. (2) The writings of Sir Francis Bacon Knt : the Kinges Sollicitor Generall : in Moralitie, Policie, and Historie. *Harleian MS.* 5106. Transcribed bet. 1607-12. (34 Essays.) (3) THE ESSAIES of Sir FRANCIS BACON Knight, the Kings Solliciter Generall. London 1612. (38 Essays.) (4) The Essayes or Counsels, **Ciuill** and Morall, of FRANCIS LO. VERULAM **Viscount** ST. ALBANS. *Newly Written.* **1626.** (58 Essays.) Three Shillings.		Vol. XIII. Bacon. 3/6
7/6			
	28. WILLIAM ROY, *Franciscan Friar.*		
	(1) *REDE ME AND BE NOTT WROTHE.* [Strasburg. 1527. This is his famous Satire on Wolsey.] (2) *A PROPER DYALOGE BETWEEN A GENTLEMAN AND A HUSBANDMAN, &c.* [Attributed to Roy] Marburg. 1530. Eighteen Pence.		Vol. XIV. Roy.
2/6			
	29. SIR W. RALEIGH—G. MARKHAM.		
	THE LAST FIGHT OF THE REVENGE AT SEA. (1) A report of the Truth of the fight about the Isles of Acores, this last Sommer. Betvvixt the Reuenge, one of her Maiesties Shippes, and an Armada of the King of Spaine. By Sir Walter Raleigh. London. 1591. (2) The most Honorable Tragedie of Sir Richard Grinuille, Knight (∴) *Bramo assai, poco spero, nulla chieggio.* [By GERVASE MARKHAM] London. 1595. [Two copies only are known, Mr. Grenville's cost £40.] One Shilling.		Fight in the Revenge. Googe. 4/
2/6			
	30. BARNABE GOOGE.		
	EGLOGS, EPYTAPHES AND SONETTES newly written by Barnabe Googe. London 1563. 15 March. One Shilling.		
2/6			
	31. REV. PHILLIP STUBBES.		
	(1) *THE ANATOMIE OF ABUSES:* conteyning a discoverie or briefe Summarie of Such Notable Vices and Imperfections, as now raigne in many Christian		

ENGLISH REPRINTS—FOOLSCAP.

Quarto. Large Paper Edit.	TITLES, PRICES, etc., etc.	Stiff Covers. Uncut Edges.	Octavo. Green C. Red Ea
	Countreyes of the World: but especialie in a very famous ILANDE called AILGNA [*i.e.* Anglia]: Together with most fearefull Examples of Gods Iudgementes, executed vpon the wicked for the same, aswell in AILGNA of late, as in other places, elsewhere . . . London. 1 Maij. 1583.		Vol.
6/6	(2) The Second part of THE ANATOMIE OF ABUSES . . . London. 1583. Half-a-crown.		Stubb 3/

32. THOMAS TUSSER.

FIVE HUNDRED POINTES OF GOOD HUSBANDRIE, as well for the Champion, or open Countrie, as also for the woodland, or Seuerall, mixed in euery Month with *HUSWIFERIE,* . . . . with diuers other lessons, as a diet for the former, of the properties of windes, plantes, hops, herbes, bees and approued remedies for sheepe and cattle, with many other matters both profitable and not vnpleasant for the Reader . . . . London. 1580. **Eighteen Pence.**

4/ — Vol. Tusse

33. JOHN MILTON.

(1) The Life of Mr John Milton [by his nephew EDWARD PHILLIPS]. From '*Letters of State written by Mr. John Milton,* bet. 1649-59.' London. 1694.
(2) *THE REASON OF CHURCH GOVERNEMENT* urg'd against Prelacy. By Mr. *John Milton.* In two Books. [London] 1641.
(3) Milton's Letter *OF EDUCATION.* To Master *Samuel Hartlib.* [London. 5 June 1644.]
One Shilling.

2/6 — Milto 3/

34. FRANCIS QUARLES.

ENCHYRIDION, containing

Institutions { Divine { Contemplative. / Practicall. / Ethycall. / Oeconomicall. / Politicall. } Morall }

London. 1640-1. **One Shilling.**

2/6 — Vol. Quarle

35. The Sixth English Poetical Miscellany.

THE PHOENIX NEST. Built vp with the most rare and refined workes of Noble men, woorthy Knights, gallant Gentlemen, Masters of Arts, and braue Schoolers. Full of varietie, excellent inuention, and singular delight. *Never before this time published.* Set forth by R. S. of the Inner Temple Gentleman. London 1593. **One Shilling.**

2/6 — The Phœnix Nes 2/6

36. SIR THOMAS ELYOT.

THE GOVERNOR. The boke named the Gouernor, deuised by ye Thomas Elyot Knight. Londini M.D.xxxi. Collated with subsequent editions. **Half-a-crown.**

6/6 — Vol. Elyot 3/

Demy Quarto.

Will be ready, about March 1871, in one Volume, 12s. 6d.

801. RICHARD EDEN.

I. A treatyse *OF THE NEWE INDIA, WITH OTHER NEW FOUNDE LANDES AND ISLANDS, AS* **WELL** *EASTWARDE AS* **WESTWARDE**, as they are knowen and found in these oure dayes, after the descripcion of SEBASTIAN MUNSTER, in his boke of vniuersall Cosmographie, &c. [London, 1553.]

II. The First English Collection of Voyages, Traffics, and Discoveries.— *THE DECADES OF THE NEW WORLD OR WEST INDIA, &c. &c.* [by Peter Martyr of Angleria.] [Translated, compiled, &c. by Richard Eden.] Londini, Anno **1555.**

1. The [Dedicatory] Epistle [to King Philip **and** Queen Mary.]
2. Richard Eden to the Reader.
3. The [1st, 2nd, and 3d only of the 8] Decades of the newe worlde or west India, Conteynyng the nauigations and conquestes of the Spanyardes, with the particular description of the moste ryche and large lands and Ilandes lately founde in the west Ocean perteynyng to the inheritance of the kinges of Spayne. In the which the diligent reader may not only consyder what commoditie may hereby chaunce to the hole christian world in tyme to come, but also learne many secreates touchynge the lande, the sea, and the starres, very necessarie to be knowen to al such as shal attempte any nauigations, or otherwise haue delite to beholde the strange and woonderful **woorkes of** god and nature. Wrytten in the Latine **tounge** by PETER MARTYR of Angleria, **and** translated into Englysshe by RYCHARDE EDEN.
4. The Bull of Pope Alexander VI. in 1493, granting to the Spaniards 'the Regions and Ilandes founde in the Weste Ocean' by them.
5. *The Historie of the West Indies* by GONÇALO FERNANDEZ OVIEDO Y VALDES.
6. Of other notable things gathered out of dyuers autors.
7. Of Moscouie and Cathay.
8. Other notable thynges as touchynge the Indies [chiefly out of the books of FRANCISCO LOPEZ DE GOMARA, 'and partly also out of the caade made by SEBASTIAN CABOT.']
9. The Booke **of Metals.**
10. The description **of** the two viages made owt of England into Guinea in Affricke [1553, 1554].
11. The maner of fyndynge the Longitude of regions.

INDEX.

.*.* An abridged analysis of this voluminous work was issued in the previous catalogue (1 Dec. 1869); which will be found bound up with 'English Reprints' issued **during this** year, 1870.

Imperial Folio.

1001. PETRUCCIO UBALDINI—AUGUSTINE RYTHER.

A Discourse concerning the Spanishe fleete inuadinge Englande in the yeare 1588 and ouerthrowne by her Maiesties Nauie vnder the conduction of the Right-honorable the Lorde Charles Howarde highe Admirall of Englande: written in Italian by PETRUCCIO VBALDINI citizen of Florence, and translated for A. RYTHER: vnto the which discourse are annexed certain tables expressinge the generall exploites, and conflictes had with the said fleete.

These bookes with the tables belonginge to them are to be solde at the shoppe of A. RYTHER, being a little from Leaden hall next to the Signe of the Tower. [1590.]

The twelve Tables express the following subjects :—
FRONTISPIECE.

I. THE SPANISH ARMADA COMING INTO THE CHANNEL, OPPOSITE THE LIZARD; AS IT WAS FIRST DISCOVERED.

II. THE SPANISH ARMADA AGAINST FOWEY, DRAWN UP IN THE FORM OF A HALF MOON ; THE ENGLISH FLEET PURSUING.

III. THE FIRST ENGAGEMENT BETWEEN THE TWO FLEETS, AFTER WHICH THE ENGLISH GIVE CHASE TO THE SPANIARDS, WHO DRAW THEIR SHIPS INTO A BALL.

IV. DE VALDEZ'S GALLEON SPRINGS HER FOREMAST, AND IS TAKEN BY SIR FRANCIS DRAKE. THE LORD ADMIRAL WITH THE 'BEAR AND THE 'MARY ROSE,' PURSUE THE ENEMY, WHO SAIL IN THE FORM OF A HALF MOON.

V. THE ADMIRAL'S SHIP OF THE GUIPUSCOAN SQUADRON HAVING CAUGHT FIRE, IS TAKEN BY THE ENGLISH. THE ARMADA CONTINUES ITS COURSE, IN A HALF MOON ; UNTIL OFF THE ISLE OF PORTLAND, WHERE ENSUES THE SECOND ENGAGEMENT.

VI. SOME ENGLISH SHIPS ATTACK THE SPANIARDS TO THE WESTWARD. THE ARMADA AGAIN DRAWING INTO A BALL, KEEPS ON ITS COURSE FOLLOWED BY THE ENGLISH.

VII. THE THIRD AND THE SHARPEST FIGHT BETWEEN THE TWO FLEETS : OFF THE ISLE OF WIGHT.

VIII. THE ARMADA SAILING UP CHANNEL TOWARDS CALAIS ; THE ENGLISH FLEET FOLLOWING CLOSE.

IX. THE SPANIARDS AT ANCHOR OFF CALAIS. THE FIRESHIPS APPROACHING. THE ENGLISH PREPARING TO PURSUE.

X. THE FINAL BATTLE. THE ARMADA FLYING TO THE NORTHWARD. THE CHIEF GALLEASS STRANDED NEAR CALAIS.

LARGE MAP SHOWING THE TRACK OF THE ARMADA ROUND THE BRITISH ISLES.

These plates, which are a most valuable and early representation of the Spanish Invasion, are being re-engraved in *facsimile*, and will be issued in the Spring of 187 at the lowest feasible price : probably HALF-A-GUINEA.

∴ *Other works may follow.*

Annotated Reprints.

By various Editors: under Mr. Arber's general supervision.

Some Texts require the amplest elucidation and illustration by Masters in special departments of knowledge. To recover and perpetuate such Works is to render the greatest service to Learning. With the aid of Scholars in special subjects, I hope to endow our readers with some knowledge of the Past, that is now quite out of their reach. While the Editors will be responsible both for Text and Illustrations; the works will be produced under my general oversight: so that the Annotated Reprints, though **of** *much slower growth,* **will** *more than equal in value the English Reprints.* E. A.

In the Spring of 1871: in Fcp. 8vo the First Volume (to be completed in Four) of

The Paston Letters. 1422-1509.

Edited by JAMES GAIRDNER, Esq., of the Public Record Office.

EVERY one knows what a blank is the history of England during the Wars of the two Roses. Amid the civil commotions, literature almost died out. The principal poetry of the period is that of Lydgate, the Monk of Bury. The prose is still more scanty. The monastic Chronicles are far less numerous than at earlier periods: and by the end of the Fifteenth Century they seem to have entirely ceased. Thus it has come to pass that less is known of this age than of any other in our history. In this general dearth of information recent historians like Lingard, Turner, Pauli, and Knight, who have treated of the reigns of Henry VI., Edward IV., &c., have found in *The Paston Letters* not only unrivalled illustration of the Social Life of England, but also most important information, at first hand, as to the Political Events of that time. So that the printed Correspondence is cited page after page in their several histories of this period.

The Paston Letters have not however been half published. No literary use was made of them while accumulating in the family muniment room. William, 2nd Earl of Yarmouth, the last member of the family, having encumbered his inheritance, parted with all his property. The family letters came about 1728 into the hands of the distinguished antiquary, Peter le Neve; afterwards, by his marriage to Le Neve's widow, **to his** brother antiquary Martin of Palgrave; on his death again, **to a** Mr. Worth, **from whom** they were acquired by Mr. afterwards Sir **John** Fenn.

In 1787, **Fenn** published a small selection of the Letters **in two** volumes 4to; **of** which the **first** edition having been sold off in a week, a second appeared in the course of the **year.** He then prepared a further selection, of which **two** volumes appeared in **1789; the** fifth volume being published after his death, in 1823. Strangely enough, the Original **Letters** disappeared **soon** after their publication: and only those of the Fifth volume have, **as** yet, been recovered. There is no reasonable doubt that they still exist and will some day be found. There is no necessity, however, to postpone a new edition indefinitely, **until they are** again brought to light: for a comparison of the Fifth volume with its originals establishes Sir John Fenn's general faithfulness **as to** the Text; and therefore our present possession, in his Edition, of the contents of the missing Manuscripts.

Three hundred and eighty-seven letters in all **were** published by Fenn; about Four hundred additional letters or documents, belonging to the same collection and which have never been published at all, will be included in the present edition.

Not only will the Text be doubled in quantity; but in its elucidation, it will have the benefit of Mr. Gairdner's concentrated study of this Correspondence for years past. Half his difficulty will be in the unravelling of the chronology of the Letters, partly from internal evidence, partly from the Public Records, and other sources. Fenn's chronology—for no fault of his—is excessively misleading. This was inevitable, from the difficulties of a first attempt, the state of historic criticism in his day, and the limited means then available for consulting the public records, &c. It is hoped, however, by restoring each Letter to its certain or approximate date, vastly to increase the interest of this Correspondence. In addition textual difficulties will be removed, and valuable biographical information afforded.

The Letters of the reign of Henry VI. will form Vol. I. (estimated at about 600 *pp.*); those of Edward IV., Vols. II. and III. (together about 800 *pp.*); and those of Richard III. and Henry VII., Vol. IV. (about 300 *pp.*). The price will be *about* one shilling for every 100 *pp.*; and the work, it is expected, will be completed in Two years.

THE undermentioned **modernized texts are** in preparation. Great care will be bestowed in their transformation into the spelling and punctuation of the present day: but the Originals will be adhered to as closely as possible.

Leisure Readings in English Literature.

The object of the volumes that will appear under this general title, will be to afford Restful Reading; and, at the same time, by exhibiting the wealth of thought and the wit in expression of our Old Authors; to predispose to a further study of our Literature: in which study these Readings will serve as First Books.

They will contain many excellent Poems and Passages that are generally but very little known.

Choice Books.

THE DISASTROUS ENGLISH VOYAGE TO THE WEST INDIES IN 1568.

Recounted in the Narratives of Sir JOHN HAWKINS: and of DAVID INGRAM, MILES PHILLIPS, and JOB HORTOP, survivors, who escaped through the American Indian tribes; or out of the clutches of the Inquisition; or from the galleys of the King of Spain: and so at length came home to England.

∴ *Other works to follow.*

These works will be issued, beautifully printed and elegantly bound, in Crown 8vo.
The above is a specimen of the type, but not of the size of page.

---

5 QUEEN SQUARE, BLOOMSBURY, LONDON, W.C.

www.ingramcontent.com/pod-product-compliance
Lightning Source LLC
Chambersburg PA
CBHW032222230426
43666CB00033B/589